Parenting Teenagers in the New Millennium

Dr. G. Scott Wooding

Fitzhenry & Whiteside

Fitzhenry & Whiteside Limited
195 Allstate Parkway
Markham, Ontario L3R 4T8

In the United States:
121 Harvard Avenue, Suite 2
Allston, Massachusetts 02134

www.fitzhenry.ca godwit@fitzhenry.ca

Fitzhenry & Whiteside acknowledges with thanks the Canada Council for the Arts, the Government of Canada through the Book Publishing Industry Development Program (BPIDP), the Ontario Arts Council and the Government of Ontario through the Ontario Media Development Corporation's Ontario Book Initiative for their support for our publishing program.

10   9   8   7   6   5   4   3   2

National Library of Canada Cataloguing in Publication

Wooding, G. Scott, (Gary Scott), 1944–
Rage, rebellion & rudeness : parenting teenagers in the new
millennium / G. Scott Wooding.
Includes index.
ISBN 1-55041-755-X

1. Parent and teenager.   2. Parenting.   3. Adolescence.
4. Adolescent psychology.   I. Title.   II. Title: Rage, rebellion and rudeness.
HQ799.15.W664   2003   306.874   C2003-900590-9

United States Publisher Cataloging-in-Publication Data

Wooding, G. Scott.
Rage, rebellion & rudeness : parenting teenagers in the
new millennium / G. Scott Wooding. -1st ed.
[392] p. : ill. ; cm.
Includes bibliographical references and index.
Sequel to: Hear me, hug me, trust me: parenting today's teenager effectively.
ISBN 1-55041-755-X
1. Parent and teenager.   2. Parenting — Miscellanea.   I. Title.
649/. 125 21   HQ799.15.   W8732 2003

Warning — Disclaimer: Parents are advised to consult a qualified counselor, psychologist, or healthcare professional prior to acting on the basis of material contained herein. The opinions expressed in this book are those of the author. The author, advisors and Fitzhenry & Whiteside shall have neither liability nor responsibility to any person or entity with respect to any loss or damage caused or alleged to be caused directly or indirectly by the information contained in this book.

Cover design by Kerry Design
Inerior design and typesetting by Daniel Crack, Kinetics Design
Printed and bound in Canada

Contents

Acknowledgements

Encouragement to write this book came initially from my former publisher, Doug McArthur. Many thanks for the time and effort he spent to complete and polish this work.

Much appreciation is also extended to the staff and students of Ian Bazalgette Junior High School in Calgary who provided not only encouragement but also most of the quotes and anecdotes used in this book. Particular thanks are extended to the former principal, Gerry Sharpe, the Language Arts coordinator, Val MacPherson, and my favorite school secretary ever, Gloria Hawken.

Major revisions were made on the basis of comments made by a number of very busy people who took the time to read the unedited text. These included Jean Hage in Ottawa. Ruth Coleman, Tara Wood and Joan Bever of Calgary, and Laurie Muir of Black Diamond. My heartfelt thanks to all these active parents.

Introduction

Most parents fear teenagers and the approaching teenage years of their own children. If you do not believe this, walk through a large shopping mall some day and objectively note your feelings as you come upon groups of teenagers. Most adults will carefully avoid these groups as well as the stores in which they are found, even though the great majority of them are entirely harmless. Why is this? The reason is found in a lack of understanding of what motivates their behavior as well as in not knowing how to deal with their adolescent conduct.

The purpose of this book is to help reduce not only the fears and misconceptions about teens, but to give clear solutions to many of the most puzzling problems that parents encounter with their children during these years. To begin this process, the opening chapter provides a brief summary of the author's first book, *Parenting Today's Teenager Effectively: Hear Me, Hug Me, Trust Me*. The ideas and conclusions about teenagers found in this first chapter form the underlying philosophy of the remainder of the book.

The second chapter then attempts to explain the common personality traits of most teens. Because their behavior is mostly driven by hormones, the majority of teenagers act similarly. By understanding what is normal for teens, most parents can relax in the knowledge that their teenager's apparently erratic behavior is actually common to the species. On the other hand, reading the second chapter may awaken some parents to the fact that their adolescent's behavior is actually outside the normal limits, and hopefully will cause them to seek help.

Next will be a look at what is different about today's teenager from teens of previous generations. This is often termed the "generation gap." While generation after generation of teens all go through the same physical and emotional changes over a period of several years, the world in which they are undergoing these changes differs. Teens of the 1940s grew up without television in their homes. Teenagers of the 60s and 70s did not have computers. These varying contexts make it appear that the adolescents are very different from their parents, when in fact they have many similarities. Both similarities and differences need to be examined to see how they relate to effectively parenting modern teenagers.

The first three chapters, then, give a general look at the world of teenagers. Once this framework has been built, the focus shifts to many of the most common problems that teenagers encounter in today's complex world. Each problem will be thoroughly analyzed as to the reason for its occurrence, with clear solutions following. This approach is unique as most books do not spend much time examining the causes of the behaviors, but simply try to give solutions. It is the author's opinion that an understanding of the causes is important so that parents can realize how they developed. This understanding helps to prevent recurrences of the behaviors both with the teen experiencing the problem, and with younger children who have yet to enter the teenage orb.

The problems examined in this book have been grouped as much as possible into common themes. This thematic approach can occasionally be somewhat arbitrary. For example, the section on teen telephone usage could just as easily have been placed into the "Common Teenage Issues" section. Arguments can be made in either direction, but the idea is to group the different problems into the general areas where parents have difficulty, so that they could read through several such predicaments and get a feeling for a general approach to handle them all.

This book, then, is somewhat of a hybrid which attempts to both provide a brief overview of the nature of teens, as well as give ideas on how to handle specific problems. The first three chapters should definitely be read together while the rest of the book is designed as a "troubleshooting guide" or "teenage encyclopedia," so parents can learn to cope with problems that may be particular to their household.

Chapter 1

The "Hear Me, Hug Me, Trust Me" Parenting Approach

"Good parents make you feel more secure.
You tend to be more confident if you have a strong family."
— Fiona

In this extremely complex and busy world, parents need some techniques and strategies to help them raise their adolescents to be responsible and self-confident individuals. They cannot rely only on the methods that their parents used on them, for these may be outdated or ineffective. Instead they need an approach to raising teens that takes into account the changing times and the increasing demands made on today's teenager. These parenting techniques need to be preventative as well as reactive. In other words, parents should not have to wait until a situation occurs to find out how to deal with it. Rather, an approach needs to be in place that can keep these crises to a minimum. Human nature unfortunately ensures that crises cannot totally be eliminated. Such factors as heredity, peer pressure, the desire to try new things and inexperience often conspire to override even the most effective parenting. However, an effective parenting methodology can prevent the majority of these emergencies, can deal with most crises as they appear and thus can virtually guarantee a relatively smooth transition between childhood and adulthood. Such an approach is the "Hear Me, Hug Me, Trust Me" method of raising teens.

Background

The "Hear Me, Hug Me, Trust Me" approach to teenagers is not a system developed by "experts" in the field of raising children. Rather, it is an approach based on what teens themselves believe are factors in effective parenting. It arose, almost accidentally, from an annual classroom exercise that the author conducted called "Design the Ideal Parents." The exercise itself was originally conceived in self-defense, as classroom discussions in a life-skills class were constantly returning to the subject of parents — specifically, how unfair they were. One day, as a challenge, the students were told to divide into groups and turn their complaints into constructive suggestions for parents. They were asked to design what they thought would be their "ideal parents." Much to the amazement of the author, they took this challenge very seriously and each group produced a very creditable list of traits that they wanted to see in their parents. Once each group's suggestions were listed, the overall catalog of parenting traits was quite impressive.

> *Most parents did not seem to have a clear idea of how to deal effectively with teenage behavior.*

For several years this exercise was conducted as a method of discussing parenting, so that the students could try to see why their parents acted as they did. For example, in analyzing what consequences were effective in disciplinary situations, the exercise gave an excellent opportunity for discussion of why discipline itself was necessary. It worked well as, year after year, the classes took it equally seriously.

Finally a class from which the author expected relatively little did a particularly outstanding job on this exercise. This class had been very difficult to teach and had not taken much of the course seriously up to then. After complimenting the class on the maturity and insight of their presentations, the author was asked why, if the students knew these things about parenting, their parents did not. It was a valid question, as it was clear from the discussion that there was some truth behind it. Most parents did not seem to have a clear idea of how to deal effectively with teenage behavior.

The class was then asked how we could get the information that they had compiled out to parents. Suggestions included parent information nights and the production of a pamphlet. Both of these were rejected because there was too much information to present in these ways. Eventually a book was suggested. Since the students had provided most of the information, volunteers were requested to help design and produce such a book, and a core of 4 or 5 students from this class came forward. They in turn brought in others who eventually formed "Doc's Book Club."

While the composition of the group fluctuated greatly over the next two years, the volunteers basically spent two noon hours a week working on the design and content of the book. Ideas were plentiful and an outline gradually appeared. The students settled on 12 characteristics of what they thought would make ideal parents, and contributed thoughts on how to get parents to develop these characteristics.

Unfortunately this was as far as the students could go. Their writing skills and work habits were simply not up to actually writing the text. It was probably too much like homework. At this point "Doc" himself took over. For the next two years questionnaires were handed out to classes soliciting details to flesh out the points developed by the "club." The quotes thus obtained are sprinkled throughout the text of the original book, *Parenting Today's Teenager Effectively: Hear Me, Hug Me, Trust Me*, published in 1995. Here, for example, is Lisa's original list of traits she feels would be exhibited by "ideal" parents:

- *considers kids' feelings*
- *includes kids in family discussions*
- *fair discipline*
- *not too picky about grades*
- *gives hugs and kisses*
- *tells you when you've done a good job*
- *easy to talk to about anything*
- *not intimidating*
- *goes places with you*
- *remembers when your special events are*
- *not too restrictive*
- *listens to kids' point of view*
- *doesn't get mad*
- *supportive*

As you can see the list is very reasonable. Lisa asks for discipline, just that it be fair. She appears to realize that restrictions are necessary, but doesn't want too many. Two of her points refer to communication, wanting parents to be "easy to talk to" and to listen to their teens. As it turns out, good communication between parents and teens was a characteristic that teens felt to be one of the most important, but that today's parents almost universally do very badly. Lisa's list was by no means unique; most of the teens surveyed covered these points. It was just that hers was one of the most complete and insightful.

The principles of the "Hear Me, Hug Me, Trust Me" parenting approach, therefore, come from teenagers themselves and not from experts in the field. Their knowledge base comes from their position as the consumers of parenting. They may not know the theory behind why the principles work; they just know what works best for them. Interestingly, most of the experts agree with them.

The 12 Characteristics of Parenting Teenagers

The core of this parenting approach is twelve characteristics that teenagers decided were essential to be an effective parent. Here is the list, in the order that teens thought them important:

- *Understanding*
- *Communication*
- *Discipline*
- *Fairness*
- *Trust*
- *Respect*
- *Responsibility*
- *Caring*
- *Honesty*
- *Humor*
- *Spending time together*
- *Setting an example*

While parents easily accept some of these characteristics, others come as a distinct surprise. Discipline, for example, practically leaps out of the book at adults. Given the protestations they get when they discipline their teens, parents find it hard to believe that the youngsters actually ask for it. They do, and they even know why it's important. Spending time together is another shocker for most parents. It usually seems that teens would far rather be with their friends — to such an extent that many parents give up trying to plan activities together with their kids. Obviously this impression, too, is incorrect. If teens ask for these things, then protest when they happen, perhaps it's the methods that are wrong and not the concepts themselves. This is in fact the case, as will become clear below.

Another concern with this list is its length. Trying to incorporate all twelve of these characteristics into a parenting style seems even harder than learning a golf swing. This was a major concern until it was realized that the characteristics cluster into three groups — Hear Me, Hug Me and Trust Me. Hence the title of the system.

In this section the headings and their respective characteristics that fall under them will be listed for your perusal only. The next sections will outline what each characteristic means and why it comes under a particular heading.

Hear Me — Communicate with Me
- *Understanding*
- *Communication*
- *Fairness*
- *Respect*
- *Honesty*

Hug Me — Show Me You Care
- *Discipline*
- *Fairness*
- *Caring*
- *Humor*
- *Spending time together*
- *Setting an example*

Trust Me
- *Trust*
- *Respect*
- *Responsibility*

Note that some characteristics fall into more than one category. This is because they relate to both groupings. For example, to communicate effectively with your teen you have to respect their ideas, although you need not agree with them. Similarly, to be able to trust your teen, you must respect their ability to make decisions. If this were mathematics the categories would undoubtedly be mutually exclusive. Unfortunately, when dealing with human nature, things are never as precise as the mathematical world is.

The overall philosophy of the "Hear Me, Hug Me, Trust Me" approach, which arises from these characteristics of "ideal" parents, views teens as a "between group" — no longer a child and not yet an adult. In one book on teenagers, the authors actually refer to them as "middlers." Children's behaviors need to be either completely directed, as in, "Time to go to bed, Jennie," or the choices have to be very limited. An example of this would be, "Would you like mommy or daddy to take you to bed now?" Adults can generally decide most aspects of their lives for themselves. Adult bedtimes are therefore decided entirely by them. Teenagers need to be treated differently than both groups. This treatment involves consulting with them whenever possible and yet being non-democratic when the occasion warrants. Staying with the bedtime analogy, a bedtime would first be set in consultation with the teen at the start of the school year. Parents would then need, in most cases, to remind the teen when the time arrived each evening. Balancing consultation with direction can be a difficult process. The "Hear Me, Hug Me, Trust Me" approach helps make this balance much easier to find.

Hear Me

> *"An ideal parent for me would be someone who listens.*
> *They just listen to my problems and then*
> *maybe suggest a solution."*
> — *Heather*

Communicating with teens has always been a difficult process. Certainly the number one complaint of the teens surveyed was that their parents don't listen to them. The so-called "generation gap" is rooted in the lack of communication and understanding between the generations. Being able to "hear" your teen will go a long way towards bridging this gap.

1 *Understanding*

> *"To me the perfect parent would be one that would*
> *understand the problems us kids go through."*
> — *Steve*

Since the entire second chapter of this book is devoted to understanding the origins of teen behavior, it will not be discussed at length here. Suffice it to say that understanding involves more than just knowing that hormones are at the basis for much teenage behavior. It involves listening to the teen's side of an issue, and having some empathy or feeling for why they feel and act the way they do. It also involves having some knowledge of key teenage worries such as peer pressure, crushes (not a teenage word anymore, but you know what I mean), passion for loud "music," strange tastes in clothing, hairstyles, and where to wear their jewelry and the importance of their friends.

To develop this empathy parents need to do some homework. The first step should be to dig out old high school yearbooks, and spend some time reminiscing. Gaze with fondness on the clothing, hairstyles and old friends that leap out from the dusty pages. Try to remember how your parents felt about them. Then try to translate those feeling to the parents of today — which would be you.

The next step is to spend some weekend time at the largest mall in your neighborhood. Start by sitting in the food fair for an hour or so and watch the wildlife cruise by. Try to determine what are the norms or standards for such things as clothing, hairstyles, jewelry placement (remember when it was just in the earlobes, around the neck or on your finger?), and even tattoos. This will give you an idea of what is normal teen behavior. When you have determined what the standards are, then pay some attention to those who go beyond the norm with bizarre clothing, hairstyles and even odder jewelry placements. These are the insecure teens who need to go beyond the standard in order to gain attention. Comparing the standard to the bizarre will give you a good idea of where your child fits into the teenage behavior continuum.

From the food fair, gravitate to the music stores. Check out the posters and advertising to see who is popular at the moment. Another way of doing this is to tune into the local music video channel and watch an hour's worth of videos at prime teenage time (after school or in the evening). This not only lets you know what music is popular with the mainstream, but also gives you an idea as to where the clothing and hairstyle fashions come from. Again, the more insecure teens will listen to "fringe" music that is not nearly as common and is usually much harder to listen to for adults.

This research will pay big dividends in the area of understanding. If you know what is common and popular in these areas, you will know whether or not you need to worry about your teenager. For example, if your son were to arrive home one day with the top of his hair dyed blond, and you've just seen a popular music group with several blond-topped members, you will realize where the desire to dye came from. Then check out your yearbooks again and compare the hairstyles with the album covers of your old LPs. A light should come on and you can bathe in the glow of your understanding. This is certainly better than getting angry and starting an argument. On the other hand, if the hair is in long red and blue spikes, then it really is time to be concerned and perhaps seek some counseling help.

Armed with this newfound understanding, parents can be empathetic with their teens rather than antagonistic. They can relax in the knowledge that their teen is just being a teen and is not an alien from the planet Ork. When the parents relax, the teens also relax and the household atmosphere becomes a comfortable one rather than a war zone. Understanding, then, is a vital component of the "Hear Me" section of this approach to parenting. You "hear" by knowing what drives teen behavior and how they think.

2 Communication

*"I feel I can't talk to my parents about certain things because
they just don't understand from my point of view. Sometimes my mom
just relates my situations to how she thinks they should be handled.
I can't talk to my dad at all —only about basketball or things that
have nothing to do with my life."*
— Laura

Understanding teenagers is a good start for parents, but it is not enough. Teens want to be able to communicate with them because they realize that, for many subjects, their friends' ideas and opinions are just not mature enough. Remember your kids before they were exhibiting teenage behavior? They would come home from school and babble like a broken water closet about the day's activities. While teenagers are not as prone to talking about their activities, they haven't changed *that* much. They still want to discuss things. It's up to parents to give them the opportunity and the "ear."

There are two aspects to communicating with anyone — talking and listening. Of the two, listening is the most important for teens. They need to vent often because there are so many confusing things in their lives. Things like why their friend is mad at them or why a certain boy doesn't like them are common concerns that teens need to discuss. Unfortunately the great majority of parents are poor listeners so teenagers eventually quit trying to talk to them, relying instead on an empathetic teacher, a counselor, a friend's parent or just their friends. Here, in brief are the **Guidelines for Listening to Teens:**

A **Make it possible for teens to talk to you by making both family time and personal time available.** You can do this by having family dinners on a daily basis, driving kids places, doing chores with them, or just sitting on the edge of their beds as you "tuck them in" at night.

B **Make eye contact and concentrate on what the teen is saying.** Teens know when your mind is elsewhere — and they hate it. Often the conversation will not be particularly stimulating, but pay attention anyway. If they can't tell you the mundane things, they certainly will not discuss the serious issues with you. Teens need to know that you are interested in what they're saying — or they won't say it.

C **Keep in touch with their lives.** You cannot listen effectively if you don't know what teens are talking about. Know what music groups they like, who their friends are, who their teachers are, and when they have tests and big assignments. If you don't keep in touch with these things you will continually need clarification, as in, "Who are the Purple Orangutans?" This will frustrate teens by constantly making them explain themselves.

D Don't interrupt. Telling a teen that there is a stain on his or her shirt right in the middle of a recitation of how the big game went is annoying. The stain will wait for the laundry. The story won't.

E Don't make snap judgments. Wait until you hear the entire story. Leaping to a conclusion is another conversation stopper, very similar to interrupting. Here is a typical example:

> Mom: *Did you take those library books back today?*
> Brian: *No, I didn't.*
> Mom: *I told you last night that they had to be back today.*
> *Don't you realize that now you'll have to pay a fine?*
> Brian: *It wasn't my fault.*
> Mom: *Of course it was. They were your books.*
> *Sometimes you're so irresponsible!*

If it turns out that Brian had tried to take the books back, but the library had been closed for renovations, then Mom would have a very angry teen on her hands. A better approach would have been to ask why he hadn't taken the books back, then listen carefully to the answer.

F Try not to show any emotion while listening, including anger, disappointment or laughter. As soon as a parent shows emotion during a conversation, communication ceases. Listen carefully to the entire story or anecdote — then comment *calmly* on the contents. An example might help illustrate this point.

> Jessica: *You should have seen Mark at the party last night.*
> *He was so drunk he passed out on the front lawn.*
> Dad (loudly): **There was booze at that party?**
> **That's the last party you go to for a long while!**

With a reaction like this, Jessica will not be telling her father anything more about what goes on in her social life. It would have been more effective for Dad to wait until she finished the story, then to have asked, in a normal tone of voice, about the presence of alcohol at the party.

G **No matter how relevant you think it is, don't relate the situation to your youth.** Teens just do not believe that anything that happened 20 or more years ago has relevance to today. If you want to test this, just start a sentence with, "When I was your age . . ." and see what happens. You will either get a groan or a glassy-eyed stare that indicates that the teen has tuned out. This does not mean that there is no relevance to your experience as a teen. By all means use it to help you understand how the teen feels — just don't say anything. It won't help and it may shut down the conversation.

H **If told something in confidence, keep it to yourself.** This can be a tricky one, especially if the teen says, "Don't tell dad but . . ." This can be difficult for mom. The basic rule, though, is if there is any chance that the story will get out, don't tell anyone. If dad can keep a secret, and not let on he knows anything, then it is usually a good idea for spouses to share the information. However, this is a far as it should go. Parents should not tell the other kids, their friends or even Aunt Martha anything that has been told to them in confidence. If you do, and the information gets out, then nothing more of a confidential nature will ever be told to you again.

For teenagers a parent who can listen is usually enough. Unfortunately, listening alone would not make for effective parenting. There are times for parents when the other part of communication, talking, becomes important in raising teenagers. There are several such times.

One of the most important is when teens are not in a communicative mood. This is often. It was mentioned earlier that teens want to talk to their parents. While this is true, it is not the case all the time. In order to find out what is going on in a teenager's life it is often necessary to ask. Even this is not usually a straightforward process with teens. Questions often receive monosyllabic answers as in, "How was your day," "Fine." The technique of asking more and more detailed questions until a conversation gets started is important for all parents of teens to learn. Teens are not good conversationalists much of the time, so parents need to get the ball rolling. To be able to ask questions, parents must know what is going on in their teens' lives. Here is an ideal conversation to illustrate the point.

Mom: *How was school today?*
Michelle: *Fine.*
Mom: *How was art class?*
Michelle: *Why?*
Mom: *Well didn't you have a disagreement with the teacher last class?*
Michelle: *Yeah. She said I didn't hand in my project and I did.*
Mom: *Well did you get things straightened out?*
Michelle: *Yes — finally. She found my project under her desk.*
It must have been accidentally knocked on the floor.
She apologized so everything's OK now.

In this case it took two questions to get communication going, and it was important that Michelle's mother knew 1) that Michelle had art that day, as options are usually not scheduled every day, and 2) that Michelle had had a problem in that class. The fine art of questioning is vital to communication and parents should not be afraid to interrogate a bit when conversation is not forthcoming.

Another time talking is necessary is when a point needs to be made. Usually this occurs when the teen has done something wrong. In this case it is important for parents to realize that their youngsters usually are well aware of what they have done wrong. There is generally no need to rehash the details of the crime in the form of the dreaded *lecture*. Instead, all that is necessary is to state the problem and quickly determine the consequences. This can be done unilaterally, as in, "You were one hour late, so you will have to be home one hour earlier tomorrow night." Another method is one of consultation such as, "You were one hour late for curfew last night, what do you think the consequence should be?" Another vital aspect of making your point as a parent is to stay calm. As soon as parents lose their temper, the teen will quickly respond in a similar manner. The next chapter will go into more detail, but suffice it to say that teenagers are highly emotional beings. You do not want to initiate a shouting match; you just want to deal with the situation effectively.

Talking is also necessary when teens fail to carry out their responsibilities. A later section will deal in detail with how to handle this type of situation. For now, strictly looking at communication, it is important to distinguish the fine line between reminding and nagging. A teenager accepts reminding, whereas nagging makes them mad. Both are methods of communicating, but nagging irritates teens (actually, it irritates everyone), whereas reminding, while not accepted joyfully, is at least accepted as being fair. The difference between the two is mainly in the tone of voice and the frequency with which the reminder is given. In nagging, parents usually use a tone of frustration and irritation that communicates itself clearly to the teen. In fact the irritation seems to spill over to them so that the teen becomes defensive and answers in a like tone. Then the parents get angry (the old, "Don't talk to me in that tone of voice," bit) and the battle is on. There is a difference also in the frequency of the communication. Reminding can become nagging when done with too short an interval between the reminders.

The most effective way to keep from nagging is to use humor in your reminders. Keep them light by making a little joke of it. The teen will get the point and will not become defensive. A simple example would be, "If the grass gets any longer I'll need a machete to get to the garden." Another line might be "I'll be back in a few minutes. I'm going out to buy some more dishes. Ours are all dirty." These lines are definitely not good enough for the Comedy Channel, but they keep the situation light while getting the message across. Teens are not good at doing chores, so these reminders are necessary until the job gets done.

While on the subject of talking to teens, there are two guidelines that should be followed no matter what the occasion is. First, parents should try to talk to their teenagers on an almost equal basis, rather than talking down to them. Basically this involves giving reasons for your parental decisions rather than just telling the kids what to do. One of the distinguishing features of teenagers is that their reasoning abilities are far more developed than those of younger children. They not only can understand more complex ideas, they virtually demand reasons for actions. Wise parents give these reasons.

The other guideline is to avoid yelling in all circumstances. Teens hate it, perhaps because it is a way of treating them like children, just as talking down to them is. They usually yell back, which results in an argument. When parents stay calm, the situation has a better chance of being resolved. The teen may lose control, but as long as the parent doesn't, hard feelings are usually avoided.

Guidelines for Talking to Teens

1 *Expand the conversation by asking more and more specific questions.*
2 *Avoid lecturing. Make your point briefly and drop it.*
3 *Don't nag. Remind with humor until the job is done.*
4 *Try not to talk down to teens. Give reasons for your decisions.*
5 **Don't yell!**

This section on communication is long because the topic is so vital. This is the real key to the "Hear Me" part of the formula. If you can communicate with teens, you don't even have to understand them that well. Listen effectively, and talk when necessary and teens will think you're a wonderful parent.

3 Fairness

"My parents are so unfair.
They never listen to anything that I have to say.
They must think I'm stupid or something."
— Billy

This is one of the traits of the "ideal parent" that falls into more than one category. It falls into the "Hear Me" section because teens often think things are unfair when their opinions are not being listened to or when they have no input into family or classroom decisions. Their desire to have an identity of their own, separate from that of their parents gives them a belief that they should have a say in decisions. In other words, teens are developing their own opinions, ideas and beliefs, and they feel that these should be heard. Their budding social conscience quickly picks up inequities in treatment and their impulsiveness causes them to point them out. If parents and teachers are not willing to listen and to take their suggestions seriously or if they are not willing to explain their actions, then they are, in teens' eyes, being unfair.

The areas of unequal treatment most often mentioned by teens are being dealt with very differently than their siblings or peers and not being seen as an individual. These areas will be reviewed in more detail in the "Hug Me" section, but the key here is that teens need to be listened to when they detect apparent inequities.

4 Respect

> **"Never look down on anybody unless you're helping him up."**
> — Jesse Jackson,
> *20th-century American political activist, preacher*

As discussed in the section above, teens are able to think more abstractly than they could as young children, and are able to develop opinions, ideas, beliefs and dreams. For teenagers, respect means that parents not only listen to their ideas but actually give them some consideration. Once again, the *listening* aspect of this trait is what places "respect" in the "Hear Me" section. Teens don't even mind if parents don't accept everything they say, as long as they at least consider it and then give valid reasons for the rejection.

For example, say a 98-pound teenage boy tells his parents that he wants to play middle linebacker on the high school football team. If dad responds "No way. You're too small," then no respect for his son's dreams has been shown. The son will probably become angry and defensive. A more respectful reply might be to ask what interested him about this position. That could lead to a discussion of the various positions, and may give dad an opportunity to tactfully mention the size problem. If no such opportunity presents itself, then the best approach would be to let the boy try out and discover the problem himself. Unfortunately it is the nature of teenagers to have to find out a lot of things for themselves.

Respect for them as real people is extremely important to teens as the story below illustrates. Listening effectively to teens' ideas and opinions is a vital aspect of showing this respect.

Jodi's Story

Respect for a teenager as a real person may not seem like a major concern. Other problems, such as communication and discipline usually appear to be more important. While this is often true, in Jodi's case lack of respect caused a major breakdown in family relations.

The local family court referred Jodi to a psychologist because she refused to see her father anymore. Her parents divorced when she was one year old, with her mother gaining custody. Her father had visitation rights on Wednesday evenings and every other weekend. At 10 years of age Jodi started trying to get out of visiting her dad by making excuses. She would refuse to talk to him on the telephone, and pretend that she was sick on his weekends. At 11 she refused to go to his place at all, and the father took Jodi's mother to court, saying that she was causing the problem by encouraging Jodi not to see him. He also felt that Jodi preferred to be at her mother's place because there was less discipline there.

While Jodi was not yet a teenager, she was certainly exhibiting many of the "symptoms." She was very mature for her age and extremely articulate. In her sessions with the psychologist it quickly became clear that there definitely was discipline in the mother's home and, while the mother was not particularly supportive of the dad, she was not denigrating him in her daughter's presence. Jodi very clearly stated that the problem was that her dad always treated her more as an object than as a person. He never consulted her about their activities together, and never gave reasons for his actions. For example, he refused to let her use the phone one day, but gave no rationale for this decision. Being treated in this way made it a demeaning experience to go to his place. When this was added to the normal teenage concerns about visitations, such as missing friends, two systems of discipline and constant packing, the result was a complete refusal to see her father any more.

Respect for a teenager as a person may not usually be the most important of the parenting traits, but in this case it definitely was.

5 Honesty

"We deserve to know the truth. Usually they don't tell you the
truth because they're trying to protect you and not hurt you.
They think we're too young to handle the truth.
I think a family would be better if everyone was open."
— *Jane*

This parenting trait is closely allied with respect. By being honest with their teens, parents are showing respect for their ability to reason and understand. This is particularly true when family problems occur. Many parents try to shield their children from such concerns as a close family member with a terminal illness or a parental job loss by denying that there is anything wrong. Unfortunately this rarely works because teens can usually tell when there are problems in the family. Often they will not know the nature of the problem, just that there is something seriously wrong. This can result in their jumping to conclusions that may be far worse than the actual problem.

Honesty is included in the "Hear Me" part of the approach because by leveling with teens about family problems it makes parents more human and trustworthy and therefore more approachable. Teens will then feel more comfortable talking to their parents and discussing their own problems.

Hug Me

"We need our parents because no matter how often they
make us mad we still need them as a sense of security.
We need to be loved."
— *Kristi*

As will be discussed in more detail in Chapter 2, the teenage years are the most insecure of a person's life. In trying to develop their own identities, teens have to cast off the role of being someone's child. The identity that once came from their daddy being a fireman or their mother being a nurse is gone and nothing has yet replaced it. Teens are in an identity "no man's land," which will not fully change until they have a set of personality traits and a career of their own.

The result is a highly insecure individual who needs the support and caring of parents. The "Hug Me" parenting traits are all ways of showing that parents love their teens and are behind them in all circumstances.

1 Caring

"Parents should once in a while give you a hug and say
'I love you' or out of the blue give a surprise party or a gift."
— Mitch

The most obvious way a parent can express their love for their children is to actually demonstrate affection. Hugs themselves are the best. These should not be reserved for when the youngster has done something good. They should be given anytime, such as when passing in the hall or while sitting watching TV. Some teens get embarrassed when hugged in front of friends, but if the family is in the habit of hugging frequently, the kids generally get used to it.

Teenagers also appreciate verbal expressions of affection. "You're a great kid," or, "I'm lucky to have you for a son," or any words to this effect will be appreciated by your children. Mind you, don't expect words of thanks in return. Most teens are a little embarrassed by open affection and will probably just say something like, "Oh mom," or, "You have to say that — you're my dad." Don't worry that this means they don't appreciate the words of affection. They always do.

"Sometimes just the little things count, like taking me to a
soccer game or driving me to the mall. Making me dinner and
washing my dirty clothes are other ways they show me they care.
Asking me how my day was and helping me with homework
or just giving me a hug are other ways my parents show
their love towards me."
— Jeannette

Another expression of affection can come by way of little treats or presents. Gifts are almost always appreciated by teens, whether or not there is a real occasion. In fact they are especially valued if there is no occasion at all. At times when gifts are expected, such as Christmas or birthdays, not giving a gift is disastrous as teens make a direct connection between remembering to buy presents and caring. In most families this is not a problem, but in divorced or separated families, the non-custodial parent can easily forget an occasion. This is very hard on teens. While gifts should never be used as a substitute for spending time with the teen, they are definitely part of the caring picture when used in conjunction with the other signs of affection.

2 Discipline

While it might seem at first that a huge mistake has been made by putting "discipline" in the "Hug Me" section, it is definitely in the right place. Parents who do not care don't take the time or expend the energy that is required to discipline their children. Even teens know that by setting rules and by giving consequences when the rules are broken, parents are displaying their love for them. While this principle seems relatively straightforward, disciplining teens is probably the most difficult part of raising them, and is the area where most arguments start. There are two main aspects to the disciplinary process, setting rules and meting out consequences.

A Rules

> *"I really hate it when I ask my parents if I can do something*
> *and they just say 'no' without giving a reason.*
> *Or if they tell me rules without giving a reason.*
> *If they just give me fair enough reasons, I will obey the rules."*
> — *Kristina*

Rules are necessary for teens both for their safety and to teach them the self-discipline that they will need in the future when there are on their own. Curfews, for example, help to minimize the chances that a teen will get into trouble by staying out too late; the longer they are out with their friends, the more chance there is that something could go wrong. Curfews also help to ensure that a teen gets enough sleep, and they help to teach time management. Along with curfews, family rules need to be in place in such areas as telephone use, TV times, bedtimes, homework, manners and chores.

Once it is realized that rules are important for so many reasons, it becomes necessary to actually set them. This is harder than it may seem. Even though teens generally understand that they need rules, and even though they are aware that this shows that their parents care about them, they will still get extremely upset if they perceive that the rules are not fair. While fairness is a highly subjective concept, there are some guidelines that need to be followed if arguments and rebellion are to be avoided. These guidelines are discussed in detail in the section called "Setting the Rules."

Rules are the bedrock on which an effective disciplinary system is built. Once clear rules are in effect, it is vital that they be enforced, and that consequences be applied when they are broken.

B Consequences

"My Mom says she will punish us but she never does.
Parents should go through with what they say they're going
to because if they don't their kids will lose respect for them."
— Laura

It's a fascinating fact of teen behavior that even when they know they need rules and agree to what those rules should be, they still manage to break them frequently. There are several reasons for this. These include peer pressure, absent-mindedness, impulsiveness and just plain testing the limits. While most of these are self-explanatory, the last is confusing to parents. It seems that sometimes teens just have to test to see if their parents really do mean what they say. Inside they want the rules to be enforced, because it makes them feel more secure and shows them that their parents really do love them. In fact, they become very disappointed if they break a rule and nothing happens. No matter what caused the transgression, consequences need to be applied as swiftly as possible. The only excuse for postponing punishment occurs when parents are too frustrated and angry to make a rational decision. Then it's best to say, "We'll talk about this in the morning."

Even though teens want consequences when they've done wrong, do not expect them to thank you after you've handed down the sentence. They'll complain, whine, argue and sometimes even shout.

Fear not! This is just the need to establish their identity kicking in. At this point the teen is reminding you that they are growing up and are not a little kid anymore, so now they can protest your decisions. This protest, assuming the consequences handed out are reasonable, is mainly a ritual, but this is when you have to have faith that you're doing the right thing. You are — and the thanks will come 10 years from now. Don't let yourself be sucked into an argument, or into losing your temper. Stay calm and firm.

As in setting rules, there are some definite guidelines to follow to make this process a little easier on parents. No good parent enjoys this part of the disciplinary process, so it makes sense to keep the process as easy on you as possible. See the section on "Sentencing the Culprit" for a complete overview of how to set consequences (relatively) painlessly.

3 Fairness

> *"My parents are never unfair.*
> *They always listen to hear my side of the story."*
> — *Jessica*

Rules and consequences for breaking them are a major component of the "Hug Me" part of this parenting approach. They are also the major cause of teens crying, "That's not fair!" Fairness was discussed in the "Hear Me" section because having their opinions, ideas and beliefs heard is important to teens. It is equally as important to listen to teen concerns when it comes to discipline, because this too shows that you care about them.

There are several areas of concern to teens when it comes to the interplay of discipline and fairness. One occurs when parents are too arbitrary or inflexible. There are some circumstances that call for leniency or complete forgiveness for the transgression. In order to determine if leniency is called for, parents have to listen to the reason why the problem occurred. Often parents are so angry when they confront their teen they are unwilling to listen to an explanation. Every once in a while the teen has a good reason for what happened and no consequences are necessary. For example, if the teen is over an hour late for curfew because the parent who was supposed to drive them home did not show up on time, then this was not the teen's fault and the punishment can be dispensed with.

"My parents are really unfair when it comes to my brothers and sister. Whenever they do something wrong my parents come to me and start yelling at me. I have no idea why."

— *Hanna*

Another area of concern to teenagers when it comes to rules and consequences occurs when there is unequal treatment of siblings. Girls are often given stricter rules than are their brothers simply because of the gender difference. This is perceived as unfair, even though parents seem to have good reasons for their decisions. Similarly, younger siblings often have much stricter rules than did the older family members when they were younger. Teens have good memories when it comes to family rules. If older brother had a bedtime of 10 PM when he was 14 and the younger child still has to go to bed at 9 PM now that he has turned 14, then unfairness is perceived. This situation often happens because parents simply do not think to change the rules on a regular basis. In other circumstances they have good reasons for their decisions, but have not shared them with the teen. Teens are not usually good communicators. They are often unable to bring up their concerns. Instead they display rebellious behavior, hoping their parents will see the light. Unfortunately this does not always happen.

When setting rules, parents would be wise to check with other parents to see what the norm is . . .

Inequalities between peers are also a common reason for the teens to cry foul. If most of their friends can stay out to 11 PM on weekend nights, and they have to be home by 9 PM, then the teen feels unfairly dealt with. When setting rules, parents would be wise to check with other parents to see what the norm is in order to have a basis for comparison. If rules are set in consultation with teens, and parents know what is most common, then this type of unfairness is unlikely to occur. If you believe that the general standards are too lax then by all means set the rules where you think they should be. Just remember that if they deviate greatly from the norm, you will have a very unhappy teen in your household, and rebellious or angry behavior may be frequently displayed.

These concerns will be discussed in greater detail in the sections on "Setting the Rules" and "Sentencing the Culprit."

4 Spending time with your teen

*"I want parents who take you places
instead of leaving you home all the time."*
— *Rashid*

Along with discipline, this is one of the parenting traits that can be very confusing. On the one hand, teens want to be more independent and to spend more time with their friends. On the other they want to spend time with their parents. Obviously, some sort of balance needs to be found. The important point to remember here is that teens do want to be with their parents, far more often than most people think. Taking the time to be with their teenagers rather than doing household chores or taking part in adult activities such as golf or committee meetings is a clear sign to teens that their parents love them. The secret is in finding that right balance.

Achieving this balance is not really that difficult. It simply involves communication (again). Teens have minds of their own and make plans of their own. If parents make conflicting plans involving their teens, then problems occur. If the parents suddenly announce plans to go camping for the weekend when a major teen party is scheduled for the same time, then the teens will complain. Parents then get the idea that their teens would rather be with their friends. Not so. They just want to go to that particular party. If, on the other hand, the parents had sat down with the teens well ahead of time to plan when they should go camping and where they should camp, then the situation would be entirely different. Then the teens would be looking forward to the trip, since they have helped plan it.

*"I'd like my parents to spend time with me when I need help
or when I'm lonely or just when I need someone to talk to. I like to do
most things with them — walking, swimming but mostly just talking."*
— *Megan*

This is not to say that spontaneous activities are not possible with teens. They definitely are. It's just that parents can't always count on their teens being enthusiastic about doing things with them if they haven't been consulted. The idea is to keep asking about spur of the moment things, but not to be disappointed if the teen has something else in mind. Going shopping together, taking walks, and going for picnics or trips to the zoo are all things that teens have indicated they enjoy. It's just that often they want these activities to be more on their terms than they did a few years previously. Parents should definitely keep asking about spontaneous things, and consult their teens about more complex trips and vacations. This strategy will not only show that they care about their teens, but will result in some great times together.

5 Humor

"A sense of humor is important in a parent. When I'm feeling sad my dad tells me a joke to get me out of my mood."
— Donna

To ask that parents be humorous seems like a very strange request. How can humor possibly relate to parenting? The answer is that humor takes the edge off many tense situations and makes them more bearable. Teens realize that parents who take the time and effort to make a joke, no matter how lame, are showing they care about them. These parents are showing a more human, or softer side, of themselves that helps teens to accept disciplinary situations. Parents who deal with these situations with anger or sternness seem not to care about the teen; they seem to care only that the job gets done or the teen is punished. Many parents believe that injecting humor into what to them is a serious situation will lessen the effectiveness of their actions. This is not so. As long as the consequences are handed out, or a lesson is learned by the teen, then being a little bit funny will only help the situation. The use of humor seems to be a small thing, but it is highly valued by teens.

Some examples might be useful. As we will see in a later section, teens know that chores are good for them, they just are not very good at actually doing them. Nagging only leads to arguments, but if humor is used in reminding teens of their responsibilities, anger and resentment are usually avoided. Saying something like, "How about taking the garbage out before the city shuts down our kitchen for sanitation violations," is far more effective than, "Take that garbage out NOW!" It is a gentler more caring approach than the dictator style. Both get the job done, but one way leads to anger while the other might even get a chuckle. The lines don't have to be hilarious; they just have to take the edge off the situation.

Another situation where humor keeps the circumstances from getting too tense is when there has been a minor disciplinary infraction. A line like, "Did your bus get hijacked to Cuba or something?" will get the point across that you are concerned about your teen's lateness. It also gives the teenager a chance to explain, since a hijacking will only rarely be the actual cause of tardiness. Yelling, "Where the ____ have you been?" sets the scene for an argument, as the youngster will immediately be on the defensive and can quickly become emotional.

The use of humor in tense situations shows that parents care about their teens because they are obviously trying to avoid confrontation. It shows their loving parent side rather than their stern disciplinarian side. Teens appreciate this difference in approach and will usually respond in kind. It is better that they be groaning at your weak attempt at humor than yelling at you for being unfair. The home will be more relaxed and the family will function far more effectively.

> *"I can joke with my parents and even present some snide comments.*
> *Of course, I have to put up with their comments back too."*
> — *Nguyen*

6 Setting an example

> *"My mom smokes and I hate it. Every time she comes to hug me or even*
> *within a 10-yard radius it makes me feel sick. She knows it but doesn't*
> *try real hard to quit. If you're a parent, don't smoke."*
> — *Stephanie*

This is one of the traits of the "ideal" parent that is often overlooked. Parents can show that they care about their teens by actually living the characteristics that they're trying to instill in their kids. Teens do not want their parents to be the same as their friends; they want them to be better. The "do as I say not as I do" approach does not work with teens because they want to know why they should not be like their parents. While there are often good reasons, when parents are smokers and do not want their kids to get hooked, actually setting an example works much better. Teens do not want their parents to be hypocrites. Instead, they want to be able to look up to them.

The areas where examples need to be set by parents were identified as fighting, yelling, swearing, drinking and smoking. These are quite basic. They don't involve any complex philosophies, they just require some basic common sense. Parents fighting either in front of the kids or in their hearing make it difficult for a teen to understand why she can't fight with her brother — especially when he's such a little brat. Dad's swearing while working on a do-it-yourself project makes the use of profanity seem justified in frustrating situations. These are not complicated issues, but they are ones that require self-control. This is exactly what teens want to see in their parents.

> *One of the most important aspects of being a parent is to pass on a set of values to the children that will help them to live productive and effective lives.*

By practicing what they preach, parents are helping to reinforce the moral code that they should be teaching to their children. One of the most important aspects of being a parent is to pass on a set of values to the children that will help them to live productive and effective lives. This should be done throughout their childhood by telling them the difference between right and wrong, giving consequences for doing illegal or immoral things and finally by setting an example by not doing these things themselves. As has been said several times, teens differ from young children in their ability to reason. They easily pick up any discrepancies between words and actions. The old saying "actions speak louder than words" certainly applies here. Teens tend to take actions much more seriously than talk, and will follow their parents' example rather than listening to what they say.

Parents setting a good example for their teens falls in the "Hug

Me" section because it clearly shows that the parent cares enough about the teen to display self-control. While this can be very difficult at times (especially when you're trying to follow instructions written by someone who already knows how to do something) self-control is certainly worthwhile practicing while the children are growing up. Teens definitely appreciate it and will learn more from this example than from any other source.

Showing teens that you care about them obviously has many facets and that might make it seem difficult to do. All it really involves, however, is some thought and planning both for and with your teens. It also involves some self-sacrifice, especially when it comes to spending time with them. All this should not really be too difficult as most parents really do love their kids — it's just a matter of clearly showing it.

Trust Me

> *"Most of my parents' rules are reasonable but a lot of them*
> *really stink. Things like, 'You're not responsible enough to do this,*
> *this and this.' But they haven't even given me a chance to prove myself."*
> — Mike

The previous section stresses the insecurity of teens and their need for signs of affection from their parents. Their need to be trusted illustrates the contrasting side of teenagers, namely their growing need for independence and the need to establish their own identity, separate from that of their parents. To find this identity teens need increasing amounts of freedom and to be able to make more and more decisions for themselves. This is one of the most difficult and frightening aspects of raising a teenager because it means that parents have to sit home worrying while they allow their teens out into the big, scary world. It is also a very important aspect of the parenting process. Without being given the chances to make their own mistakes, teens will not grow up to be confident, secure individuals. Instead they will need to rely on others to make their decisions and to tell them how to live their lives. The development of trust is therefore a vital constituent of raising teenagers.

1 Trust

Building trust between parent and teen has several key components. The first is to actually *tell them that they are trusted.* That seems simple enough, but typically teens have to hear it often, and parents have to find places to fit a statement of trust into a conversation. It is also important that parents really mean it when they tell their teens that they are trusted. Adolescents can see right through insincerity, so if parents don't really mean it, they will only make the situation worse.

Another important part of showing teens that they are trusted is to *keep questions about their activities to a minimum.* There are three main questions that *do* need to be answered before a teen goes out. These are: "Where are you going?" "Who are you going with?" and "What time will you be home?" These questions are important because they help parents if something actually does go wrong. Parents will know where to look for their kids if they don't come home on time and what other parents to call to see if they know where their teens are. Teenagers should be trained to automatically provide this information and be given the reasons why it is required.

Other than the "Big Three," questions should be limited. When teens get home it is certainly permissible to ask if they had a good time, but otherwise it's best not to make the questions too specific. This is especially true if they went to an activity that they had not previously been allowed to go to, like a rock concert or a mixed party. *If you do not find out otherwise, assume all went well.*

> **"Parents shouldn't be so nosey. I'm sick of them asking me about**
> **every single thing that happens in my life. Maybe sometimes**
> **I don't want to tell them. Do parents really need to know everything?"**
> — *Erica*

Another important component of developing trust between parents and teens is to allow them to make as many decisions on their own as possible. These decisions should be ones that do not involve danger to them, like what to spend their allowance on or what clothes to wear each day. If a fifteen-year-old were to ask to go to an all-night dance party, or "rave," the answer would have to be NO. There are too many chances for things to go wrong at this type of event. Otherwise, let their decisions stand, and allow natural consequences to teach them when the decisions were right. If they spend their entire allowance on a CD right after they receive it, then the natural consequence is that they have no money for the rest of the week.

Kimberly's problem is typical: "I never get to fill out my option form at school. My father always does and all the options he makes me take I'm bad at and I don't like." Not only is Kimberly not allowed to choose her own options, she does not even get any input into these choices. You can imagine how well she does in these subjects.

It's often difficult for parents to know for certain whether or not an activity is potentially dangerous. If in doubt, homework needs to be done to check it out. Call other parents, the school counselor or the teen's favorite teacher. This is especially true in the case of younger teens. Otherwise, whenever possible allow the kids to make their own decisions.

Finally, when teens are allowed the privilege of going to new types of events, parents should not check up on them. Checking can be in the form of calling another parent the next day to see if your child really did do what she said she did, or it can be actually "dropping in" to the event to see if your teen is there. Neither is in the spirit of building trust. If you don't hear anything after an event, assume all went well. Teens will, of course, occasionally make mistakes in judgment. In such a case hand out consequences and start trusting again. It is only when a pattern of errors develops that parents need to start worrying and perhaps seek professional help.

> *"My freedom is important to me and I know what's*
> *right and wrong and usually make the right decisions.*
> *Why can't my parents realize that we are more mature*
> *than they think most of the time so they should trust me?"*
> — *Nadine*

Trust has to start somewhere and it should be with the parents. If teens are not given some privileges so that they can show that they can be trusted, how can parents possibly learn to trust them? The rule for parents is that they should **trust first**. It should not be up to the teens to somehow prove that they can be trusted so that they can be given these privileges. This is one of the most difficult aspects of being the parent of a teenager. Parents tend to remember all the things they did as teenagers that their parents didn't know about, and many of these were probably dangerous. They naturally want to prevent their children from trying dangerous things. Unfortunately, to try too hard will not only not help the teen to become an independent person, but will be seen by the teen as an attempt by their parents to prolong their childhood. Protection of the teen is the reason for the family rules. Once these are set each year, parents must allow their teenagers more and more freedom as they get older and trust that they have raised them well. In other words, as long as the adolescent is home by the curfew, and parents have not heard anything to the contrary, they have to trust that everything happened as the teen says.

The Trusting Process

1 *Tell them you trust them.*
2 *Trust them first — don't make the teens **prove** they can be trusted.*
3 *Let the teens make appropriate decisions.*
4 *Don't ask too many questions.*
5 *Don't check up on them.*
6 *Keep your fingers crossed.*

2 Responsibility

"I babysit, empty the dishwasher and set the table.
I think that's fair because both parents work and they need help."
— *Courtney*

Responsibility is a form of self-discipline where you do not have to be told to do necessary things. If the kitchen dishes have piled up a responsible person does them without being prompted. When the grass insists on growing too long, then it must be cut. A responsible person does this automatically, if not entirely happily. Teens are not yet responsible people. They do need prompting before they will do necessary but not usually enjoyable tasks. While this prompting can be a painful process for parents, it is a necessary if a teen is to develop into a responsible adult.

It is also a necessary process in the development of trust between parent and teen. The more responsible a teen is, the greater the chance that his parent will trust him. In order to display this responsibility, the teen has to have some regular chores and duties. The number and type of these duties will be different for each household. The more children in the family, the more the chores can be spread around. If both parents are working, the teens need to pitch in more than if one parent is home all day. Whatever the circumstances, every teen should have some responsibilities around the house to help them to develop self-discipline.

> *"I have to clean my room and sometimes vacuum.*
> *I also have to take out the garbage. I think I have just enough chores."*
> — *Kent*

Trust develops from responsibility as teens become more and more proficient at doing their chores with minimal prompting. Rare is the case, however, where no reminding at all is necessary. Parents should certainly strive for the situation where all household duties are done automatically; they just shouldn't expect it. The less prompting to do chores that is necessary, the more comfortable parents can be about allowing their teens freedom and privileges.

Included in household responsibilities are homework and school marks. In fact, school performance should be considered a teenager's main responsibility. As with household duties, effective school performance helps to develop trust for teens as it shows that they are taking this responsibility seriously. Parents can then have a higher expectation that, when given a privilege, the teen will act responsibly.

Because of the importance of both home responsibilities and schoolwork, later sections will detail systems for ensuring that both areas are handled effectively by teens.

3 Respect

Respect is one of the traits of good parenting that falls into two categories. Its relevance to the "Hear Me" category has already been discussed. In that case it involved listening to teen opinions, ideas, beliefs and dreams with consideration. In the case of the "Trust Me" group it involves taking a similar approach to their decisions and explanations.

Allowing teens to make their own decisions has already been discussed. If your son insists on dying his hair chartreuse, respect that decision and let his peers make the judgment. This does not mean that you have to agree with his color choice. It is certainly appropriate to give your opinion, just don't forbid the action. Humor is one of the best ways to get your opinion across without breeding defensiveness. A comment like, "I had curtains that color once. It looked great on them but I'm not sure it's you," will make your point without starting an argument. Hair color alone is not life-threatening so why worry about it. One of the best ways to get that color to stay longer is to raise a fuss. Rebellion will then kick in, just to show you that he is his own person.

> *"It's hard to talk to them when they think you're lying but you really are not and they still don't believe you."*
> — Lisa

Explanations for apparent rule infractions are another place where respect is important. If your teen arrives home an hour late for curfew, you are entitled to an explanation. If it sounds reasonable, accept it. There are definitely times when circumstances conspire against teens and cause things to go wrong. Listening carefully to these explanations, and accepting them when they seem reasonable is a sure way to develop trust with your teen. Naturally, common sense needs to be used when accepting explanations. If the same thing happens several times in a row, it means either the teen is lying or she's not learning from past problems. Consequences are probably in order. Also, if the explanation is too difficult to believe, then checking on it is entirely logical. In the main, however, it is best to respect the teen's explanation whenever possible.

Because of the incidents that parents read about in the newspapers and see graphically displayed on TV, they worry about the things that could happen to their teenagers. The natural response is to try to protect them from all these possible harms. Unfortunately there is only so much parents can do. If they do not develop trust in their teens, then the youngsters will either rebel or they will not develop into self-confident, independent adults. The "Trust Me" part of this parenting approach may be the most frightening aspect of the formula, but it is as vital a component of the parenting process as the "Hear Me" or "Hug Me" sections.

When the "Hear Me, Hug Me, Trust Me" Parenting Approach Does Not Work

There are times when despite trying to be the best parent possible, teens get out of control. In these instances it may be that parenting methods are not the problem. There are other reasons that, while rare, may explain your teenager's behavior. Included in this list are such causes as schizophrenia, severe depression or sexual abuse by a relative or family friend. If you are firmly convinced that you are doing everything possible as a parent but you are still having serious problems with your teenager, then it is time to seek professional help. Most of these issues will be dealt with in later sections; read these and try to determine whether or not the problems are a result of your parenting methods or are coming from some other cause. If the latter, get help from a counselor or psychologist.

Chapter 2

What is a Teenager?

In Chapter 1, an important part of the "Hear Me, Hug Me, Trust Me" parenting approach involved understanding teenagers. Knowing the origins of behavior that usually changes radically from when they were preteens helps to remove much of the fear adults have of teenagers and some of the anger that results from their behavior. The power of understanding can be illustrated by the example of the eclipse. Hundreds of years ago, eclipses caused great fear and consternation when they appeared because no one fully understood why they were happening. For lack of any other explanation, eclipses were seen as evil omens or signs of anger by a deity. Now that we know that they are caused by a planet or moon coming between the Earth and the Sun, we actually look forward to seeing them. This is a complete turnaround in attitude caused by knowledge. The same can be true of teenagers. Although they are much harder work than watching an eclipse, and they last much longer, knowing the causes of their behavior, and understanding the stresses they are under, helps parents deal with their behavior more effectively and be less worried about them.

As a friend and I walked down the street one warm spring day, we noticed a lady pushing a baby carriage across the street in front of us. Behind her, pushing an identical carriage but in miniature, was her 4-year-old daughter. My friend turned to me and said, "Isn't that cute. What happens to them when they become teenagers?"

In fact, quite a bit happens as children move into adolescence. Although many parents feel like the process that changes their darling young children into snarling

36

adolescents is the work of an evil being, such is not the case. If it were, a simple exorcism would end the problems created by these would-be adults. Alas nothing this straightforward will work because, rather than being possessed by evil spirits, adolescence is a natural sequence of events that is initiated by the body's hormone system. Incredibly, this process actually has a purpose, which is to prepare the bodies of these young people for reproduction.

Adolescence would not be a problem for either parents or teens themselves if the hormones injected into the child's unsuspecting system only prepared them physically to perpetuate the species. Unfortunately nature is much more complex than this. The problems parents experience with teens generally occur because these same hormones also initiate changes in the personality. These personality changes are mainly directed towards helping teenagers become independent from their parents, which is a necessity if they are eventually to live on their own and raise their own children. Unfortunately, this striving to become independent creates considerable friction in most households, as neither parent nor teen is either fully prepared for these alterations in personality or completely understands why they are happening. This is the origin of the fearsome reputation of the teen years.

Let's examine in detail, then, the complex series of personality changes that these hormones initiate. Later in the chapter there will also be a brief discussion of exactly what these hormones are, and how they work.

What is a Teenager?

Teens Are Highly Emotional

> *"In the last 2 or 3 years my attitude has changed*
> *a lot towards things, especially my parents.*
> *I find myself getting in more arguments with them."*
> — Carly

Apart from physical changes, the clearest sign that your child is becoming a teen is rapid mood swings, characterized by instant anger or tears, as the occasion requires. A towering rage can be touched off by the simple act of disagreeing, no matter how nicely, with the developing adolescent. The unfortunate thing about this is that parents rarely seem to understand the emotional nature of teens, and constantly get sucked into arguments, many of which become very hurtful. Here is a typical example:

Your daughter comes into the room in a very short skirt and belly shirt and the conversation follows this path:

Daughter: *Mom, is this outfit OK to wear to the dance?*

Mom: *Well, it is rather revealing.*

Daughter: *What do you mean "revealing," it's what everyone is wearing.*

Mom: *I don't think you should wear that, the boys will get the wrong idea about you.*

Daughter: *Are you calling me a slut?*

Mom: *No, of course not. You asked me what I thought and I think that it is not an appropriate outfit.*

Daughter: *I hate you. You **never** like what I wear.*

From this point the argument can quickly deteriorate into a shouting match where each side tries to say something hurtful about the other. This can result in several possible actions, including daughter running to her room in tears, mother banning daughter from going to the dance or father stepping in and getting both women mad at him. It is one of many possible examples of no-win situations with highly emotional teenagers. The daughter was in this case either trying to get some attention from her parents or peers, or she was looking for approval. The mother didn't realize this and suddenly she was drawn into an argument that she didn't know how to get out of.

Teens are not staying up late at night planning ways to upset their parents. They just react quickly in highly emotional ways to things that appear to threaten their attempts to become independent.

Hurt feelings, resulting in tears or mild depressive behavior, also easily occur during the teen years. A careless comment from a friend or a member of the opposite sex is all it takes to upset them. This extreme emotionality is responsible for much of the dread that parents have of teenagers. Parents must mentally prepare for the fact that teenagers are going to be very emotional and not take the anger or tears personally. Teens are not staying up late at night planning ways to upset their parents. They just react quickly in highly emotional ways to things that appear to threaten their attempts to become independent. A clear understanding of the emotional nature of teens is necessary for parents, as this will help them to keep from becoming too emotionally involved and thus be able to deal effectively with the crisis at hand rather than becoming a part of it.

"I think I have changed a lot in the last few years because I want to do things and my parents won't let me so I get really mad at them."
— *Chandra*

They're Extremely Insecure

"One thing I would change is my self-esteem,
which will probably get better as I get out of school.
But junior high is hard. You try to be perfect but no one is."
— *Sheena*

Despite a constant façade of thinking they know everything about everything, the teenage years are the most insecure time of a person's life. No teen feels tall enough, smart enough, slim enough, athletic enough, or popular enough. This is why you constantly hear 5 foot 8, 120 pound girls complaining about being "too fat." Unless the teen has an eating disorder, this type of remark is made to get reassurance from peers and parents. Teens can never get enough of this type of support, as they truly feel inadequate most of the time. This insecurity is another result of the teen struggle to gain independence. In trying to establish an identity separate from that of their parents, teens arrive in a never-never land between being an extension of their parents and developing their own persona. They don't yet have a clear idea of who they are, and this makes them feel like a nobody. In defense, they often cover up their insecurities with either a "know-it-all" attitude or an "I don't care" stance. Don't let these cover-ups fool you; inside teens are extremely insecure.

It is this very insecurity that causes them to need the support of their parents so much — right at the time that they seem to be trying to push them away. This is baffling to parents. Their teenage child wants to spend more and more time with friends, and complains whenever you plan an outing, but really wants your love and support? How does this work? Very delicately. A balance has to be found between spending time with your teens and supporting their activities, and giving them the freedom and space they need. Most parents find it hard to believe that teenagers' insecurities cause them to need their parents more than ever; they are confused by all the "pushing away" signals they keep getting. Here is a typical example of teen behavior that illustrates this point.

Monday
Dad: *When is your game this week?*
Son: *Friday night.*
Dad: *Do you want your mom and I to come?*
Son: *It doesn't matter.*

Friday
Son: *Are you coming to my game tonight?*
Dad: *I don't think so, we are probably going over to the Brinkleys' to play bridge.*
Son: *Aw! You never come and watch me play.*

Here we see the "pushing away" signal in the son's apparent lack of concern about whether the parents come to his game or not, and his chagrin when he finds out that his parents took him seriously. He needs to maintain the outward appearance of nonchalance to display his independence. But teens very much need support in all forms — verbal reinforcement, physical signs of affection and attendance at games, recitals and school events. Such support helps to compensate for their profound insecurity at this stage of their lives.

A Teenage Wish List

Here are some of the comments that teens made when asked how they would change themselves if they could:

- I'd have more confidence.
- I'd be taller, even though I'm 5'8".
- I'd have sideburns like Jamie's.
- I'd have more friends.
- I'd be smarter and a better listener.
- One thing I would change is my body. There are many minor things about my body I would like to change.
- I'd change my looks. Even though everyone tells me I am not ugly, I think I am. I have to get a higher self-esteem before I will convince myself.
- I would like to be shorter or be more intelligent.
- I'd change my weight, my figure and my hair.
- I'd change the way I think sometimes, because sometimes I forget to think about my actions before I do them.
- I wish I wouldn't worry about what others think of me.

They Crave Independence

As has already been mentioned, in their struggle to become fully adult teens demand more and more independence. This comes in the form of wanting to make their own decisions about how they spend their spare time, how they spend their money, what clothes they wear and what music they listen to. Teens begin to think of themselves as mature at a relatively early stage because they recognize that they are changing even if their parents often don't. This supposed maturity causes them to think that they are capable of making more of their own decisions than they actually can handle at this age. Tiana's statement provides a clear example of this: "I think I have changed quite a bit because I have matured and become more responsible than I was 2 or 3 years ago. I have learned about responsibility and the troubles of growing up."

Unfortunately, teenagers' lack of maturity and experience in the world causes many of their decisions to be poor ones. Some are made as a result of peer pressure; others are done impulsively. Their insecurities cause them to fiercely defend their choices, no matter how wrong they were. This is a real dilemma for parents as they are often initially reluctant to allow their teens to make their own decisions; they are accustomed to the kids being too young to do this. Growing up catches many parents off guard. When they do, begrudgingly, start to allow their children to make up their own minds about things, they are often rewarded by some poor decisions. This is very discouraging, and leads to frequent arguments.

Bad Choices

Katrina, a tall, attractive 13-year-old was referred for counseling by her father because she was "going downhill." When the counselor investigated this apparent behavior change it was discovered that Katrina had skipped school one day at the insistence of a friend, and during the course of the escapade she had been caught shoplifting a set of false eyelashes. She had been arrested (an unusually severe reaction by the store), and had had to call her father to pick her up at the police station. When asked the reasons for doing these very uncharacteristic things, Katrina replied, "I don't know why I did them, I guess I just made some bad choices." The desire to make her own decisions coupled with teenage impetuosity and some peer pressure gave her a day that she will long remember.

A balance is needed. Parents need to be aware of their teens' need for independence and allow them to make their own choices in areas where the decision can't hurt them. Choosing their own clothes is an example of a choice teens can make with no serious consequences. Setting their own curfews, on the other hand, can lead to dangerous situations and cannot be allowed, at least in the early teen years.

They'll Argue that Black Is White

The combination of teenage emotionality, insecurity and need for independence creates a very dangerous mix. The result is that they argue almost daily. In fact, arguing is often one of the first signs that teenage behavior is beginning. Let's examine how this mixture operates.

As has already been discussed, the need for independence means that teens want to make their own decisions. If a decision or request is questioned by parents or a teacher, as they so often are, teens become defensive and begin to argue their case. The argument is a result of the teens belief that their parents are either not allowing them to make decisions or that their decisions are not being properly respected. Teenage insecurity causes them to feel threatened when their decisions or requests are questioned and they dig in their heels even further. The reasons for this probably revolve around the idea that since they don't have much confidence in themselves socially, it is especially galling when their parents, whom they rely on for security, don't seem to have any confidence in them either. The result is anger when instant agreement is not forthcoming.

The final ingredient in the mixture, their emotionality, usually results in the teen exploding very soon after a decision is questioned or a request is denied. This reaction is virtually reflexive, and generally beyond a teen's control. Tannis recognizes this when she states: "My bad temper would be the first thing to go if I could change anything about myself, because I get so frustrated so easily it sometimes scares me.

Parents need to practice staying calm when their teen explodes. It's not easy, but if the parent can't keep cool when the teen blows up, the result will be a very ugly scene where nasty things get said and no one really comes out the winner. It is important to understand that it is not a personal attack on the parent when a teen begins to argue; factors within the teen are the cause. Keeping this fact in mind will help parents to remain calm in the face of their exploding teen, and the situation will get resolved much more amicably.

> *It is important to understand that it is not a personal attack on the parent when a teen begins to argue. Factors within the teen are the cause.*

They Can't Look Ahead in Life

One of the most puzzling aspects of teenagers is their inability to look ahead in their lives. Their lack of experience in life, combined with their blustering, apparent overconfidence, leaves them without the ability to plan for their futures. Teens, especially younger ones, live for today, and belittle any attempt to get them to look forward. Ask any ninth grade class what careers they would like and the most unrealistic answers result. Of a class of thirty, five want to be lawyers, four others doctors, and the rest just want to be rich. There is a definite readiness factor associated with the ability to plan ahead, and most teens are not yet there.

Parents need to realize that because most teens are incapable of planning ahead, they are not yet ready to take control of their lives. Arguments based on reason and logic about the future, designed to either convince a teen to stay in school or to better his or her grades, will not work. This means that parents must maintain more control over their children's lives than they might expect. Teenagers are not yet ready to make major decisions about what courses they should take in high school, whether or not to drop out of courses, or even how long they should work on assignments or study for exams. Parents must therefore stay heavily involved in any areas that might impact their child's future.

They Spend Too Much Time with Their Friends. Why Do They Wear Those Clothes? And Turn Down That Music!

While hormones initiate teenagers' need for independence, this need actually shows itself in several ways, all of which seem to appear at about the same time. The intense desire to be with friends is one of the clearest and most puzzling for parents. Suddenly friends become so important that the teens see them all day in school, visit them after school then talk on the telephone with them as long as their parents will let them. Many parents become resentful, feeling that these teens are replacing them in their child's affections. There are several possible explanations for this phenomenon and these will be discussed in detail in a later chapter. For now it is enough to state that parents need to be aware that the change in status of friends is a normal component of the teenage years and that, while there need to be some controls put in place, the situation need not be resented.

"Friends are really important to me because good friends will always be there for you no matter what happens. You have fun with them and they'll always help you. Without them the world would be a total wreck."
— *Amanda*

Another way in which teenagers attempt to establish their own identities is through their choice of clothing. Not only do they become very fashion conscious, but the fashions they choose need to be very different from what their parents might choose for them. This extreme fashion sense eloquently states, "Hey look at me. I'm a separate person Practical sweaters from Aunt Edna, and warm sensible jackets carefully selected by mom and dad, remain in the back of the closet, while whatever is the present rage (usually what is worn by rock stars, actors or professional athletes) is worn again and again. Often clothing becomes the focus of a pitched battle when parents decide to take a stand, only to be confronted by a near-hysterical teen who just knows that to wear what her parents suggest would be social suicide. Teens rarely see that in striving to be different, they are all wearing the same type of clothing — in fact, they are conforming with each other. Even if they would admit this, the conformity is far less important than being seen to be different from the adults. Teens are subject to peer pressure, as Michelle very candidly states: "Well, like everyone else I want to fit in with the crowd. Your friends tell you if you look good or not and if it's in style or if it's cool, so I guess they do have an influence on what I wear.

While clothing is only occasionally the focus of teen/parent conflict, music almost always is. Both the style and the volume frequently become the subjects of major disagreements. This has probably been the case since Mozart's parents told him to play his harpsichord more quietly. To be popular with teens, music has to be disliked by parents. This helps the teens to be different and to establish that all-important identity. Fortunately there has never been any evidence that music corrupts young minds — just their eardrums. Parents are well advised to steer clear of this area, unless the tunes have lyrics that are clearly in violation of the family moral code.

The change in status of friends, wearing "fashionable" clothing and listening to loud, weird music are all signs of children trying to become adults. When understood and when subject to some necessary guidelines, these behaviors become less threatening and more tolerable. The understanding of all three of these subjects is so vital to family harmony that they will all be discussed in detail later in this book.

They Begin to Notice the Opposite Sex

The one aspect of teenagers that parents usually do expect is their developing interest in the opposite sex. They expect, and indeed even hope, that their children will have an active and enjoyable social life, as parents can remember many of their own adventures with the opposite sex. What they don't expect though, are all the difficulties that surround this interest — and there are many of these.

One of the first noticeable signs of a burgeoning interest in having a boyfriend or girlfriend is the increase in telephone traffic, often surrounded by considerable secrecy. Calls will rarely be taken on the kitchen phone if others are present; teens instead will migrate to the telephone with the most privacy. Parents with just one telephone line beware — it will be busy a lot, and calls will almost never be for you. Calls will no longer be strictly informational, as in, "What are we doing tonight?" they will now become social, as in, "Did you see what Cindy was wearing today?" All subjects will be discussed at great length to the detriment of homework, chores and your own telephone time. Of course the phone traffic would increase with the teen years anyway, as they come to rely more on their friends, but with the addition of calls to and from the opposite sex, the telephone time can easily double. This trend, although it may seem trivial, can actually cause huge arguments. Parents need to have a policy in place, and then expect the unexpected if they hope to have telephone peace in the family.

A less anticipated side effect of the developing interest in relationships with members of the other gender can often be a change in friends. This generally occurs more often in females, but can happen to males as well. This change, from friends of many years' standing to a completely new group, is usually the result of differing rates of maturity. If one teen starts becoming interested in an active social life, including parties and dances, while the other members of the group still prefer their own company, that teen will soon find others who share the same interests. This can be devastating for teens who are left behind as they rarely understand what they have done to lose an old friend. The fact is they have done nothing, the friend has just started to change interests, again due to hormonal changes. Depressions and crying spells can be the result, and parents need to have some understanding of this type of situation if they are to be able to help their teen cope.

Depression can also result in another, more easily understandable way — being dumped. Teens do not maintain relationships long. Most are measured in days. Nevertheless, being dumped still hurts. Remember that teens are highly insecure and a relationship that ends unsatisfactorily is seen as a rejection. Parents who trivialize the importance of the incident, while trying to help their teen overcome the resulting depression, can do more harm than good. Each failed relationship is seen at the time to be the end of the world, even though parents know that recovery will likely be swift. A sympathetic response from parents to these earth-shattering events can do no harm, and will help to develop good communication with teens. This can be extremely useful later if serious events do occur.

A Typical Telephone Tale

It was 7:30 PM and Jeannie had been on the telephone with a friend for almost an hour. Her dad, who was expecting a call, was becoming increasingly frustrated and the conversation went as follows:

Dad: *Jeannie, is your homework done?*
Jeannie: *Not yet dad.*
Dad: *Well, get off the phone and get it done.*
Jeannie: *OK, dad.*

15 minutes later:
Dad: *Jeannie, are you off that phone yet.*
Jeannie: *Just a minute dad.*
Dad: *No more "Just a minutes," I need the phone.*
Jeannie: *But Chrissy was just telling me something really important.*
Dad: *I don't care how important it was, get off the phone.*
Jeannie (begrudgingly): *All right.*

10 minutes later:
> Dad: *Jeannie get off that phone right now.*
>
> *Jeannie: Dad, I told you it was important.*
>
> Dad (loudly): **Your homework isn't done and I need the phone —
> get off now!**
>
> *Jeannie: Why do you have to be so mean? You never let me talk to
> my friends.*
>
> Dad (even louder): **What do you mean never? You've been on the
> phone for almost an hour-and-a-half.**
>
> *Jeannie: You never understand. You don't care about my friends.*
> **I hate you!**
>
> Dad: **That's it! You're grounded for two weeks.
> Go to your room.**

*A simple incident turns into a family battle. How to handle telephone
problems will be discussed in detail later in the book.*

They Need Their Privacy

*"I really need my privacy sometimes. My parents always want me
to be with the family, but I don't see any need to build relationships.
I just need to be alone sometimes."*
— Carrie

Carrie speaks for many teenagers with these words. Whether it's the
relatively frantic pace at which they live, or whether it's just a physical
necessity brought on by their hormones, it is a fact that teens need
frequent "time-outs" from the world. This usually takes the form of
barricading themselves in their rooms with the stereo blaring, but it
is still a form of withdrawal from social contact. The apparent need
for privacy is very puzzling for parents. Indeed, it often angers them,
perhaps because they take it as a personal rejection. After all, it was
just a few months ago that their children stuck to them like a zebra
mussel. Suddenly they are disappearing into their rooms for hours
on end — often doing nothing at all.

Once again it is important for parents to recognize these retreats as a normal part of teenage existence. There is no personal message of rejection. As long as homework and chores are being done, and obligations such as music lessons and practices are being attended, there should be no problem letting them "veg out" for a while.

Disorganization Is a Way of Life

While there are always exceptions, most teens live in a world of relative chaos. Bedrooms are usually the most obvious sign of this trait. Others are lost assignments, forgotten lunches (although sometimes this is on purpose), and notebooks that look like rats' nests. Boys are usually more disorganized than girls, but all share this attribute to some extent. In fact, parents should worry more about "neat-freaks" than disorganized and messy teens, as the few that are extremely organized are often tense and anxious as well.

The reason that most teenagers are disorganized is probably rooted in their emotionality and relatively short attention spans. Thinking sequentially, which is necessary to being well organized, seems to be extremely difficult for them. Suggesting to a teen that he should make up a study schedule for the upcoming exams thus becomes a baffling task. Teenage brains seem to jump around a lot, rather than following a sequence of steps.

Understanding this aspect of teens helps parents to keep from getting angry when their teenager's disorganization creates family problems. It does not mean that parents should do the organization themselves. Instead it means that patience is required to teach and re-teach organizational skills. Detailed discussions of messy bedrooms and learning to do chores are found in later chapters.

Dumb and Dumber

An inescapable fact about teenagers is that they often do "dumb" things. For a variety of reasons they miss curfews, shoplift, get drunk, skip school or drive wildly. When questioned after making such a mistake, they can almost always tell you why what they did was wrong. This really confuses parents — if they know after the fact what was wrong with their actions, why did they still do it?

The answer to this question goes back to two of the basic attributes of most teenagers — they are emotional, and they are insecure. The same hormones that often are responsible for anger and depression can also cause impulsiveness and acting without thinking. Flip Wilson would have explained this tendency by saying, "The devil made me do it." The teens themselves don't understand it, and therefore cannot explain why they took the action they did.

The Flood

Walking down the hall of a local junior high school, a teacher noticed water running out from under the door of a science room. The door was locked, and by the time he had located the classroom teacher, the entire room and a large part of the hallway had been flooded. The cleanup took the caretakers and teachers over an hour. An investigation by the vice-principal quickly unearthed a surprising culprit. Jimmy, a quiet A-student, had caused the flood by turning on the tap of the teacher's sink as he left the classroom. He didn't notice that the sink was plugged with discarded paper towels, and so had not intended to cause a flood. When asked why he did such an atypical thing he could only reply, "It just popped into my head."

Insecurity becomes a factor in what we will now call "impulsive acts" when others influence teens into doing them. This is often called "peer pressure." While in fact, many parents blame this phenomenon on teens' behavior more often than they should, it certainly does occur. Teen insecurity often makes it difficult to say no to what they perceive to be a more popular friend. When the friend suggests an action that the teen would normally not do, the teenager does it anyway, just to keep the friend's favor.

Whether teens do impulsive things on their own or because of others, it is important that parents understand that it is part of their nature to do them. This does not mean that the act is merely shrugged off with a "teens will be teens" kind of attitude. They must learn not to do things that hurt others in some way so consequences need to be imposed for these actions. However, the difference is that parents do not have to get mad or defensive. Instead, they need to deal with the situation in a calm, supportive manner indicating that while they still love their teen, he or she must accept the consequences of their thoughtless actions.

They're All Walking Hormones

Parents and teachers often talk about "raging hormones" to explain any teenage behavior that they either don't like or don't understand. Unfortunately few of these adults understand anything about these complex chemicals. In fact the interaction between the various hormones is so complex that even with today's advanced research techniques, scientists still do not understand the entire mechanism. While this book is by no means scientific in nature, it might be interesting to briefly examine how these hormones work, just to get an understanding of the incredibly complex changes which occur in a teen's body.

The mechanism that begins puberty is not yet understood. It is known that somewhere between the ages of 8 to 13 for girls and 9 1/2 to 14 for boys a "central clock" somewhere in the upper part of the brain sends a message to the hypothalamus deeper in the brain. This causes the pulsing release of gonadotropin releasing hormone, which in turn stimulates another brain structure, the pituitary gland, into releasing two more hormones, luteinizing hormone and follicle-stimulating hormone. These travel through the body fluids to the primary sex organs, the testes in males and the ovaries in females, causing them to start the production of the sex hormones. In the male the hormone is testosterone, produced by special cells in the testes. The female counterpart is estrogen from the ovaries. Supporting hormones, called adrenal androgens are produced in the adrenal glands on top of the kidneys.

These hormones have dramatic effects in two areas. The first is on the body itself. Growth is stimulated not only in height and bulk but also in the enlargement of the primary sex organs. This is most easily noticed in the breasts of females. Sperm begins to be produced in the male testes and eggs in the female ovaries. The secondary sexual characteristics, deepening voice and facial and pubic hair in males and underarm and pubic hair in females, also begin to develop.

The least understood area of development stimulated by the hormones is psychological. Pubertal changes result in increases in adolescent moodiness, which take the form of anger in males, and anger and depression in females. They also cause an increasing desire for greater physical and emotional separation from parents. Somehow, these hormones — again, mainly testosterone and estrogen — affect the personality at least as much as they affect the body. Naturally the effects on some are greater than on others. This depends partially on when puberty begins. Early maturation in boys appears to be an advantage, while in girls it seems to work the opposite way. According to researchers, boys who reach puberty early are viewed as relaxed, independent, self-confident and physically attractive to the opposite sex. Early maturing girls tend to be below average in popularity, more withdrawn and lacking in self-confidence and do not tend to be leaders. These findings appeared in a study by Mei-Fang Cheng, and were reported in the journal *Bioscience* in 1996. They are easily corroborated by a visit to any junior high school.

Another factor that controls the effects of hormones on behavior is parental reactions to the changes. Those who are not prepared for these alterations in personality often tend to either overreact or under-react, which makes the changes more pronounced. For example, parents who insist on choosing their teen's clothes may breed rebellion. The teen will simply keep extra clothes at a friend's or at school and change after leaving home. Lack of any clear reaction to a teen's newfound need for independence and support can in turn lead to attention-seeking and angry behavior. Teens whose parents pay little attention to their emotional needs may turn to vandalism or bullying to act out their anger.

Hormones may be the main culprits in the behavioral changes of teens, but they need not cause disharmony in a family. If the changes are understood and expected, parents can enjoy the teen years even more than those which precede puberty.

A Sense of Morality Begins to Develop

"Ethics is a code of values which guide our choices and actions and determine the purpose and course of our lives."
— Ayn Rand,
20th-century Russian/American novelist and philosopher

This is another aspect of teenage personality development that tends to catch parents off guard. Throughout the teen years a growing sense of what is right and wrong begins to develop in teenagers that sometimes puts them at odds with their parents. Naturally much of this moral sense comes from the parents, and rightly so. However there is a portion of this developing moral sense that apparently comes from their environment outside the home.

Parents often discover this part of a teenager's makeup by coming into conflict with it. For example, bringing office supplies home from work can bring an admonition from the teen because they know this is wrong, as can drinking and driving or failing to point out a clerk's error (in the parent's favor) at the supermarket. The vehemence of the teenager's reaction is usually a surprise for parents, who are used to their children looking up to them and not being critical of their actions.

One place where this moral sense can become a major problem is when separated or divorced parents bring their new love interests home for a sleepover. Most teens react to this with outrage — even when they themselves are already having sex. This can actually be the start of the teen taking an intense dislike to the parent's new partner and can weaken the relationship between the teen and the new partner, or even destroy it.

Another common problem occurs in families where the parents have grown up in another culture and are trying to raise their children with a set of values that is alien to those of the culture in which they are living. These teens see the clash in moralities and often have great difficulty accepting their parents' ideas. The usual result is rebellion and family turmoil.

The area of moral development is so important that Chapter 7 is devoted entirely to the discussion of moral issues.

Why Are Parents So Unprepared for the Teen Years?

It is no secret that teenagers are very different from younger children. After all, their reputation does precede them. The characteristics of teens have been known for thousands of years, as we know from the following quotation:

They (young people) have exalted notions, because they have not been humbled by life or learned its necessary limitations; moreover their hopeful disposition makes them think themselves equal to great things — and that means having exalted notions. They would always rather do noble deeds than useful ones. Their lives are regulated more by moral feeling than by reasoning — all their mistakes are in the direction of doing things excessively and vehemently. They overdo everything — they love too much, hate too much, and the same with everything else.

Except for the rather flowery language, this passage could have been written yesterday. Instead the Greek philosopher Aristotle wrote it over 350 years before the birth of Christ — or about 2350 years ago. Teens' lack of practicality and their emotionality are both clearly described. Yet despite the known facts about teenagers, most parents have no idea what to expect when their doting child enters puberty. All parents even have the advantage of having been teenagers themselves, yet they are usually unprepared when their children reach these years. Even many junior high teachers (see "One Teacher's Viewpoint" below), who deal daily with children in the 11–16 age range, often have little understanding of the causes of teenage behavior and misbehavior and become angry when teens act like kids instead of being reasonable and logical like adults.

What causes many parents and teachers to be so unprepared, despite the vast body of knowledge that exists about teens? It appears to start from the amazing ability of the human mind to forget pain and painful experiences. The mechanism of how information is stored in the brain is not well understood. Even less well understood is how and why information is removed from memory, or forgotten. Somehow the brain decides which memories to keep and which ones to eliminate. In fact it's uncanny how often it removes just that piece of data that you need, allowing you to remember that William the Conqueror defeated King Harold at the Battle of Hastings in 1066, but causing you to forget your boss's wife's name at the annual Christmas party. The fact is, however, that the brain does tend to eliminate painful memories. If it didn't, most women would probably have only one child after experiencing childbirth. The result of this mental forgetting facility, combined with the passage of years, is that most of the more agonizing experiences of the teen years tend to be forgotten, while the pleasant ones remain. Memories of fights with parents over rules and infractions of rules, of being dumped by the opposite sex and of being ostracized by peers all become fuzzy and muddled, making it very difficult for parents to empathize with their highly emotional teens. This not only results in parents being puzzled by their teens' behavior, but it also makes communication very difficult. It is not easy to talk to someone whose behavior you can't understand.

Another major reason that parents are unprepared for teenage behavior is a function of the nature of family life when children reach the teen years. When children are first born, most parents are relatively young and have the time and energy to focus on their children. They are often new to their neighborhoods and to their careers. As the children grow, so do parents' careers and responsibilities. Usually responsibilities increase, requiring more time to be spent at the job. Parents develop ties in their neighborhoods in the form of committees and volunteer activities, and they develop recreational interests such as golf, tennis or bridge. In short they are busier when their children reach the teen years than they were when the kids were younger. With the busyness comes a lack of time and energy for parenting.

One Teacher's Viewpoint

A few years ago a teacher on staff came to check with me about a student but saw that I was busy counseling that very student and left. Later she stopped me in the hall to ask how the session had gone. Kim's major problem was chronic lateness, but she also had low marks and often displayed a "chip-on-the-shoulder" attitude. I explained that I would probably not be able to help much as the problem was mainly centered in the home, and the parent was not very effective. Kim was a very intelligent girl but had a learning disability in the area of language. She was very articulate verbally, but had difficulty writing. The problem had been first noticed in Grade 1, but little had been done about it. The result of these writing problems was that Kim did not enjoy school, at least the academic part.

> *Kim's lateness was a result of the fact that her single-parent mother worked nights and didn't get home until around 2 AM. She then slept until late in the morning. Kim was responsible for getting herself up, dressed and fed. Since school wasn't enjoyable for her, she tended to fall back asleep on many days after shutting off her alarm. With no one to remind her to get up, she often didn't, coming to school an hour or more late. When told this, the teacher's response was, "Well I have to get myself here on time, why can't she?" Clearly she did not understand the nature of teenagers. They just do not have the self-discipline that adults do. On her own Kim could not overcome the problems she faced. She needed an adult's guiding hand both at home and at school.*
>
> *If the teachers who work with teens every day do not understand them, it's no wonder that parents don't.*

This lack of time and energy means that parents often do not do the research they should to learn about their teenage children. Prenatal classes are always full. Night and weekend classes about toddlers are well attended. But offer a course on teenagers, and the bare minimum to run the course show up. In fact many programs get cancelled. The shelves in bookstores tell a similar story. Where there are 10 books about babies and toddlers, there is only one about teens. Parents have more time and energy to learn about their young children, and the book market reflects this.

This combination of selective memory and lack of time and energy to do the necessary research means that parents rarely understand the needs and motivations of teenagers. Parents are also often under the impression that because teens are obviously striving to become more independent, they don't need them as much. As the teens give cues that indicate they don't need their parents as much, parents interpret these actions to mean that they are not wanted in their teens' lives. The opposite is in fact true. As has been discussed earlier, the early teen years are the most insecure of a person's life. This is when parental support and guidance are needed the most. Unfortunately, due to misunderstandings and misconceptions, this is when parents often step back from parenting. The result is the generation gap and a lot of fighting.

Armed with the above knowledge about the nature of teenagers, the onset of this behavior should not catch parents unprepared. While teens change radically during puberty and throughout the teen years, these changes can actually be enjoyed by parents who understand what is coming and are prepared to deal with it. The teen years need not be like the eclipses were to people of the Dark Ages, but instead should be seen as a natural progression on the way to adulthood. This understanding is a key component of the "Hear Me" part of the overall "Hear Me, Hug Me, Trust Me" parenting philosophy.

Chapter 3

How Are Today's Teens Different?

In the passage quoted in the previous chapter, Aristotle gave us some clues that teenagers are not much different now than they ever were. The effects of puberty, both physically and emotionally, are the same on today's teen as they were on the ancient Greek adolescent. If the world external to the teen were still the same as it was in 350 BC, then teens today would indeed be identical. Their clothes would be much simpler too. Unfortunately this is not the case. The world has changed greatly, and these changes do impact teenagers. It is the opinion of most experts that the changes in modern society that have resulted from technological advances and social revisions have increased the stressors on everyone, teens included. The result of increasing the stress levels of an already highly emotional person is inevitably an even more emotional person. In other words, teens today are physiologically the same as those of Aristotle's day, but they are different in that they appear to be under more pressure than previous generations. This extra pressure often results in teenagers being angrier and more explosive than ever before. It is worthwhile to examine where these new stresses are coming from so that parents can help to minimize them and maintain calmer, happier households.

D-I-V-O-R-C-E

"I don't like not having a dad."
— Kate

Probably the biggest stress-inducing change in society today has been the increased divorce rate. Somehow, out of the Vietnam War era of the late 1960s and early 1970s, a "Me Generation" developed.

58

Many adults of this generation appear to have abandoned the self-sacrifice that is so often needed to raise children and instead adopted a philosophy that personal happiness is all-important. Political pressure from this group has resulted in the slackening of divorce laws, to the point where any reason to abandon a marriage is acceptable to a court. Rather than work through the problems that can occur even in the strongest marriages, the "Me" person chooses to abandon the marital vows. There is no problem with this philosophy as long as children are not involved. When there are kids, especially in the range of 8 to 15 years of age, the emotional effects are devastating. Parents tend not to want to believe this, thinking that because they are rid of the cause of their unhappiness, the children will also be happier. This is far from the truth.

The problems associated with divorce are many. Single parenting is hard on children because funds are usually more restricted than they were while the marriage was alive. The resulting cutbacks in lifestyle and the increases in tension that money problems bring add to the tensions that arise with the onset of puberty. Another problem is that with just one parent there is no one else to share the load when teens become difficult or when the custodial parent is tired and stressed out. Custody arrangements can also be hard on children as they are often constantly going back and forth between households, with different sets of rules and expectations. As well, their social lives go on hold when it's their weekend to be with the other parent, since the parents are usually well separated from each other, living in different neighborhoods. Worst of all, children almost always miss the non-resident biological parent. Most children appear to need both their parents, and they become both sad and angry at various times as a result of their perceived loss.

Having said this, it should be recognized that there are times when divorce is necessary, such as in abusive or alcoholic relationships. In these cases, even though divorce will have its effect on the children, it is certainly preferable to remaining in the marriage. In most other circumstances, it should be avoided if at all possible when children are involved. The effect of divorce on teens is usually so devastating that an entire book could be devoted to this topic alone. While this is not possible in this volume, Chapter 9 will try to cover the main problems as experienced by teens.

Remarriage

The majority of adults need companionship, and this seems especially true when they are single parents. The result of this need is that at some time after the breakup of their original marriage, the parents begin dating again. Usually, remarriage is the result. With the possible exception of the death of a parent, nothing is more traumatic for a teen than having a stranger enter the household. Not only is this new person usurping the position of the biological parent, he or she is also partly taking the one remaining parent from them. This comment by Michaela is typical: "My mother is more distant now that she has remarried. She depends on her husband more. He doesn't mind his own business. He steps into confrontations between me and my mother. He doesn't pull his own weight around the house."

The anger generated by this situation is generally directed at the newcomer, who is usually surprised, then angry, at this welcome to the household. Despite being adults, stepparents often react to this apparent dislike defensively by being stricter and more authoritative. This approach generally tends to backfire, as it fuels the natural rebelliousness of most teenagers, resulting in constant tension within the household. The situation becomes even more complicated when each parent has children of their own, resulting in a "blended" family. Stepparents need to understand that resentment to their presence is a normal reaction that will die down in time, given a more understanding approach. This approach will also be detailed in Chapter 9.

Parents Are Busier

The lifestyle portrayed in the old television sitcom *Father Knows Best* probably never did really exist. This consisted of father being the sole wage earner in the family, coming happily home each day to his stay-at-home wife and his three children. Never did the show portray father coming home in a bad mood from a difficult day at the office. Nor did it show mom as a bored housewife taking her frustrations out on her unsuspecting family. While the show might not have been completely true to life, it did represent a lifestyle that was far more common in the 1950s and 1960s than it is today. Now most families have both parents working, usually for "economic" reasons.

Exactly what these reasons are is sometimes hard to tell. In some families the cost of living dictates the need for two salaries. In many others it is a lifestyle preference, either to afford more consumer items, like automobiles and larger houses, or so that both parents have an opportunity for a career.

No matter the reason, having both parents employed has several negative effects on teens. The first effect is a relative lack of time and energy to spend with the children. Where once there was one parent at home, relatively free from the stresses of employment, now there is no one. After a full day of work, most parents just want to relax — not help their teens with their homework or attend their events. This lack of energy can also display itself in the avoidance of discipline by parents. It takes energy to stand up to teens when they become demanding, but a tired parent will often give in rather than expend the energy on overseeing chores or following through on a discussion. The resultant lowering of disciplinary standards is very unsettling for teenagers, giving the impression that their parents don't care about them.

A second negative effect is parental tension levels when they do arrive home. After the stresses and worries of the working day, parents often arrive home with short tempers. This mixes very badly with the emotional and often explosive nature of teens. If neither side can stay calm in a dispute, very nasty scenes result. It is vital that parents stay as calm as possible when their teens are upset. If they cannot, due to their high stress levels and frayed tempers of the working day, then their relationship with their teenagers can become very strained, and family life can be a constant state of tension.

It is not just both parents working that makes parents busier. Community and social activities also take up time and valuable energy. Granted, some of these activities are in support of the teenagers, but many are not. While some of this activity is also a result of the "Me Generation" discussed above, much of it parents seem driven to do. There are so many committees, good causes and associations out there that parents just seem to be sucked into them. While some hobbies and recreational activities are definitely necessary for parents, restraint should be exercised throughout the years the children are growing up. They badly need time spent with them, and this time should be enjoyable, not tense. The busier parents of the past

2 or 3 decades are definitely adding to the tension in their children's lives.

More Violence

"I think the area of life that is more difficult now than in previous generations is violence. Before if you didn't like someone you would fight then it would be over. Now if you even look at someone the wrong way, people want to fight and bring their friends to jump in and they're not going to stop until you're dead or seriously hurt."
— Helen

There seems little doubt that violence in our society continues to rise. While statistics give varying pictures of exactly how much this violence actually has increased, its incidence has definitely risen. Present day society is more violent than were previous generations. The causes of this phenomenon are complex, but they probably involve a combination of larger urban centers, less parental discipline, broken families and economic disparity. No matter the causes, the media is full of it and this is where the teens get their information. Murders, rapes, family beatings, teen shootings and wartime massacres in foreign lands all occupy the headlines and newscasts, often in real time. Weapons are now common in schools, often requiring a police presence that was not necessary 20 years ago.

This violence worries parents and teens alike, as the teenagers are now mature enough to recognize the dangers. Not that this stops them from wanting to go to all night "raves," and pressuring their parents to stay out late at parties; they are still emotional, impractical beings who tend to think they are invulnerable. Nevertheless, in their saner moments, teens recognize that modern society does have many dangers, and this is of concern to them. This realization definitely adds to the stress of teen living, as they feel they have even less control over their lives than did previous generations. They understand that the increased violence in society limits their movements, especially at night, and they resent this. Added to the normal teen emotional load, then, is a mixture of fear and resentment. As most veteran parents can testify, teens do not need any extra emotional pressure, they are already volatile enough.

"My mom told me she used to go to the fair all by herself
and no one worried. I can't even walk to the corner store
at night without some kind of fears."
— Melissa

Drugs and Alcohol

"There's more peer pressure for teens
nowadays, especially drugs."
— Anna

Like the increase in violence, drug use among teens continues to rise. Again this is a complex phenomenon that has yet to be satisfactorily explained by social scientists. What is clear is that where two generations ago only alcohol was readily available to teens, now there are a wide variety of drugs easily obtainable. Something changed in the late sixties and early seventies to cause young people to want to use more mind altering substances, and teens feel pressured to use them.

Even alcohol use has spread into the lower age groups. When the drinking age was 21 in most states and provinces, older teens could obtain alcohol in various fraudulent ways, but younger teens had difficulty obtaining it in any quantity. Now alcohol is commonly present at parties in grade school, before the children have even reached their teens, despite the fact that most jurisdictions have now raised the legal drinking age back to original levels. Again the pressure to partake is present, causing considerable confusion.

This confusion is very hard on teens. They usually cannot discuss this issue with their parents because they realize that the parents will not only be adamantly opposed to drug use, but they may become angry if the subject is even brought up. This despite the fact that most parents use alcohol themselves, and many used, or at least tried, drugs in their youth. Thus they are left to resolve their confusion themselves, or with their friends. Few friends have the maturity to find solutions to peer pressure, so many wrong decisions are made. The stress load this creates can be very hard on teens, especially the more insecure ones.

> *"I feel that when my parents were young the world wasn't*
> *as corrupt as it is right now. Now teens can go out and get*
> *weed (marijuana) almost anywhere they please."*
> — *Alex*

Another problem created by the use of drugs and alcohol by young teens is the amount of trouble this leads to. The majority of serious disciplinary and legal situations that teens get into can be directly attributed to the use of these mind-altering substances. Consider the Diane's story, which is typical:

> *I was at this party and everyone was drinking so I had a couple of coolers. I wasn't really drunk, but I guess I wasn't thinking straight because I decided to walk home. To save time I took a shortcut through this park near my house. I never usually did this 'cause the park is all dark and scary. When I was away from the street this guy jumped me from out of the bushes. He tore my clothes almost off but I kept screaming and finally he ran away. That was the dumbest thing I ever did.*

Diane was lucky that she managed to get away, but nevertheless the experience was traumatic for her. Typically she was afraid to tell her parents, but her school counselor persuaded her to do so and to call the police. Incidents such as this, and much worse, are repeated every weekend. Despite the rapes, whether by strangers or friends, car accidents, house trashing, and vandalism, teens continue to get drunk and stoned and to pressure those who really don't want to partake. Why this powerful interest in these substances?

The probable reason for the relatively heavy use of these drugs (alcohol being the most common) involves the very pressures on teens that are being described in this chapter. While most teens will experiment periodically, the frequent users of mind-altering substances are those teens experiencing the most stresses. After all, drugs have been used to relieve stress and tension since time began. The difference is that throughout history, mainly adults have used them. Now, with the stresses of society being felt at younger ages, drug use has migrated to these lower age levels. While many think that education about the effects of these drugs will solve the problem, the situation is unlikely to change until the pressure on teenagers is reduced considerably.

> *"Today we have more addictive drugs*
> *and we are less afraid to try new things."*
> *— William*

Sex

> *"I don't think teens should have sex. I say this because I think*
> *that a person hasn't reached full maturity until they are in their 20s.*
> *I also believe this because I think that if a girl gets pregnant,*
> *the baby's parents will have no way of supporting the baby and*
> *the teens' young lives are as good as garbage."*
> *— Ahmed*

The change in premarital sexual habits has occurred like an avalanche, starting slowly in the late 50s and early 60s, then growing faster and faster throughout the 70s and 80s. It has taken most of a century for the puritan morals of the Victorian era to be carried away by this avalanche of change, but today we have a society where the average age of loss of virginity occurs at 15. This is a major change from the 1960s when sex during the early teens was a relative rarity.

There are several aspects of this trend that increase the stress on teens. The first and most obvious is that despite the improvements in birth control and the introduction of sex education in schools, pregnancy still occurs. In fact, the rate has stayed relatively steady for many years. This indicates that teen hormones override the education and knowledge provided by sex education programs in the schools. They have the facts, but not the maturity level. So, while in most states and provinces less than 10% of the births are to teens (see chart below), the possibility of getting pregnant is still there, causing teenagers to worry about their hasty actions with the opposite sex. The unstable nature of teen menstrual cycles heightens these fears as teens equate missed periods with pregnancy and often worry needlessly after a sexual encounter.

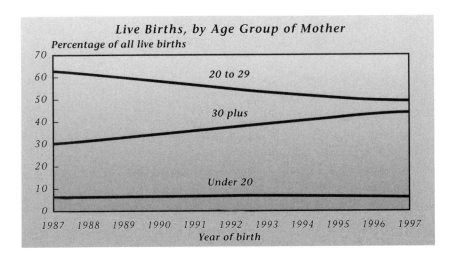

Canadian Birth Statistics

Another obvious stressor in the area of teenage sexual activity is the very real threat of contracting a sexually transmitted disease. In past generations, when teen sex was infrequent, this was not a realistic concern. Now that adolescent sex is relatively common, it causes teens considerable worry. Another aspect of this problem is the increase in the number of diseases that can be contracted. In the past only syphilis and gonorrhea were major threats and these were relatively easily controlled with antibiotics. Now chlamydia, genital herpes, human papillomavirus (HPV) and AIDS have been added to the original two, and the latter two of these not only have no cure, they are potentially life threatening. While this knowledge is unfortunately not enough to cause teens to abstain from sex, it is enough to create concern and fear after the sexual act. These fears are heightened when one of their friends actually contracts an STD, an occurrence which is becoming increasingly frequent.

> *"I don't think there's really a right time or age for teens to have sex.
> I think that when you're ready you know. You have to be ready to
> accept all the responsibilities that come with it. But right now I think
> that most of us are definitely not ready because a lot of us couldn't
> handle the emotional problems that come with it."*
> — Melissa

A less apparent cause of stress related to sexual activity in teenagers is the awkwardness that results between participants after the act. Sex changes relationships radically, a fact that even adults often have trouble resolving. Teens, being far less mature, find the pressure arising from encounters with former sexual partners extremely uncomfortable and often deal with it badly. This is particularly true in the case of casual sex such as that resulting from alcohol or drug use. Sex resulting from a relationship is less embarrassing at first, but becomes so when the relationship breaks up. Friends are often lost and barriers arise between acquaintances as a result of the sexual activity.

Sex among teenagers generally creates more problems than it solves, adding to the burden of stressors on them. Unfortunately, it is almost impossible to stop the avalanche of activity created by the more liberal sexual mores of today. Parents need to play a more active role in sex education as only they can have the influence on their children that is required to have them think before they act. Schools are just not enough. More on this will be discussed in Chapter 7.

Technology

> *"Keeping up with the new technology in*
> *life is hard and a lot of stress."*
> *— David*

There is a myth in modern society that children are all good with computers, VCRs, video games and other such technology. As with all myths, there is a grain of truth involved. Children do tend to be less inhibited by technology and are usually more willing to try the simpler things — like setting the time on the VCR or learning a new video game. However the truth is that most youngsters are just as afraid of the more complex aspects of technology as are adults. This is particularly so in the case of computers. While most kids enjoy playing video games on them, only a very few want to learn to program them or to take them apart. Unfortunately, most teens realize that technology will inevitably play an important part in their lives, and they are worried about how hard it will be to learn how to use it.

A second aspect to this technology concern is that teens realize that the increasingly technological world in which they live, with its massive amounts of information readily available, will require a higher level of education than was necessary for previous generations. One of the reasons that teens are aware of the need for more education today is that their parents and teachers are constantly telling them this. Joanne recognizes this fact when she states: "Life is more difficult for teens today because there is more pressure on us to do well in school."

Parents have always wanted their children to do well in school, but these days there is an almost frantic pressure being applied to teens because of both parents' and teachers' awareness of how complex the world has become. Both groups are themselves struggling with technology and information so they want their children and students to be able to understand it. One result of this pressure is an emphasis on homework. There is considerable evidence that more homework than ever before is being piled onto students, and they feel this pressure. In a recent survey conducted by the author, over 50% of the respondents named homework as one of their major stressors. Here are some of the comments:

"Tests and homework stress me out a lot because you try so hard and don't always get the best marks."
— Nicole

"I get stressed out by homework because sometimes I don't understand it and my parents don't know how to do it, but they tell me to do it anyway and when I tell them I can't they yell at me. If I yell back they blame me for arguing."
— Erica

"The thing that stresses me out most is homework. Sometimes the load is incredible and I worry that I won't get it all done in time. The teachers all seem to give assignments the same night or ones that are due at the same time. I wish they would talk to each other and space things out so we don't have so much to do at once."
— Josh

A later chapter will detail how parents can help reduce the stresses of homework and help teens to get better organized, since their natural lack of organization is also part of the problem. As Mindy says:

"I always leave everything to the last minute so I either rush to do it in the morning or at lunch. I'd rather clean the litter box than do homework or study. Sad but true."

While there is little doubt that homework is a valid educational strategy, the method of administering it may need to be re-examined by educational authorities. Teachers are only trying their best to help their students to succeed in this highly technological world. Unfortunately not all kids are capable of understanding the complexities of the computer world, but they feel the pressure anyway. The myth that all kids are good at technology fools adults into believing that grasping technology is easy for youth. This is just one more small pressure that adds to the burden of stresses placed on teens today.

Urban Life

With the bulk of the population now living in cities, and with the population of these cities continuing to grow, pressures unique to urban dwelling have become major stressors of adults and teens alike. Noise, pollution, traffic, crowds and crime all wreak havoc on the nervous system, adding to the list of pressures already being experienced by teens.

> *"I get stressed out by very loud noises, screaming, yelling, running and crying (the crying is from the kids I babysit)."*
> — *John*

One example of these urban pressures that is relatively recent is bussing to school. Where once each neighborhood had a school that children could walk to, now, for economic reasons, the majority of children must take a school bus through city traffic. Often they are three to a seat as bussing is costly. School starting times can be up to an hour earlier than the traditional 9:00 AM so that the same bus can make two trips, morning and afternoon, to different schools. Bussed students cannot go home for lunch, so they must endure the crowding, noise and indifferent food of school lunchrooms. While it is true that rural students have been bussed for a longer time than urban children have, they don't have to endure the traffic problems and double shifting that their city counterparts do.

A contributor to the violence in modern society, discussed earlier in this chapter, can be the stresses of living so close together. While crowding alone rarely causes violence, the noises, rudeness and selfishness of people living in close proximity to each other add pressures that can set off a person who is prone to being violent. Road rage is a classic example of this phenomenon.

With the bulk of the population now living in ever-growing cities, both adults and teens feel the stressors that city life creates. This adds to the growing number of pressures on the youth of today.

Teens Are Busier Too

"I hate having to do things all at once i.e. soccer practice and homework and friends. It's hard to have to keep up with all those things because it would be nice to get good grades and be a good soccer player and talk to friends but I usually have to commit to one thing."
— Jay

Many teens of today would agree with Jay. In fact many are busier. Some juggle two sports and music or dance lessons as well as schoolwork and friends. The result is frazzled and tired teens who often don't do as well at any of their activities as they could. What has happened to bring about these busy young lives?

One cause of teenagers being as busy as many are is the burgeoning recreational opportunities offered by communities. Where once only a few sports, such as basketball and hockey were offered, and these only for boys, now there are a wide variety of community sponsored leagues in many more sports. Football, volleyball, soccer, swimming and gymnastics are now available for both sexes, while hockey and even rugby have opened up for girls. Athletically inclined youngsters have more opportunities than ever before to participate in these activities. When these opportunities are added to those already offered by school athletic programs, their number becomes very large. Since these opportunities exist, many teens overcommit themselves in the typical teenage belief that they can handle anything. The result is that many young people find themselves eating a sandwich left over from lunch for their supper, while their parents drive them frantically from an after school activity to a community sport.

It is not just teenage overenthusiasm that causes them to become involved in so many activities. Parental ambition is just as frequently the culprit. Parents have always wanted their children to do well in life, but with today's huge salaries for professional athletes many parents push their kids to do well in sports in the hope that they will make either the big leagues or the Olympics.

Sports are not the only areas of extracurricular involvement. Music lessons, dance lessons, riding lessons and the martial arts are all common activities for today's youth. Such lessons were once only available to wealthier parents, but in the affluent society we live in, they are within the budgets of most families. Again, parents usually involve their children in these activities because they want them to become well-rounded individuals in later life. There is no more active group in a school, for example, than the Band Parents. They tirelessly raise funds for the school band, holding garage sales and bingos and selling chocolates. They are willing to work so hard because parents realize a musical background is good for their kids as both a discipline and an art form.

All these lessons, sports and other activities are indeed good for teens, in limited quantity. But as their number increases, and scheduling becomes more and more complex, then teen stress levels rise. It is up to parents to balance the load, as young people are not only poor organizers, but believe they can handle anything. The key is that they are enjoying the activities they are involved in, and have time for all the things they really like to do.

Katherine's Story

Katherine was one of those students that all teachers love to have in their class. She was bright, athletic and had a sparkling personality. It seemed as if she should have no problems in the world. This was not the case. She was frequently in the counselor's office complaining of being "stressed out." The problem centered on her activity load. Besides her school studies, which she took very seriously, she was on the basketball team, played community soccer, was in the Science Fair Club, and took piano and dance lessons. Things were not helped by the fact that her parents were not getting along and only communicated with each other through Katherine. Both parents were well-educated professionals who did their utmost to spend time with Katherine.

Since she could not control her parents, the answer to reducing her stress load was obviously to cut down her activity load. This proved more difficult than the counselor thought. It turned out that Katherine really enjoyed her sporting activities, tolerated dance and hated playing the piano. In response to the suggestion that she quit dance and piano, or at least piano, she replied that she couldn't because her parents would be disappointed.

Throughout the two years that Katherine continued to see her school counselor, she maintained her heavy schedule and her high stress level. All the counselor could do was teach her relaxation exercises and give her a chance to vent her frustrations. Her fear of disappointing her parents was just too strong.

The Consumer Phenomenon

An interesting phenomenon has been occurring in our society for at least the last 30 years. The relative affluence of our modern culture has made it possible for families to have more "things." Two cars, several televisions, summer cottages, boats, snowmobiles and riding lawn mowers are just some of the possessions that many people now have. The phenomenon is that the more we have, the more we seem to want. This is not just an adult preoccupation. Teens seem to have caught the consumer bug as well, and they too want more of their own "things." While parents tend to be generous, they cannot usually afford the cars, expensive stereo sets, video games, designer clothing and other paraphernalia that teens feel they need.

To get the money for these goods, teens often have to get part-time jobs. This is where the problem occurs. With all the other activities that are available, and given that schoolwork should be the prime focus, jobs add a large measure of stress to teenage lives. Employers like having student help because they can either pay them a special student rate or at least the minimum wage. The tendency is often to give the students more hours than they can adequately handle, as it is economically beneficial for the employer.

Forty-hour workweeks, on top of school, are not unusual. This not only creates stress, but often sleep-deprivation as well. This topic is also explored in greater depth in a later chapter.

While there are probably other sources of teen stress, the picture is already quite clear. The world is very different not just from Aristotle's generation, but from that of even one generation back. These pressures make life harder for teens, but need not make it impossible. They are highly adaptable, given the support and security that they need. In other words, if the family is stable and loving, today's youth will survive the teen years in fine fashion. If the supports that they need are not there, the result will often be seen in anger, depression and general unhappiness. Good parenting is obviously a huge factor in this equation.

Chapter 4

Discipline and Rules

Few aspects of the parenting of teenagers are as misunderstood as the development of rules and the application of discipline. And yet, a thorough grasp of the principles involved is vital to raising a self-confident and self-disciplined teen. Rules and discipline fall into the "Hug Me" section of the "Hear Me, Hug Me, Trust Me" philosophy of parenting teenagers. Parents who set rules and enforce them effectively are clearly demonstrating to their teen that they love them and care what happens to them.

Unfortunately, as a result of a complex shift in the values and attitudes of modern society, many parents have come to neglect this aspect of parenting, thinking that discipline is punitive and that friendship between parents and their children is more important. Nothing could be further from the truth — as even the teens themselves will tell you.

The benefits of setting household rules, delegating household responsibilities and enforcing these rules and responsibilities with appropriate consequences cannot be overemphasized. The result will always be closer families with happier, more self-confident teenagers.

Doing the Chores

"I feed my pets, babysit, get things for my mom, clean up my room,
do the dishes, make my bed and vacuum the house.
This is fair because I'll turn out well in the future because of this."
— *Branden*

Branden is not alone in his thinking. Most teens surveyed agreed that they should have household chores and, like Branden, most understood that the chores would be good for them in the future. Unfortunately most parents would have a hard time believing this because teen thinking and teen actions are two very different things. Getting adolescents to actually do the chores they have agreed to is one of the most frustrating parts of parenting. Let's take a brief look at why responsibilities are necessary and what problems these create.

The Problems

There are several reasons why teens should have chores to do around the house. The major one is to teach them responsibility, organization and time management. These are skills that will serve teens well not only in school but throughout their entire careers. Another reason is simply to help out tired and harried parents, most of whom work. Finally, teens learn household expertise that will serve them well when they become householders. Such skills as learning to operate a power lawn mower or dishwasher or basic automobile care will come in handy in adult life.

The main problem associated with these responsibilities is that even after several years of having the same chores to do, teens rarely do them without reminding. This puzzles and frustrates parents who feel that the reminders should not be necessary. Teens, in turn, often view this reminding as nagging which causes them to become defensive and angry. When the teenager becomes sarcastic or flippant, parents get angry and ugly scenes result.

Another parental concern is the lack of attention to detail that teens give to their tasks. Despite constant reminders, their internal quality-control mechanisms often appear to be turned off, resulting in slipshod performances. Parents often view this as a personal affront, as if the teen is purposely trying to upset them by not doing a good job. Again, angry scenes are the result.

The frustration levels created by trying to get teenagers to do chores are often so high that parents give up and do the jobs themselves. While this is understandable, it is certainly the wrong approach. The skills and attitudes that are taught by having household responsibilities are too important to ignore.

Chore Avoidance Theory

"I have to set the table, brush and bath the dog,
feed the animals and clean my room. I think that's fair but
as well I think I should have more to do."
— *Megan*

The quote from Megan is just to remind parents that teens really do have a sense of responsibility. Why then don't they follow through and actually start their chores without prompting? Why do they rarely complete them properly? There are several aspects of teenagers' personalities that interfere with this process.

One of these is teenagers' natural lack of organizational ability and time management skills. This is a major area of misunderstanding between parents and teens. Adults forget that their own organizational skills developed over a number of years and were not, as a rule, an innate feature of their personality. Teens literally do not know where to start their chores and what order to do things in. Their skills in this area will take years to develop, just like those of their parents did. The more complex chores, like washing the car or mowing the lawn are often difficult for them unless parents outline the steps *many times.*

Time management is another weak area for teens. Most do not have an accurate sense of how long chores take and how much time should be allotted to them. This causes the youngsters to either over- or underestimate the time necessary to complete the tasks. An overestimate makes them not want to do the task at all for fear that it will interfere with some aspect of their social lives. An underestimate often results in their starting a task, but failing to complete it due to prior plans with friends, or even a favorite TV show that is coming on. Time management is a skill that even some adults don't have. To expect teens to be born with this ability or to somehow develop it on their own is too high an expectation of adolescent capabilities.

Another factor that interferes with teenagers getting their chores done is their impulsiveness. Teens tend to act without thinking. This tendency is probably related to the emotionality created by the secretion of new hormones into their systems. Whatever the cause, rational thought does not usually precede their actions. For example,

Sally may have full intentions of actually tidying up the kitchen when her friend Jennifer calls and wants her to go to the mall. Zip! Sally is out the door within seconds, all thoughts of a clean kitchen having disappeared with the ring of the phone. In most cases, teens do not weigh the benefits of a clean kitchen against the pleasures of going to the mall. They just act. This tendency seems to baffle teens as much as it does their parents, and they are totally unable to explain why they acted as they did.

Generally teens seem not to have the ability to critically examine their work, even when they're not trying to rush off to a social event.

Another puzzling trait of most teens is their poor quality-control mechanisms. They seem to be unable to distinguish between a thoroughly done task and a slipshod one. Often they will be heard to say, "That's good enough," when to the adult eye the job has not been done at all satisfactorily. This does not appear to be a rationalization. Generally teens seem not to have the ability to critically examine their work, even when they're not trying to rush off to a social event.

All these inherent traits of teenagers interfere with their ability to get their chores done. Once again, understanding these traits will help parents to keep their anger and frustration in check. Unfortunately it will not help the teens to get their jobs done. Knowing that it is important for teens to learn responsibility, parents need more than understanding to do their parental duty. They also need some critical skills.

Parental Actions

The skills necessary for parents to teach their teens responsibility, and in the process get some help around the house, can be summed up in three words — "patience," "persistence" and "humor." For short let's call it the **PPH approach.**

Patience is necessary so that parents can stay calm throughout the tedious and frustrating process of getting their teenagers to do their assigned chores. In the early stages of teen development, parents need to realize that chores are going to take a while and just be a little more patient than they might be with a fellow adult. Staying calm is a major part of this process. Getting angry will only cause the teen to respond in kind. Remember that the teens do not know why they can't get their tasks done to their parents' satisfaction. There is no point in calling them "lazy" or in lecturing them about the evils of sloth. Instead just relax and calmly see the process through.

Being patient and staying calm has another important benefit. It allows parents to be instructors and to teach kids how to start and follow through on tasks. Since most teens don't have the organizational ability to know where to start a task and what steps to follow to complete it, parents need to walk them through the process. Showing teenagers how to do the job once is not enough, it will take much repetition before most youngsters will be able to complete the tasks without guidance. This is where patience becomes invaluable. The example below will illustrate this process in more detail.

Cutting the Lawn

Here is a typical process that parents need to teach their teens in order to get the lawn mowed properly:

1 Get the lawnmower out.
2 Check the gas. If it's low (first show them what low is), then refill the tank from the can in the garage. Put the can back in its place.
3 Get a garbage bag for the clippings.
4 Start the mower.
5 Do the back lawn first. If you have a particular mowing pattern that you prefer, specify it.
6 Empty the grass catcher into the garbage bag.
7 Mow the front lawn, in the appropriate pattern.
8 Empty the clippings again.
9 Put the lawn mower away.
10 Put the bag(s) of clippings in the garbage area.

You will need to go through this process **many times**, and check periodically while the job is being done. Eventually you will get to the point when all you will have to say is, "Do I need to buy a goat, or will you cut the lawn today?"

The second skill parents need is **persistence**. Expecting a teen to complete a task after being reminded just once is expecting far too much. Stay with it. Persist with reminders until the job is done. Keep in mind the poor organizational and time management skills of teenagers. They really do struggle with these tasks, no matter how straightforward they seem to adults. There is a strong tendency for many parents to give up and do the jobs themselves. Some feel that this will make their teenagers feel guilty so that they will do the chores themselves when they realize how hard mom or dad is working at the teen's task. This is unlikely to happen. Other parents simply feel that the energy necessary to get the teen to do the job is greater than actually doing it themselves. This may be true, but it teaches the teen nothing about responsibility. The only lesson they will learn is that if they wait long enough, their parents will do the job.

The final skill in this PPH approach may be the most difficult for some parents. Using **humor** to remind teens of their assigned chores is by far the most effective way of being persistent. The humor does not have to be the sidesplitting variety of the professional comedian. It just has to take the edge off the reminder. The use of humor shows that you are not angry or upset, you just want the job done. Simple lines like, "I don't hear any cleaning sounds coming from the kitchen," are corny but effective. A groan from your teen is far better than an angry shout. Take the time to phrase your reminder in as humorous a manner as possible; it will certainly pay big dividends.

What about jobs that are supposed to be done before parents get home from work? Such tasks as walking the dog or making the beds are daily ones that cannot wait for the weekend. In this case the use of "sticky notes" is recommended. Those little colored pads (they used to be yellow but now they come in various colors, including fluorescent ones) with the glue on the top edge are excellent for use when parents cannot be on the spot. Put several in prominent locations — especially on the telephone and fridge — all with slightly different messages. Again, try to make them humorous by using witticisms or little drawings to get your reminder across. If you arrive home and the jobs still aren't done, make sure nothing else happens until they are. No phone calls or TV, just have them get at it.

By understanding the basic nature of teens, then using this understanding to stay calm while employing the PPH approach, the chores will get done and the family atmosphere will be much more relaxed.

The Perfect Chore Defense

When teens are reminded to do their chores, the normal response is a groan or complaint. This is expected and tends to signal to parents that they need to start their reminding and supervising. The author's son found a far more effective approach to avoiding chores. When reminded, he always agreed immediately and cheerfully — then went right back to what he had been doing. This agreement tended to throw off the parents by setting up their expectations that the job would be done very soon, so reminding and supervising was initially not seen to be necessary. When eventually his parents realized he had not started, they would remind him. Again the response was cheerful agreement. Again the parents would be lulled into a false sense of security and would usually forget about reminding him for a considerable period of time, sometimes completely. You would think that clever parents would catch on to this technique very quickly, but not so. The cheerful agreement technique is so pleasant that it worked to postpone tasks for years.

The Bedroom

"My parents and I always argue about my room being clean. Seriously, my mom wants my room to look like no one lives in it."
— Darren

Few things typify teenagers as clearly as the state of their bedrooms, and few subjects create more arguments between teens and their parents. It seems amazing that such an apparently simple thing could create such tremendous friction between parents and teens.

The Problem

The problem in this case seems very straightforward. Parents want teens to keep their rooms clean and teens, although not usually disagreeing outwardly with the concept, seem incapable of doing it. It's not that the rooms are just untidy, they're disaster areas. Clothes are strewn about, CDs are everywhere, usually not in their cases, and far too often dirty dishes, potato chip bags, and gum wrappers are intermingled with the mess.

Most parents have learned over the years that tidiness works better than a random distribution of goods and garbage. Clothes stay neater and cleaner when hung up. Articles are found more easily when they are returned to their proper places. More importantly, the household is healthier when potential microbial growth areas, such as leftover food and other garbage, are removed. Parents not only want to pass these effective habits on to their children, they want the bedrooms, which they rightly consider to be part of their homes, to be as clean and neat as the rest of the place.

It's not just the mess that bothers parents; it's the décor as well. Teens often want to decorate what they see as their space in ways that tend to offend parents. Posters are some of the main offenders. Life-size pictures of scruffy looking singers and actors, scantily clad ingénues or advertisements for bizarre goods or banned substances beam down from the walls. In stark contrast are the stuffed animals and toys that would be more appropriate in the room of a younger child. All this is combined with shell collections, bottle collections, autographed napkins and the occasional stolen street sign. Altogether it's enough to make a parent cry.

Another concern parents have about teen bedrooms is the amount of time they spend in them. Parents wonder why anyone would want to spend so much time among so much chaos. Many take it as a rejection of themselves, which adds to the myth that teens do not want to spend time with their parents. Others wonder if they're doing something illegal or immoral in there. Most parents are just plain puzzled as to why their kids want to isolate themselves.

Teens appear to be happier amongst chaos. They rarely respond with alacrity to a parental request to clean their rooms, and more often than not, actively resist the concept. They decorate in bizarre fashions and try to cram way too much into way too little space. They spend more time than they used to in these messy, weird places. The result is major arguments and considerable unrest in the households of the great majority of teens. Is this behavior a worldwide teenage plot to drive parents crazy or is there a reasonable explanation for this phenomenon?

Messy Bedroom Theory

*"I think it's important to keep your room clean because it's
more comfortable and you can find your stuff easier."*
— Corey

There are several factors that conspire against parents in the eternal struggle for bedroom order and cleanliness. The first, and probably the main, cause of the problem is teenagers' need to develop an identity of their own. In order to show themselves to be different people from their parents, they need to act differently. Since most parents are neat and orderly, most teens become the opposite. This is not a conscious decision, and it definitely is not done with the idea of upsetting the parents. It just feels more comfortable for the teen to live in chaos than in sanitary organization. The chaos puts their personal stamp on their area and makes it different from the rest of the house. Interestingly, teens with messy parents hate this trait and once again tend to take an opposite approach. They usually keep their area clean and tidy.

> *The worries, fears, stresses and just plain stimulation of their environment wear down even teenagers. They want a place where they can relax and escape from it all for a while.*

The quest for an identity of their own is also behind the décor teenagers choose for their rooms. The posters they select tend to be either heroes of theirs, be they musical, athletic or thespian, or things they believe in. They are their dreams and aspirations and are therefore part of the teens themselves. The other things in their rooms represent parts of their lives past and present, including childhood toys and collections from the present. Their rooms are part fantasy and part reality and are an attempt on the part of the teens to describe themselves. They are also a place of sanctuary for the adolescent. The worries, fears, stresses and just plain stimulation of their environment wear down even teenagers. They want a place where they can relax and escape from it all for a while. The tendency is to try to make their rooms as comfortable and relaxing for themselves as possible. Unfortunately, what is relaxing for a teen can be very stressful to a parent.

Another factor that precludes most teens from having tidy rooms is their natural lack of organizational ability and time management skills. Thus the order to, "Go clean your room," is not as simple for teenagers as it sounds. This was discussed in detail in the "Doing the Chores" section. Similarly the impulsiveness that characterizes teens was also discussed in the previous section. They simply forget completely about their rooms in the excitement of more interesting events. Adults do not normally react in this impulsive manner. As with the organizational skills, this is an area that parents have difficulty understanding. They do not remember that they were once impulsive and prone to acting without thinking a process all the way through. Teens are impatient. They want to do things immediately — and they do.

It can be seen from these explanations that what appears at first to be a simple problem is actually a complex one that is rooted in the basic nature of teenagers. Understanding this nature does not get the bedrooms clean, but it does take away the anger that usually results from finding your teen's room looking like the aftermath of a hurricane.

> *"I sort of think it's important to keep your room clean because then you can find stuff easily. But I don't like to clean up all the time — that's so boring."*
> — *Tabbie*

Parental Actions

Understanding the problem does not solve it. Parents would be shirking their duties to simply ignore the problem as a passing phase. There are good reasons to be organized and teens need to learn them. Let's start with the décor before tackling the more the difficult cleaning problem.

A good rule to follow when considering how a teen decorates his or her room is that unless it's morally offensive to you, leave it alone. Posters of nudes or marijuana plants may be a statement of your teens' dreams or values, but they do not represent the morality you want to teach. Don't just order that the poster come down, though, as that will inevitably lead to an argument. Instead, sit down

. . . unless it's morally offensive to you, leave it alone.

and discuss the reasons why the material is offensive and let the teen know that, while the room is his or hers, the house is yours and in it your morality will prevail. Hopefully the teen will understand. If there is nothing offensive, let the room be truly theirs by allowing them to decorate it in a fashion that is comfortable and/or pleasing to them.

Occasionally, the material will be placed there just to test you and see what your parental reaction will be. It's part of teens' checking to see if you are paying attention to them. Thus, while they may protest your action (again to display their separate identity), they want it and expect it. Teenagers can certainly be complex creatures.

The "sanctuary" aspect of the teen's room bothers many parents. They cannot understand why youngsters spend so much time there. In fact, many take it personally that their teen would rather spend time in his or her room than be with them. Parents have even been known to remove the door from the bedroom because they were either angry that their adolescent sought refuge there or were worried about what might be going on in the room. The answer is that the teen is usually just escaping from the pressures of being a teenager for a while. There is no conscious intention to avoid the family or shirk responsibilities. No sinister plots are being hatched. The best approach is to simply leave the teen alone unless its time for dinner or you need something. The teen will appreciate the break, and you will not have an argument on your hands.

The cleaning and organizing aspects of teen bedrooms is a more complicated problem. The first suggestion would be to not try to have the room neat and tidy on a daily basis. Daily cleaning and organization is possible but will take a tremendous amount of parental energy. A more effective method of dealing with the problem would be to set a weekly cleaning day. Saturday would be a good choice. On that day the room is to be cleaned before the teen leaves the building or begins any other activity. Parents need to realize that supervision and reminding will be necessary. The PPH process that helps to get chores completed is detailed more completely in the "Doing the Chores" section. It basically involves staying calm and keeping after the teen, as humorously as possible, until the job is done to your satisfaction. The patience involved in utilizing this approach would almost qualify most parents for sainthood — but it's worth it. The entire process of getting a room cleaned to a parent's satisfaction could take several hours. Prepare mentally for this each time you initiate the cleaning ritual. A typical room-cleaning scene might be as follows:

Dad: *OK son, time to clean your room.*
Sean: *Aw dad, I'm in the middle of this game.*
Dad: *Sorry, the game will have to wait. Let's get at it.*
Sean: *Oh, all right.*

20 minutes later:
Dad: *Sean, are you working on your room.*
Sean: *I'm just about to start.*
Dad: *Let's get it done so you can get back to your game.*
Sean: *All right.*

another 20 minutes:
Dad: *How's your room coming.*
Sean: *I'm starting now.*
Dad: *They could have cleaned the entire Parliament buildings by now. Let's see some progress.*
Sean: **All right. All right. I said I was starting.**
Dad (Ignoring the tone of voice): *OK. I'll expect to see it finished. Soon.*

15 Minutes later dad checks on the progress:
Dad: *What's with the video game? I thought you were supposed to be cleaning this room.*
Sean: *Well I started but I guess I got distracted.*
Dad: *All right. Start by hanging up your clothes and putting the laundry in the hamper. Then make your bed and put your CDs away.*
Sean: *I know. I know.*
Dad. *Right. I'll check again in a few minutes to see how it's going.*

The keys are patience, persistence and humor. Try to either ignore any sarcastic or angry retorts or to rebuke them mildly. Don't get angry or give up, and don't take over the job yourself. Improvements in the time taken to complete the cleaning and in the quality of the job will be slow, but if you stay with it, they will definitely be seen. During the week, while the room is in "chaos" mode, just close the door and grit your teeth.

Passing the Laws

"My parents' rules are fair and usually I don't break them.
Except when I go out with my friends and I forget to call
that I'm going to be late."
— *Julie*

The world would certainly be a much more pleasant place to live if there were no need for rules. Unfortunately they are required for our own protection. For example, if there were no traffic laws, everyone using the roads would be at the mercy of careless and reckless drivers. If adults need laws for their protection then teenagers, who are usually far less mature, certainly need them. Rules protect teens from their own immaturity and impulsiveness. It would be far easier for parents if they did not have to make and enforce these rules. It takes tremendous amounts of parental energy to monitor the activities of teens and hand out consequences for infractions. Fortunately setting rules and enforcing them when broken pays huge dividends by teaching teens self-discipline and preparing them for life as independent adults.

"I wish my parents would be more strict.
They let me come and go whenever I want and I hate it."
— *Amber*

Fortunately for parents, teenagers almost unanimously agree that they need rules. They aren't always sure why they need them, but they do realize that by setting rules, parents are showing they care about them. Once again, it's the "Hug Me" part of the philosophy. Knowing that their teens are not opposed to limitations helps, but setting rules is still difficult for most parents. How many should you set and how strict you should be are questions that spring to mind for neophyte parents of teens.

The Problems

One major dilemma for parents of today's teenagers is that despite what is written in the previous paragraph, a strong movement has slowly developed over the past generation or two that questions whether teenagers should have rules and subsequent consequences for breaking them at all. Somehow concerns about corporal punishments for children have been translated into concerns about there being any discipline at all. Where not long ago many parents lived by the old saying, "Spare the rod and spoil the child," suddenly not only was there no rod, but no real discipline either. Either through misguided philosophy or sheer laziness many parents have taken a laissez-faire approach to raising children which uses a "kids will be kids" kind of thinking. *This does not work.* All children need rules and this is even truer for teens than it is for the younger children.

The teen years are the most insecure of a person's life. Teenagers need regulations so that they do not have to constantly be making decisions. They are highly unsure of themselves and their decision-making capacities and rules help them to feel more secure. They need to know where the limits are so that they do not have to set them themselves. Teens also need to know that their parents care about them, and they know full well that parents who don't care don't bother to set limits. While there is no room in an effective discipline system for corporal punishment, rules and their enforcement are a vital component of raising teenagers.

Rules may be necessary for teenagers to feel secure, but whenever the word "rules" is mentioned to teens another word becomes immediately associated with it. This is "fair" or "fairness." Teens will accept rules readily if they think they are fair, but will react strongly against any limitation that they think is unjust. The problem for parents is determining whether the teen's concept of what is fair is in line with the purpose of the rules, which is to protect the teens from harm or injury. Parents need to find a balance between being too strict and not strict enough so that both sides can live comfortably with the regulations. This is not easy, but it is achievable.

Parental Actions

The first step parents should take in setting rules as fairly as possible is to do some research. Whenever you're at a gathering of adults, such as a school activity or an athletic event, ask other parents what rules they set. Check out the curfews, bedtimes and allowable activities that these parents have determined. This will give you an idea of what the common practices are. This practice has two advantages. The most obvious is that it gives you reference points from which to set your own family regulations. The other advantage is that you are prepared when your teen cries, "But all the other kids get to stay out 'til . . ." If you know what the norms are you can't be pressured in this way.

. . . you do not need to set your family rules the same as the other parents in your area. It is your family and you make the final decisions as to how best to protect your child.

It's important at this point to state that you do not need to set your family rules the same as the other parents in your area. It is your family and you make the final decisions as to how best to protect your children. However, you need to understand that if your rules are much stricter than those of your child's peers, you will need to expend considerably more parental energy enforcing them. Your teen will be constantly comparing and complaining. As long as you are prepared for this, and can handle the constant pressure, then carry on. It's your house and they are your children.

Once you have some reference points, it's time to actually set the rules. The most effective method is to sit down with each teen on a regular basis and discuss rules and rule changes. Remember that teens' idea of fairness is that they have some input into the situation. It is also important to remember that the development of trust requires that the rope be let out slowly but steadily, so the rules should be relaxed accordingly.

Generally, teens who break rules on a regular basis are indicating that they have problems, and counseling may be necessary to diagnose and remedy them.

Frequent rule changes are confusing to teens, so once a year is usually often enough for these discussions to be held. The best time for them is before the beginning of the new school year as this is a natural starting point, but birthdays or New Year's Day can also be utilized. At these discussions it is most effective for parents to ask what rules the teen thinks should be changed. It may be that no changes are required. On the other hand, if the youngster believes that alterations are necessary, reasons need to be given. If the reasons are acceptable, then the rule can be changed.

Much will depend on the teen's track record for the past year. Occasional misdemeanors should receive consequences at the time, but should not be brought up at rule meetings. Teens make mistakes for a variety of reasons, and they should be treated as such. Frequent transgressions are a different thing altogether. In this case the rules that are being repeatedly broken cannot be changed until they can be followed. Generally, teens who break rules on a regular basis are indicating that they have problems, and counseling may be necessary to diagnose and remedy them. This counseling should involve the entire family, as few teen problems are specific to the teen alone.

Parents should try to keep the number of rules to a minimum. The more there are, the harder it is for the teenager to remember them all. Rules need to be set where problems occur or are likely to occur. For example, if the teen automatically goes to bed at a reasonable time, there is no need to set a rule. On the other hand, if the adolescent has frequent problems getting up in the morning, an earlier bedtime is indicated. There is definitely a place for common sense in the rule-setting process.

There is general agreement between parents and teens that rules need to be in place. If they are set fairly, and consequences are given when they are broken, the teens will feel more secure, and parents can sleep more soundly with the knowledge that they have done their best to protect the teen and to teach him or her self-discipline.

Areas Where Rules May Be Necessary

1 *Curfews.*
2 *Chores. Who does what and when?*
3 *The telephone.*
4 *The computer.*
5 *Bedtimes.*
6 *Homework hours.*
7 *Use of the family car.*
8 *TV hours and/or programs that can be watched.*

Summer Holidays

It was stated above that once rules are set, they should not be changed again that year. There is one major exception to this rule about rules. That occurs during the summer holidays. Once summer vacation rolls around, adjustments need to be made, particularly for teens who do not have jobs. Without the twin horrors of homework and early mornings to worry about, many of the rules can be relaxed. On the other hand, since parents no longer can be sure of where their children are during the day, it is important that new guidelines be added to ensure that the whereabouts of the kids are known at all times. This is particularly true in today's society where both parents are usually working. Another area that must be looked at is who your teens are allowed to have in the house during the day, how many can come over at a time, and what they are allowed to do and eat when they are there.

This sounds complicated, but it really isn't. The idea is to sit down with teens at the start of the vacation and calmly discuss the areas of concern. Curfews are one major discussion topic. Teens often feel that they should be allowed to stay up as late as they want, since they can sleep in in the morning. They tend to forget that working parents have to get their sleep, and don't want to be disturbed by the nocturnal wanderings of their children. A compromise might be that the teens have to be home and in their rooms at a certain time, but don't necessarily have to be asleep. They can then read, listen to music (with earphones only unless the bedroom is very isolated) or play video games, but they are not to disturb the parents. The discussion can then turn to any other important topics, until all points have been discussed.

The important point to remember is that this is a dialog. Getting the input of the teens is vital. For example, on the topic of a summer curfew, it is a good idea to ask teens what they think is appropriate. If the suggested time is, in your opinion, unsuitable, simply make a counter-offer. Try to avoid adding emotion to the situation by saying something like, "Get real," or, "Don't be stupid." Teens appreciate it when their suggestions are seriously considered, even if you cannot accept them without modification.

Remember to try and keep the process simple. Don't try to cover every possible contingency; the rules will get too complicated and hard to remember. For example, you don't have to outline every place they are not allowed to go. Simply make a rule that they should call you and let you know where they are going whenever they leave the house. If you don't approve, you can let them know at the time. Similarly, rather than trying to list which friends they are allowed to have over, just have them call you for permission each time. If you disapprove (and have a good reason) let them know then.

Summer should be a time of fun and relaxation for teens. New rules for this new season will help to ensure a safe, enjoyable and relaxing time for everyone.

Rules for Setting Rules

1 *Set rules by meeting with your teens individually.*
2 *Make them only in areas where they seem to be necessary.*
3 *Ask what rules or rule changes the teen thinks are necessary.*
4 *Explain the reasons for each rule clearly.*
5 *Once in place, don't change the rules until the next meeting.*
6 *Modify them in the summer where necessary.*

Telephone Tension

Alexander Graham Bell may have made communication between people much easier, but most parents of teenagers wish that the telephone had never been invented. More family arguments center on the telephone and its use than almost any other single issue. Why should this marvelous invention have to create so much difficulty for parents?

The Problems

Like teenage behavior itself, most parents are caught unawares by the telephone problem because it sneaks up on them. Children learn to use the telephone early and make use of it frequently throughout elementary school. However, they do so much like adults in that they convey their message, then hang up. Teenagers use it very differently.

They call friends for no particular reason, and talk for hours to someone they had just been with at school for the past six hours. Parents wonder what they can possibly have to say to each other. Even more amazing is when two teens are on the phone to each other and aren't talking at all — they're just breathing. Despite this, they complain vociferously if you insist they hang up. The interesting fact is that parents were no different when they were teens. This telephone behavior was clearly and cleverly captured in the 1960s Broadway musical *Bye, Bye Birdie*, and it had already being going on for at least a generation by then. How strange that parents forget so quickly.

Remembering what they were like as teen telephone talkers would be helpful, but whether parents do or not, the problems that telephones create are numerous and the amount of family turmoil that results is onerous. The main problem is the length of time that the family telephone is tied up. Parental calls can't get through, and younger family members can't get on it at all. This creates stress for all unless solutions are found.

Another major problem is that chores and homework tend to get ignored when the telephone rings. No true teenager would automatically defer a call until these tasks were done — the teen might miss something *really* important, like a breakup or some similar snippet of gossip. Unfortunately parents rarely realize the importance of receiving this information immediately, and by insisting that the chores be done instantly, find themselves in conflict with the garrulous teen.

One cause of telephone conflict that was not present when Conrad Birdie was being inducted into the army was the connection of the computer to the phone lines. The use of the Internet, and "chat lines" on the Net, is important enough to rate a section of it's own. It relates to the telephone usage problem when the computer is connected by modem to the virtual world. In this case, the computer uses the same lines as the telephone does, tying them up in a different way. No voices are on the line, but instead a series of 1s and 0s. Unfortunately it doesn't matter in what form information is being sent down these lines, it ties them up for lengthy periods of time.

Problems that can be equally vexing but are encountered less frequently include excessive and expensive long distance calls, calls to toll numbers, like the ones with 900 area codes, and "pranking." The long distance problem does not normally occur until a close friend, of either sex, moves to a distant location. Then it can suddenly become expensive as teens rarely realize how quickly costs can mount up. Toll numbers are similar. They are a fascinating "game" for a while, but they too can become extremely expensive. While these problems are usually short-lived — they tend to stop suddenly when a several-hundred-dollar phone bill arrives — they certainly create some major tensions at the time.

"Pranking" is the practice of calling other teens for the purpose of playing jokes on them. It may be as simple calling at 3:00 AM and hanging up when the phone is answered (usually by very angry parents). It can also be very vicious, such as anonymous calls where very crude language is used, or threats or accusations are made. These calls are rarely made by close friends, but instead are made by acquaintances who are jealous of the victim or feel that the victim has slighted them in some way. The calling is often done in groups, so that the teens can gain courage for the prank from peer support. Parents should not smugly feel that their teenager would never do such a thing. It's amazing how cruel teens can be to each other at times, and most are capable of this behavior.

A relatively new problem area has developed since the mobile telephone has become relatively inexpensive. Many teens want them as they provide a measure of independence from the restrictive telephone cord and they make it possible to be in contact with friends no matter where they go. The difference with these phones is that charges are not fixed with the monthly fee. An extra charge is levied for the time they are used, no matter whether the call is outgoing or incoming. The danger in this is that teens are forgetful and tend not to remember to keep the calls short. Charges mount up in a hurry, especially as many of the calls are made during prime billing time.

From the teen's end of the telephone, a major problem is having parents listen in on their conversations. They take this as an invasion of privacy and see it as a major trust issue — which, of course, it is. Parents who eavesdrop will have major battles with their teenagers. They may feel this practice is justified, but that only points to the fact that there are bigger problems in the family that need to be addressed.

Telephone Theory

The telephone is not just important to teens, it is seen as a vital component of their lives. The importance of friends has been mentioned in Chapter 1, and is discussed in gory detail in Chapter 8. The telephone is basically a lifeline to these friends when they are not present. Friends comfort teens when they are upset or stressed out, whether it be by parents, homework or other friends. They reassure them that the actions and decisions that were taken during the day were appropriate. They also keep them right up-to-the-minute about current social happenings. When friends cannot be present, the telephone is the next best thing.

Insecurity is also a factor in the teenage obsession with phones. They need to check constantly that nothing has happened they didn't know about. Being left out of the information loop is frightening for a teen. They interpret this as people not wanting to tell them things, and this makes them feel unwanted and highly insecure. On the other hand, having a friend call the instant an event occurs, or the instant it has been relayed to that friend, makes teens feel important, a vital cog in the information wheel. They are in the group, and that makes teenagers feel secure.

Understanding why their teen clings to the receiver like a drowning person clings to a rescuer helps parents to realize that this behavior is normal. Knowing that virtually all teens are similar when it comes to telephone use allows parents to relax and deal with the inevitable problems in a rational way. Unfortunately it does not solve them.

Parental Actions

> *"I don't mind having rules about the telephone,*
> *but I wish they wouldn't listen in to my calls. It's not like*
> *I'm planning to blow up something or anything."*
> — Billy

Nothing need be done if your teens are reasonable about their telephone use. If problems start arising, parents need to nip them in the cord by setting some rules to cover the areas where conflicts are arising. The following are some rules that teens have suggested be made:

- *set time limits for each call*
- *set limits for chat line or Internet use*
- *no use of the phone after certain hours*
- *no pranking*
- *no 900 numbers*
- *no telephone until the homework is done*
- *no really long calls (this will have to be defined for each household)*
- *ask before using long distance*
- *no eavesdropping*

These are all very reasonable and variations of these should be made in every household. Use the discussion method outlined above for setting the telephone rules. That is, sit down with your teens and negotiate with them. Then enforce these laws by withdrawing the privilege when it is abused. You don't have to be a dictator, standing by the offending instrument with a stopwatch in your hand. Simply use the rules as guidelines. For example if your daughter's homework is done and no other family member needs the phone, then don't worry too much about how long she is spending on it. Try to make any requests to cease use in calm and reasonable tones, at least at first. Teach the teens to respond quickly to any requests you make for them to get off the line, in the interests of family peace. On the other hand, if a violation is flagrant or repeated, then the consequences should be swiftly applied and adhered to for the period determined.

It is also important that your teens train their friends in the family phone laws. Friends tend to learn quickly and generally respond well in a relatively short period of time. Don't let the teen "blackmail" you by insisting that their friends won't call them if they have rules. They still will.

If parents make frequent use of the telephone, either for business or personal reasons, then whenever possible they should seriously consider getting teens their own line. Teen calls are then only allowed on that line. Do not allow both lines to be used for teenage communication, especially if you have more than one teen, or you may have the same problems but twice the bill. On this topic, if at all possible, teens should pay at least part of the monthly charge for the second line. To appreciate the privilege they have, they need to realize the cost. Like the rules themselves, the amount charged in each family should vary with the circumstances, and should be negotiated.

Other alternatives, such as call waiting and voice mail should also be explored if these options will help to solve the problems. Teens do need to be trained, though, in the proper use of these alternatives; if they are not used correctly, they won't help at all. For example, if your son won't answer the call waiting "beep" when he is talking to his girlfriend, then there is no point in paying for it. Similarly, if the voice mail is never checked, then no messages will get passed.

The idea of a mobile or cellular telephone for a teenager is generally a poor one. There is little need for them to have their own such phone on a permanent basis. There is more of the status symbol in this idea than need. Instead, parents should give the teen *their* cellular phone when there is a possibility that they might need to contact home. An example would be if there is some doubt that the teen will have a ride home. Give them the cellular so that if no ride materializes, they can call home. The teen should be cautioned that the cellular is for emergency use only, and is not to be used casually. Parents can then feel secure that if arrangements do not work out, the teen will not have to hunt for a telephone and have the correct change for the call.

Contrary to the opinion of many parents, the telephone was invented by Alexander Graham Bell and not by the devil himself. Teens need to use the telephone to maintain their lifelines to their friends. If the proper technology is present along with rules and guidelines for its use, then most of the problems will be solved.

Shannon's Telephone Tale of Two Cities

Shannon was in Grade 9 when she met Shawn. He was the coolest guy she had ever met, and he obviously must have thought the same about her because they started going out. Shortly thereafter, Shawn moved to a small town about 100 miles away. Shannon was devastated, but she was soothed somewhat by the knowledge that she could still talk to him by telephone. So she did. Every day she called him and talked for at least an hour. Her parents were unaware of this as Shannon called before they got home. She was not worried about the cost because Shawn didn't live that far away.

The problem began when her parents got the bill at the end of the month. Shannon had accumulated over $200 worth of long distance charges. Naturally her parents hit the roof and harsh words were spoken. This should have been the end of the problem except Shannon's parents, realizing that she had simply not realized how expensive the long distance charges were, did not impose a penalty — they just lectured her. The result was that Shannon resumed making the calls. She tried not to make them as long or as often, but her resolve melted whenever she talked to Shawn. As the end of the month loomed, she realized that she had talked just as long and often as the previous month and that the bill would probably be about the same.

That's when Shannon came to the counselor for a solution. Unfortunately there was no easy one and the counselor convinced her to "fess up" and face the music. He contacted the parents and suggested that Shannon be made to pay for as much of the charges as she could, on a time payment plan. This time the calls did stop, and the relationship (which was doomed anyway but Shannon didn't want to believe this) withered away. It was an expensive lesson for parents and teen alike.

The Computer

The digital world is new to most parents of teenagers, as home computers were not available during their teen years. This means that even if they do remember their teen years well, they have no reference points on which to base their decisions about how and when to use the family computer. These machines certainly do amazing and useful tasks and progress has now reached the point where most homes really do need one. Unfortunately, while they are generally a positive influence, the use of the computer needs to be regulated, as there are also many negative aspects to them as well.

The Problems

In many ways the home computer can be viewed by parents as a big, expensive, more complicated telephone. This is because many of the problems that occur with the computer are similar to those with the telephone. Overuse by one family member, for example, can frequently be a problem, and so time limits need to be set. Using the computer too late at night is also a problem similar to the telephone, so hours of use need to be set. Being on the machine when homework or chores are not done is another concern that equates to those of the telephone. If a modem is used to connect to the Internet, then the problems actually become telephone problems as modems use the same lines. Rules to cover these contingencies are relatively easy to set if you have already done so for the telephone. Regrettably there are a number of new problems presented by the computer that also need regulating. These can be much more complex, and therefore more difficult to deal with.

These new problems stem from the versatility of home computers. The telephone has just one use — communication. The computer does this and much more. It is also a productivity tool, a research tool, a games machine and a stereo set. The use of the computer as a productivity tool, for word processing and graphic design, presents no new problems for parents. It is just a question of whose turn it is to use it to produce essays and cover pages. The other uses are the ones where serious problems can be presented.

The computer can be used for communication through chat lines. These are Internet sites where people log on and talk to each other via the keyboard. While it is slower than a telephone, it allows interaction between people from all around the world at no more cost than the monthly charges from the Internet service provider. This can be very exciting and interesting. In fact it can be addictive. Like the telephone, teens can spend hours "chatting" either to complete strangers or friends just down the block. This creates a problem similar to overuse of the telephone, but adds the addictive factor. Even adults become addicted to chatting, with marriages breaking up over this problem and new romances being created. If adults are into chatting it is even harder to get teens off the lines, especially when no one else is at home. There is another, more dangerous aspect to chat lines. Some people use them for unscrupulous purposes. Adult pedophiles, for example, use chat lines to get the names and addresses of teenagers, then try to lure them into sexual encounters. Teens need to be aware of this danger and avoid giving any personal information over the lines.

The research potential of the Internet is an exciting one. Where once it took volumes of encyclopediae and many trips to the library to find information for an essay or assignment, now this information is available from your keyboard. Not all the information is positive though. Pornography is also readily available from the home computer and teenagers, with their hormones flowing, are susceptible to logging on to these sites. Hate literature, in graphic form, is also prevalent on the Internet. Parental oversight is obviously required to be aware of the Web sites that the teen is viewing.

Computer games have become a huge problem for parents. These are colorful, exciting and also highly addictive. Many teens will play games right through the supper hour and into the wee hours of the morning if allowed. Once again an area that needs supervision is presented. There are also more serious concerns with computer games. Many are also very violent. While there is no evidence that violent computer games turn teens violent, a preference for this type of game might indicate problems. It may show that the teen is very angry, and needs to vent this anger through the computer. If other symptoms of internal anger are present, such as refusing to go to school, bullying or extreme defiance, then counseling help should be sought. Even if it's not a symptom of other problems there is some evidence that violent games leave teenagers tense and stressed. If the violence of the games bothers parents, then restrictions and subsequent supervision will be necessary.

Two other problems for parents are also created by the home computer. One is the superior computer skill shown by most teens over their parents. Many parents do not know much more about computers than how to turn them on. This makes it difficult for parents to understand what their youngsters are doing with the PC, and they may actually avoid the computer rather than display their ignorance. This leaves teens free to do what they want with it.

The other problem is financial. Although computers have come down in price considerably in the last few years, they still are a major purchase for most families. Once purchased, they tend to become outdated quite quickly due to the speed of development in the high-tech industries. This often causes teens to want newer and more powerful computers long before parents are able to afford them. Parents have to balance the uses they have for their computer with the technology that is available, in order to know when to upgrade their machine. This is not easy, especially for parents who have little knowledge of computers.

At this point it almost looks like computers present more problems than they solve. This does not have to be the case if parents do their homework and use their common sense. With clear rules and effective supervision, the home computer can be a tremendous asset in any home.

Parental Action

"Parents should know what you are doing on the computer because us teens would rather play games than do homework."
— Amber

As with the telephone, it is not necessary to make a complex set of regulations for the use of the computer if no problems exist. However, it is extremely important that parents monitor computer use to see if there are any concerns. To do this, try to set up the computer in an area of the house where it can be easily seen. This may not be easy in many houses but if there is such an area, it is much simpler to see how and when the computer is being used — or abused.

Here are some of the rules that students have suggested be applied if parents feel they are necessary:

- *never give out your real name, e-mail address or any other personal information while chatting*
- *no "adult" Web sites*
- *set time limits for each person*
- *only acceptable games (acceptance being determined by the parent)*

These rules need to be set by meeting with the teens who will be using the computer and by openly discussing the issues.

If the computer intimidates parents there are several possible avenues that can be taken in order to be able to effectively monitor the machine's use. One is to have your teens teach you the various aspects of the computer that you don't understand. Let them show you how to play their games, use the chat lines, download music or surf the Web. This not only helps you to understand what their interests are and whether you need to worry, but it gives you some time together. This is a potent combination that your teen will really enjoy.

The other avenue is to take courses in computer use. They are readily available everywhere from a wide variety of sources. The cost for basic courses is usually low and since everyone in the course is at your level, they are not intimidating. Just leaving the computer to your teens to use in any way they want can be too trusting. Since there are real dangers involved with the use of computers, it's far better for parents to know what their teens are doing with it.

The financial problems caused by the rapid obsolescence of personal computers are also very real ones for most parents. When to buy a new computer or upgrade an old one can be difficult decisions since the technology changes so fast. The key is how the machine will be used. Most modern desktop computers are powerful enough to send a rocket to the moon. If the only uses being made of them are word processing and Internet research, then no upgrade is likely necessary as most computers easily handle these chores. If there are specialized music or database applications that need to be used, perhaps more horsepower is necessary. The key here is to listen carefully to your teen's arguments for a new machine, then talk to people you can trust who know the field well. If you decide against a new machine, explain the reasons for this decision, then stick to it. Parents really have to do their homework or they will be buying a Ferrari when a Chevrolet will do.

When used properly, the computer is a fantastic tool. Unfortunately it requires regulation to ensure proper and fair usage. A few simple rules and some basic knowledge will ensure that the computer remains a tool and not a potentially dangerous weapon.

Sentencing the Culprit

One of the most difficult aspects of the discipline process for parents of teenagers is deciding if, when and how to give consequences when rules are broken. It is so difficult that parents often avoid the issue entirely. The following true story illustrates this point:

A parent of a 12-year-old Grade 7 student met with the school counselor and police resource officer to discuss the boy's recent school disciplinary problems. Besides being in trouble at school, the lad was also in serious trouble with the police for a particularly severe housebreaking in which the place was heavily damaged. In the course of the conversation the parent revealed that his son had sneaked out of the house the previous night at about 2 AM. The father then stayed awake until the boy returned just after 5 AM. The counselor then asked what the father had done about it. He replied that he had not done anything and that he did not want his son to know that he knew about the nocturnal adventure. When asked why not, the father answered that he did not want to upset his son.

Unfortunately this story is all too common these days. For a variety of reasons, parents are often afraid to give consequences for broken rules or do not think they are necessary. Even when parents do hand out consequences, they do not always have the intended effect. A thorough examination of this area is definitely in order as there is little point in making rules if they are not effectively enforced.

The Problems

One of the main problems involved with modern parenting seems to be an outgrowth of the movement to ban corporal punishment. The argument over whether or not to spank a young child has been swinging towards the "not" side since the writings of Dr. Benjamin Spock. This argument has tremendous validity for many reasons. Unfortunately many parents seem to have extended it to include all consequences for misbehavior. This laissez-faire disciplinary policy, or lack of it, is responsible for many well-educated parents firmly believing that misbehavior is just a stage, and the child will eventually grow out of it. This e-mail from a concerned parent clearly illustrates the point:

> *Dear Dr. Wooding,*
>
> *I am becoming very concerned with my teenage son's behavior. He stays out well past curfew, even on school nights. He argues with both of us constantly. His marks are poor and he skips classes frequently. He has come home smelling of alcohol on several occasions. He says that it's his life and if we try to control him he will run away from home.*
>
> *Our friends say that this is just a phase and will soon pass. They advise us to ignore his behavior and he will eventually come around.*
>
> *Are our friends correct, or should we be trying to do something about this behavior?*

These parents and their friends were responsible middle-class people with college educations. Nevertheless they were obviously confused as to whether or not to discipline. This is an extremely common parenting dilemma today.

Another large group of parents is in a similar situation for slightly different reasons. This group fears that disciplining a child will destroy the relationship they have with him or her. They believe that discipline results in angry children who will come to hate their parents. Again this philosophy is often adopted by relatively well-educated parents who have taken college courses which stress humanism and non-violent approaches to conflict. Non-violence is indeed the best approach to parenting, especially with teens, but this should not be extended to non-action when discipline is called for. The opposite of what this group believes is actually the case. Teens want and need consequences when they misbehave, and become anxious and angry if they don't get them.

Parents who do fundamentally believe in giving consequences for misdemeanors have problems of different types. One of the main problems for these parents is giving consequences that are ineffective or inappropriate. These have the effect of making teens angry rather than teaching them a lesson. Two examples come immediately to mind. One occurred when a teen of divorced parents refused to go to her father's house for her biweekly weekend. She had an important basketball tournament that weekend, and she was a starting player. Her father insisted that she could not change her weekend and that she should stay at his place as scheduled, even though he lived in another town. When she did not show up, he drove to her place to get her. She still refused. On the next visitation weekend, he made her write a letter of apology and she had to pay for his gas out of her allowance when he drove to her place. These consequences infuriated the teen, as she did not feel she should have to apologize for his inflexibility.

"Punishment is a good way of getting your teenager disciplined. It's not the punishment (because we know we need it) that bothers us, it's the way of punishment. Parents don't seem to know that times have changed and just because you don't know how to punish your teenager doesn't mean you should treat them the way you were treated."
— Lisa and Sally

Another example of inappropriate consequences happened when a teen brought home a report card with marks lower than those of her previous term. Her parents grounded her until the next report card, two-and-a-half months later. This teen was also furious, as she saw no connection between her lower marks and her ability to go out on weekends. The result was a long period of arguing and sulking, which made the entire family miserable. Both of these families created difficulties for themselves by giving inappropriate consequences. In fact neither action deserved a consequence at all. Both were problems that could have been handled outside of a disciplinary situation. However, in cases where consequences really are warranted, the wrong ones can cause more harm than good.

Another problem that causes well-meaning parents endless grief in disciplinary situations is when tempers are lost and the two parties begin yelling at each other. This becomes a no-win situation because whenever anger enters the situation, reason and logic leave. A yelling match in which the primary objective becomes to verbally wound the other party is the usual result. It is very easy for this to happen. Usually when a teen has broken the rules or done something wrong, parents become very worried. They worry that they have failed as parents or that their teen is headed in the wrong direction. This worry is a form of stress, and when stressed it takes very little for the worry to turn to anger. Something as simple as the teen's tone of voice when confronted or a defiant or sarcastic comment can tip the balance from concern to fury. Once this happens, the consequences can escalate well out of proportion to the offence. The following conversation illustrates this point.

> *Dad:* *Where have you been? You're over an hour late.*
> *Sean:* *I was at James' house. He had a bunch of kids over. We were having so much fun I forgot what time it was.*
> *Dad:* *You forgot. Do you realize how worried we were? We had no idea what happened to you.*
> *Sean:* *Here we go with the worried routine again.*
> *Dad:* *Don't you get flippant with me. This is our house and we pay the bills.*
> *Sean:* *What's that got to do with anything?*
> *Dad:* *Everything you ungrateful little snot.*
> *Sean:* *Well at least I'm not a rotten parent like you.*
> *Dad (yelling):* **Get to your room right now! You're grounded for a month with no TV or telephone.**

It can happen that fast. In fact this is a relatively mild example. With all the bad language that teens are exposed to today, it would be more common for some very ugly swear words to quickly enter the conversation. Losing tempers is probably the most common problem that parents face in disciplinary situations.

It is clear from this discussion that giving consequences for teenage infractions is a difficult process for parents, either because they do not believe they are necessary, or because it is so hard to stay calm and then mete out an appropriate sentence.

Consequence Theory

As discussed in Chapter 1, teens want and need rules and they become disappointed and angry when they receive no consequences for breaking those rules. An effective system of discipline helps teens to feel secure during these years of very high insecurity by setting limits that make decisions unnecessary. By setting a curfew, for example, teens do not have to decide when to leave an activity — the decision is already made for them. Rules can even help them to bail out of uncomfortable situations. A typical situation might be a party that is getting out of control. A curfew makes it unnecessary to come up with a phony excuse for leaving. The teen just pleads the curfew.

Rules and consequences also show teens that their parents love and care about them. It takes time and effort to set rules and hand out consequences for infractions. Teens know that parents who don't care about them will let them do whatever they want. Since teens really need to know that their parents care about them, they want to be disciplined.

This does not mean that they will cheer when you hand out a consequence. If it's to be effective, they won't really like it. They may even argue and protest. However, teens know when they have erred and expect consequences to result. If these are "fair" in their eyes, then they will accept them with only mild protestations. The protestations are usually just to remind you that they have a mind and identity of their own, and not really because they don't accept their justice.

Parental Actions

> *"My parents' punishments suck. They mainly yell and hit.*
> *If I do one little mistake that everyone would laugh at,*
> *they ban me from my friends."*
> — Hanna

While hitting has fortunately become far less common in recent years, the point that parents have difficulty in selecting appropriate consequences is well made. This process is not easy and it requires thought and practice. To make the practice of setting consequences easier, we can break it down into a 4-step process that should be followed whenever your teen breaks the family rules.

1 Be Flexible

> *"My rules are OK. They aren't really set — like you*
> *can bend them but not break them."*
> — Stephanie

A rule should be considered as a guideline, not as something fixed and absolute. This is especially true for teenagers. Their typical characteristics of being disorganized and poor time managers cause them to forget what time it is and what they were supposed to be doing. They don't usually mean to do this, it just happens. This knowledge helps parents to relax and be a little flexible with the rules. If a teen occasionally misses curfew by just a few minutes, no consequences are really necessary. Parents can certainly mention the tardiness, or give a meaningful glance at the clock, but they do not need to discipline. If the lateness becomes a frequent event, then the teen is pushing the flexibility too far and consequences will be in order. Similar flexibility can be shown with telephone calls and chores. Allow them to miss by a bit, but not by a lot.

A Listen to the Explanation

> *"If it's a minor offence the parents' shouldn't punish but*
> *rather listen to the kids because that's probably why the kid*
> *broke the rule — to get the parents attention."*
> — *Kham*

Actually, while Kham definitely has good advice, it's not just minor infractions that require a parent to listen. Occasionally circumstances conspire against teenagers and cause the best of plans to go awry. In these cases teens become very upset if their story is not listened to and they receive consequences anyway. If their misdemeanor is serious enough that you can't afford to be flexible and let it go, the next step is to listen to the teen's explanation before you move to the consequences.

Most caring parents become very upset when their teen does something wrong. They worry that a trend may be developing, or that their parenting is not being effective. The tendency at this point is to overreact to ensure that the problem does not repeat itself. However, it is never a good idea to act before you have heard the full story, just in case the circumstances were not in your teen's control, and she was just as upset as you by what happened. Shannon's story is typical:

> *Lena and I went to the mall one day. On the way there she asked to borrow my backpack. She said that she had to buy some things and forgot to bring hers with her, so I gave her mine. We went to two or three stores but we weren't always together because I wanted to look at some things too. When we left the last store a security guard stopped us and asked to look in the backpack. There was a lot of stuff in there that Lena had not paid for. The security guard asked whose pack it was and Lena said it was mine. The security guard took me into the office and took my picture, then called my parents. Now I'm banned from the mall and grounded for a month. It's not fair.*

Shoplifting is very scary for parents, even though most teens try it at one time or another. Parents tend to worry that their lessons have failed or that a trend towards thievery is developing. Nevertheless, the best approach would have been to listen carefully to the story, check it out if necessary and then decide on the consequences. In Shannon's case just being involved with the law was extremely frightening for her and she really needed her parents to be supportive. Instead they made the problem worse.

By listening to the full story before reacting, parents not only get a clearer picture of whether to give out consequences, but they show their teen that they are trying to be fair. For a refresher on listening skills, reread the guidelines for listening to teens in Chapter 3.

B Discuss and Negotiate

> *"I think parents should talk to the child, hear the story, then discuss the punishment with them."*
> — *Sarah*

Once the story is heard, and you have decided that consequences are necessary, this is the time to discuss the lesson you want the consequences to teach. Usually the teens know what they did wrong, but just to be sure, restate the reason that their offence is receiving consequences. Keep this part short. The tendency here is to lecture. Parents state their position, then, if the teen does not show sufficient reaction, they restate it — often several times. Avoid this. Keep the sermon short. Just ensure that your reasoning is clear. Let's look at a brief example.

> Mom: *"I realize that you were frustrated and angry, but swearing at the store clerk and throwing the money at her was not an appropriate solution. She may have been rude because she was having a hard day. Next time just hand the item back and leave. I'll help you sort it out later. Your consequences are to apologize in person to that clerk, and you are banned from going to the mall for two weeks."*

That is all that is needed. You've made your point and sentenced the guilty party, now let it go.

It may even happen that no consequences are really necessary. Sometimes during this discussion it becomes clear that the teen really is sorry for the misdemeanor. In this case, the lesson is learned. Why overdo it? In other cases, where the offence is too serious to ignore, use this discussion technique. The following are some instances in which you have no choice but to dispense consequences:

- *when the offence is very serious, such as drinking, using drugs, shoplifting or vandalizing*
- *when the offence is deliberate, such as when the curfew is ignored because the teen was having too much fun*
- *when it is a repeat offence — earlier discussions and consequences had no effect*
- *when no remorse is shown for what you know to have been a serious circumstance*

Once the discussion is finished it's time to decide on the consequences. This is often the most difficult part of the procedure. We have already discussed how the situation can be made worse by setting the wrong penalty, so it's best to set them as appropriately as possible. The best way to do this is to start by asking the teen what the consequences should be. This is the negotiation part of the process. Many parents omit this step because they feel that the teens will suggest either a very light penalty or none at all. In fact the opposite is the case. Teens are often harder on themselves than the parent would have been.

There are two advantages to letting teens suggest the consequences. The first is that when they suggest them, they tend to protest much less and accept them much more easily. They also tend to follow through on the consequences better because, after all, it was their idea. The other advantage is that it takes the onus off you to come up with something appropriate. If the teen suggests it, then he must think it's appropriate. That makes it "fair" and, again, there will not be any protestations.

If the penalty suggested by the teenager appears to be too light a sentence, then it is certainly the parental prerogative to increase it. There is no requirement to accept the teen's suggestion; it's just good practice to hear the idea first. Before rejecting the teen suggestion though, try asking why they think this is appropriate. There may actually be a good reason that will change your mind about its effectiveness. If not you can still reject it, giving your reasons for doing so. This turns the whole scene into a dialog instead of a rant and gives little or no chance for anger from either side to cloud the picture.

This entire discussion and negotiation procedure is designed around the idea that consequences are given to teach, not to "punish." If reasons are first listened to, then given for actions, then the point will be made. If instead, the procedure is conducted in an arbitrary fashion, the only point the teen will take is that you are unfair. Anger and/or sulking result instead of a learning experience.

C Do It Immediately

> *If it were done when 'tis done, then 'twere well*
> *It were done quickly.*
> — *Macbeth,* Act 1, Scene vii

Macbeth had a good point, even though he was speaking about assassinating the King. If you are going to hand out consequences, *do it as quickly as possible,* and have them end as soon as is feasible. There are two reasons for this advice. First, the penalty will be far better associated with the misdeed if the sentence is passed immediately. Teens who are forced to wait to find out their penalty do not then link it with the act. This becomes self-defeating, as the purpose of the whole scenario is to teach the teen not to do it again. Further, they will not accept these consequences as easily as they would have at the time. Where once it seemed fair, now the penalty seems harsh.

The second reason is associated. The longer the consequences drag on, the less the teen will remember what it was for. Teens have relatively short memories for feelings. They will remember what they did, but rarely does this recollection include how upset or worried the parents had been. They really don't recall what was so bad about their transgression. The result is that they will complain and sulk when the consequences go on longer than their memory of the severity of the offence.

There is one key exception to this basic rule. If the teen's offence was so serious, or her attitude too negative for you to maintain your temper, then postpone the penalty until the next day. Do not give consequences when you are too angry to think. The result will almost always be unsatisfactory for everyone.

Sample Consequences

My object all sublime
I shall achieve in time —
To let the punishment fit the crime.
— *W.S. Gilbert,* The Mikado

Such a noble object, but so difficult to do. To actually set consequences that neatly fit the misdeed is extremely difficult, especially under the stress of the moment. Often it is difficult to think of any type of penalty, much less one that fits the crime. The following are some samples that can be drawn on.

Offence	Consequence
Late for curfew	Not very late — talking to. Very late — short grounding (a week is usually enough).
Property damage	Restitution (from own money) and an apology.
Defiance (swearing, refusal)	Loss of a privilege — TV, Nintendo, having friends over, computer.
Telephone abuse (refusal to get off, too long, bad language)	Loss of use of telephone for up to a week.

Offence	Consequence
Failure to do a chore	Must do it immediately after the omission is discovered. If repeated, this plus loss of a privilege.
Violence	Longer grounding. Discussion with a police officer about consequences of violent acts.
Rudeness	Apology.
Fighting with a sibling	Both parties to their room. If repeated, loss of a privilege for each.
Drinking or drug use	Two-week minimum grounding followed by severe restrictions on social activities such as no parties for a further month.

These are only suggestions since every case is a bit different. However as a general guideline, try to stay away from grounding except in the case of serious offences. Grounding does not work well because of the short memory problem teens have. Try to remove a privilege instead. You may not even have to decide for yourself if your teen can suggest a consequence that you can live with. Basically, don't get hung up trying to think of something that "fits the crime." Just levy the penalty and move on.

> *"If I do break my parents' rules, I'd like to be taught the right way so that I wouldn't do it again. Grounding is OK or restricting certain things like the phone, TV or computer. However, hitting and yelling wouldn't be as good because it just makes children want to do even more bad things."*
> — Brittni

Out of Control Teens

All too often in recent years some parents have suddenly discovered that their teen has stopped responding to their rules and demands. These teens come and go when they please, defy their parents' authority and become rude and abusive when challenged. These parents are usually at a loss to explain what has gone wrong. Worse, many convince themselves that this is just a stage of normal teen development and if they wait long enough, the teen will emerge from it. If you are still not sure what constitutes an "out of control" teen, read the following:

Subject: hot-tempered teenage daughter

Dear Dr. Wooding:

I am writing to you out of desperation and want to know if what we are going through is pretty much normal. We have a 14-year-old daughter who insists on spending all of her free time with her friends. And I mean every spare minute — from the time she gets home from school, till 9:00 or 10:00 PM every night. She doesn't make homework a priority at all, and gets very mouthy with her father and me when we ask her to do any-thing around the house. (Which isn't very much at all.) She may come in when it is convenient for her to grab a bite for dinner, but doesn't eat regular meals, either. I am very concerned about her health because of this. We just had a major blow-up tonight because she was home sick from school today (with a cold) and she knows that if she is too sick to go to school, she cannot just "be well" when it is time for her friends to come home. Because of her attempting to be out with her friends, and not lis-tening to my requests to get her homework done, I ended up grounding her — the only way I have been able to keep her in the house long enough to talk to her. The situation only escalated when I attempted to talk to her again about her homework and she didn't answer me. This is usually what happens — she either ignores us, or uses a really disre-spectful and sarcastic tone when it is something she doesn't want to deal with. I, for one, do not want to be talked to that way, and said if she would be a little more co-operative, things would change, and I would not be on her case all the time. I said she would only end up being grounded for a longer time. She blew up and said grounding doesn't work — it only "pisses her off" and she flew out the door. (With her friends who were waiting on the front lawn.) I would like to know how we can understand her better, and not only open up the lines of communication, but even get her to be receptive to the idea of attempting to communicate with us, and respect us. Unfortunately, I have a much stronger view of this than my husband, whose only advice to me is "leave her alone." Our daughter has a hot temper and usually uses it to get her way with her father, who tries to avoid confrontation at all costs. I really want to listen to her — but I feel she doesn't have her priorities straight — schoolwork, her health, and even helping around the house (once in a while!) all should come before her friends. I just don't want it to come to a point where she is run-ning away from home because I tried too hard with her. Can you help me?

Thank You.

This situation has all the earmarks of a teen who is running her own show. She stays out with her friends every night, ignores her homework and chores, comes to dinner when it is convenient and even defies her mother's grounding and leaves anyway. This parent not only wonders if this is normal behavior but worries that if she tries to do anything about it her daughter will run away. This sad tale is absolutely typical of this type of situation. How do parents come to find themselves in this situation?

The Problems

Parents who have teenagers like the one described in the e-mail have no difficulty explaining what the problem is — their households are tense and chaotic. Teens who demand things their way, who come and go as they please and who refuse to conform to household standards are usually major sources of worry and concern to caring parents. Families in this situation can't make any plans that include the out-of-control child, as they never know where the teen will be. They can't have family dinners, as they are not sure if the teen will even be home at meal times. They are constantly being yelled at and argued with. Other children in the family often feel neglected because so much parental energy is being expended on the problem teen, so they often become sullen and resentful. Basically the home becomes a constant battleground for the entire family.

Parents of teenagers who are out of their control are fairly sure they are doing something wrong. They realize that most households are not in situations where the tail is wagging the dog. In other words, they know that the teen is controlling the household rather than the parents and that this should probably not be the case. The word "probably" is used here because some parents are not sure that their situation is really abnormal. They wonder if their lack of control is not just a stage that parents of "strong willed" teenagers have to go through. In fact they often hope that this is the case, because then the problem is not one of their making. When seen as a natural phase of teen development it takes the onus

Teens need many obvious signs that their parents care about them, and when these signs are not clear enough, they become angry and resentful.

off the parents to find a solution. They feel that if they wait long enough the stage will end and the problem will go away. This is definitely not the case.

The majority of these parents, however, realize that they are doing something wrong but they have no idea what that is. There are actually many possible causes, but these causes usually have similar roots (see below — "When Parenting is Not the Problem" — for exceptions to this) — the teens feel that their parents do not care about them. In a minority of cases this may be true, but in most the parents do care, but they are not showing it clearly enough to the teen. As was discussed in the "Hug Me" section of Chapter 1, the teenage years are the most insecure of a person's life. Teens need many obvious signs that their parents care about them, and when these signs are not clear enough, they often become angry and resentful. This anger can be displayed in many ways. One of these ways is to push the home limits until the parents take some action that displays their affection. Out-of-control teens start this way. They push and push hoping their parents will do something that will show they really do care. If these signs are not forthcoming, they push harder by engaging in more and more illicit activities. They need to know that their parents care enough about them to take the time and energy to set and enforce limits. They also need the limits so that they do not have to make difficult and potentially dangerous decisions, like whether to go to an all-night "rave" or whether to drink or use drugs. If these limits do not exist, teenagers become tense and anxious. They try increasingly negative behaviors to see what their parents will do. They are basically testing the limits until they find them.

Unfortunately this limit testing puts them into conflict with their parents. The parents will usually yell, argue and threaten, which causes the highly emotional teen to yell and threaten back. These arguments often become so frequent and intense that the house becomes too much of a battleground and either the teen leaves or the parents kick the youngster out. Unfortunately, this does nothing to resolve the issues.

In order to find solutions to the anger that causes teens to get out of control, it is first necessary to examine the causes.

What Causes the Anger?

There are a number of reasons why teens get so angry that they eventually get to a position where they are out of control. Several of these reasons involve ineffective disciplinary systems. These were discussed in "Sentencing the Culprit," but here is a brief review. First, many parents hold philosophical beliefs that children should not be "punished" and that any form of discipline is a form of punishment. These beliefs are an outgrowth of the movement to eliminate corporal punishment, or hitting children. The original idea is correct — there is no need to hit children. Unfortunately the extension to include all types of consequences is not. Teens who find themselves in a situation where their parents do not levy penalties for misbehavior become anxious and concerned that their parents don't care about them. It has been said earlier that teens need discipline due to their insecurities. They need to know that their parents care enough about them to take the time and energy to set and enforce limits. If they do not find any limits, their anger and frustration begins to grow.

Other parents feel that giving consequences for rule infractions will destroy their relationship with the children. They feel that the aim of parenting is to be friends with your children and that disciplining them will ruin this friendship. These ideas appear to have come from well-meaning theorists, often at the university level. It certainly would be wonderful if we could raise children without resorting to rules and consequences, but unfortunately we can't. Simply explaining where a teen has gone wrong will work in cases of a minor infraction, such as being a few minutes late for curfew, but is not sufficient where more serious violations have occurred. Teens expect consequences as signs that their parents are truly worried about them. A "talking to" gives the appearance that they are not really worried about the teen and therefore that they don't really love him or her. Anger is again the result.

Finally, many parents are just too busy with work and leisure activities to control their kids. Discipline takes emotional energy and will. A large percentage of modern parents don't have this energy because their priorities are their careers and making money. Their focus is on paying for their huge home, their two cars and the many other assorted toys that are so prevalent in our consumer society.

These parents come home from work tired and stressed, and all they want is to rest and relax. The result is that they avoid disciplining their teens whenever possible. They just do not want the tension that results from these confrontations. Instead, the teens become tense and resort to any behavior that will get their parents to pay attention to them. Some are fortunate enough to find healthy outlets such as sports and academics. Most just do whatever they can to get attention, which usually involves pushing the limits. The problem with this behavior is that when the parents do react, they tend to overdo it. In other words, they explode and a massive confrontation often results. This just tends to increase the teen's frustration, and their anger multiplies.

> *The problem for teens is that they are highly emotional. They aren't sitting down and plotting their strategy rationally. Instead they are doing whatever they can to get immediate attention.*

Parents and teachers often wonder why teens don't channel their energies effectively. For example, why push the limits by doing poorly in school when it would be more positive to excel and get attention that way? The problem for teens is that they are highly emotional. They aren't sitting down and plotting their strategy rationally. Instead they are doing whatever they can to get immediate attention. They discover by trial and error that misbehavior is faster than building up a positive academic record. They do what feels best, and not what would be the most positive for them. In many ways they are actually trying to hurt and upset their parents. Possibly they fear that even if they did do well in school or sports they still would not be noticed.

While ineffective discipline systems are a prime cause of parents' losing control of their teens, there are other situations that cause teens to become angry enough to push the household limits. A main culprit these days is the various situations that result from families splitting up. Divorce alone is enough to make teens very angry. The evidence is mounting rapidly that divorce is far harder on children emotionally than most people have thought. While this fact has been obvious to anyone working closely with teens, it is one that most parents who are in the process of splitting up do not want to hear. They seem to feel that since they will be happier without the spouse, their children will be too. This is not so. Divorce is devastating on children, especially those in the 10- to 15-year-old range. Many become resentful and angry — often with both parents. They then begin the pattern of pushing the limits to let the parents know something is wrong. They resort to this behavior because they are too immature to sit their parents down and explain the situation. Indeed, many quite rightfully believe that the parents won't listen to them even if they had the maturity to handle the situation this way. Their anger can be manifested in many ways. They can misbehave, break the law, do poorly in school or even refuse to attend school. They will quit organizations that they know their parents want them to belong to, such as athletic teams, the school band and Scouts or Guides, and change to a far less desirable type of friend. These teens are trying to send a message, but unfortunately their parents rarely realize what the real message is. Even when told, they prefer to believe that the teen will get over it, rather than directly address the problem. As the teen tries harder and harder to gain parental attention, eventually they get to the point where they are out of control.

Children generally dislike intensely any stranger who is brought into the family.

In many cases the divorce can be at least partially accepted, but the situation may go downhill when a new partner is brought into the home. As will be discussed in much greater detail in a later chapter, children generally dislike intensely any stranger who is brought into the family. They see this as an attempt to replace the real parent; children, especially teens, usually hate this. The action of bringing in a stepparent is also resented because it makes the breakup much more final. Until a new partner enters the picture, most teens secretly hope that their parents will reunite. These hopes are dashed with the arrival of the stepparent. Again the anger and resentment builds. If not dealt with early, an "out of control teen" can result.

While ineffective discipline and atypical family situations are the root cause of the majority of teens getting out of control, there are others. These include physically and sexually abusive parents or relatives, alcoholic or drug addicted parents and severe emotional disturbance, such as schizophrenia. In all but the latter, anger is the source of the problem, followed by inappropriate or ineffectual parental response. The question then becomes, What is the proper parental response when signs of deep-rooted anger are detected? The next section has the answers.

> ### Causes of Teen Anger
>
> - *Parents who believe children should not be disciplined.*
> - *Parents who do not use consequences for fear of losing their teen's friendship.*
> - *Parents who are too tired to discipline.*
> - *Divorce.*
> - *Remarriage.*
> - *Severe emotional disturbance.*

Parental Actions

The first step in the process of dealing with a teenager who is out of control is to *make sure that you really do have a problem*. Like the story related in the e-mail, some parents are unsure how radical teen behavior can become and still be within normal limits. Below is a list of symptoms that should set the alarm bells ringing, particularly if three or more are present:

- *New (and less desirable) friends*
- *Radical new hairstyle or piercing*
- *Change of clothing style — again usually to a more radical look*
- *Loss of interest in activities that had been important*
- *Persistently argumentative*
- *Greater than normal need to be alone*
- *Consistent rule breaking*
- *Sudden drop in school marks, refusal to attend school or persistent skipping*
- *Abrupt change in type of music*
- *Insomnia or the need for unusual amounts of sleep*
- *Frequent alcohol or drug use*
- *Sudden changes in eating patterns*
- *Persistent lying or stealing*

If you look back at the sample e-mail, you will notice that the 14-year-old was argumentative, she frequently broke the household rules, she wasn't working at school and her eating habits were sporadic. That is definitely a teen who is out of control. Parents need to take immediate action if their child is displaying a similar symptom pattern. This is not easy, as most parents have no idea where to start. It is basically a three-stage process

Stage 1 — Discussion and Compromise

Having determined that a serious problem really does exist, the next step is to *try to find out what is causing the behavior.* You can't remedy the situation until you know why it is happening. The best approach is to sit down with the teen and try to get him to tell you what is the matter. This step is very difficult, as the gulf that has developed between you will be so wide that the teen is usually angry and suspicious. You have to keep in mind that the teen does not want to be that way. They too want to solve the problem but they have no idea how to do this. Much of their behavior has been directed at trying to get your attention. This knowledge will help you to persevere past the initial resistance to try to get to the bottom of the problem.

Another reason that initiating a discussion is difficult is that many parents do not want to hear the explanation. Deep down they probably are already aware that they are the root of the problem. Since they don't want to hear this, they either avoid the issue or send the teen to a counselor to be "fixed." There is no need for parents to be this defensive. Even though the majority of problems with teens are the result of either their parents' action or inaction, they are rarely done intentionally. There are few courses in parenting children and fewer on parenting teens. If mistakes are made, they are usually the result of not understanding enough about children. Parents do not need to feel defensive or guilty. That will just interfere with solving the problem.

To get a discussion going, pick a quiet moment when the household is relatively calm and the teen is not angry or tense. Often the best time is just as the youngster is going to bed. Will yourself to stay calm no matter what you are going to hear. Start the conversation with an "I" statement. This means that you are going to tell your teen how you feel about the state of war that exists in the household and not point the finger of blame in any direction. An example would be, "I'm really concerned about how things have been going between us lately and I'd like to try to improve the situation. Have you any suggestions?" Don't expect an instant dialog. Instead be gentle but persistent. Try not to react to any anger or rudeness. Instead, focus on any emotion that you detect and make a leading statement like, "You seem pretty frustrated," or, "You seem really angry at me."

Once a response has been generated, do not try to defend or justify any of your past actions. The accusations will eventually come thick and fast, but you want to find out what is wrong, not validate yourself. That will only lead back into an argument. Concentrate on really listening to your teen. When all the reasons seem to be on the table, it is your turn. Explain how you feel about the situation and which behaviors of the teen are upsetting to you. Do not accuse or condemn, just clearly state why you are upset and what changes you feel need to happen.

Consistent with this "listening" or "Hear Me" approach, the next step is to ask for your teen's suggestions as to how to solve the problems. They will almost always have some, and many will be very practical. You need to be prepared with some suggestions of your own. To come up with these you may need to consult some experts. This can be in the form of a counselor, a book or a friend who is not having the same kinds of problems. In any case, once the suggestions from both sides have been heard, then it's time to compromise on a final set of guidelines. The answer almost always lies in a compromise, where both sides are willing to give a little to get a lot. If necessary, write down the compromises you have decided on and refer to them frequently. Both sides have to stick to the bargain if progress is to be made.

This is the ideal way of solving the problems created by a teen who is out of control. Unfortunately many parents fail at this level, usually because emotions are just too high for reasonable discussion to take place. Communication sessions tend to break down into yelling matches. If family difficulties cannot be solved by this approach, it is time to move to the second stage.

> ### *Steps to Discussion and Compromise*
>
> - *Pick a quiet moment.*
> - *Start with an "I" statement.*
> - *Focus on any emotion detected and reflect it.*
> - *Listen carefully — don't try to justify your actions.*
> - *Ask for suggestions.*
> - *Look for areas of compromise.*

Stage 2 — Mediation

If discussion and compromise cannot solve the problems, it is time to get *professional help*. A person trained in mediating disputes, and hopefully in parenting teenagers as well, can keep the emotion out of the discussion. This usually means a counselor or a psychologist. The trick is to find one who can relate to both sides. Not all professionals can establish rapport with teenagers, which is a necessary condition if the problem is to be solved. Most teens will not want to see a "shrink" either because of the stigma that is still attached to emotional problems or because they know that it will upset their parents if they refuse. Fathers also can be a problem as many consider it "unmanly" to get a third party to solve their problems. If the teen and father can be convinced to go for help, the key for the counselor is to establish a relationship with the teen first. The parents are usually already motivated to solve the problem (and they are paying for the sessions), so they are usually willing to listen. The teen is usually sullen and resentful and does not want to be there.

To find a good professional, start by getting recommendations from school counselors, friends who have gone through the process or a church minister. If finances are a problem there are a number of agencies that have either no charge or charge on a sliding scale according to your resources. The problem with these organizations is that they are often overwhelmed by requests for their services and have lengthy waiting lists. In any case, check that the professional you choose is registered as a psychologist in your state or province, as these people must conform to standards of training, ethics and behavior.

You will know if you have the right professional after one or two sessions. Both sides must respect the counselor if the process is to work. If you find that the psychologist is not right for your family, do not hesitate to ask for a referral to another. Otherwise the process will not work and you will have wasted your money.

A good counselor will have no trouble getting the teen to open up and to relate what the problems are. Once he or she has heard both sides of the problems, recommendations will be made to

> *For the teen to change, parents usually need to change first.*

solve them. The key is for the parents to follow these recommendations carefully. Amazingly, they often fail to do so. Many parents go to counseling expecting the professional to find a solution to the family problems and apply it to the teen. They do not realize that *they* are the key to the problem. For the teen to change, parents usually need to change first. Counseling is doomed to failure for any parents who do not understand this. Remember that the root of all these problems is usually that teens do not feel loved and cared about. If they don't see their parents trying the counselor's recommendations, it is just confirmation that they really don't care. Then they won't try either and nothing gets solved.

In rare cases, counseling does not work, usually because the parents don't follow the recommendations, counseling is not instituted soon enough or a good counselor was not found. In some cases, as will be discussed below, there may not be a solution. In any of these cases parents have no choice but to go to the third stage.

Stage 3 — Tough Love

If parents have given stages 1 and 2 a fair trial and there still has been no improvement in their teen's behavior, there is no alternative but to move to a much more drastic level. It cannot be emphasized enough that this is a last resort. Parents should not shortcut the system and move directly to this stage. They need to be secure in the knowledge that all other options have been tried. However, once both stages have been tried to no avail then it is time to adopt a unilateral approach.

This stage is designed to obtain peace in the family. Up to this point the out-of-control teen has been dominating family life. The worrying, arguments and counseling sessions have taken a disproportionate amount of time. The parents' lives have been disrupted and the other children have not been receiving their fair share of the attention. It's time to cut the losses and to restore some semblance of normalcy to the household. To do this, parents have to take a very tough and unified stand.

The first thing to do is to draw up a list of rules that you want the teen to follow. These should be relatively fair, but should now lean towards the parents' ideas of reasonable rather than the compromise that might have been made before the problems started. Next, sit down with the adolescent and outline these new rules. At this point it is not a discussion — it is an edict. Then state that if these rules cannot be followed the teen will not be able to live at home. The final step is to rigorously enforce these rules. This is the hard part — especially for parents who have had difficulty setting and enforcing rules in the past.

> *Always make it clear that you love the teen and he or she can return any time they are willing to follow the rules.*

The idea is to have clear consequences for any infraction and to apply them every time. If a consequence is given and the teen refuses to comply, then the teen must leave. Always make it clear that you love the teen and he or she can return any time they are willing to follow the rules. Try to ensure that you know where they can be reached. Then show them the door. A sample conversation may make this process clearer.

Dad: *Where are you going?*

Jamie: *I'm going to a party at Elise's.*

Dad: *No you are not. You were grounded for a week for being late last weekend.*

Jamie: *I'm going and you can't stop me.*

Dad: *No I can't, but if you leave you can find another place to stay for the next three days.*

Jamie: *Yeah right!*

Dad: *This time I mean it. Are you going to stay home?*

Jamie: *No way.*

Dad: *OK. Give me your house key. Are there any clothes you*

> *want to take with you? (Note: If Jamie refuses to give up*
> *the key, you can always change the locks)*
> Jamie: *You're just bluffing.*
> Dad: *Not this time. If you leave the house, you are not to return for*
> *three days. Either you follow the rules or you cannot live here.*
> Jamie: *Oh all right. I can't believe you're this mean.*
> Dad: *I'm not mean. I just want you to follow the rules.*
> *Beyond that you still have the same freedom you did before.*

There are three keys to making this approach work. The first is that the parents cannot waver. They must stay calm, but look and act like they are serious, because if there is any wavering at all the teen will win. The next key is that both parents must present a unified front. The teen must not be allowed to play one against the other. The third is the hardest. Parents must be ready to follow through if the teen will not comply. There can be no hesitation. The teen is out of the house until ready to abide by the household rules.

To be able to use this approach, parents must be convinced of several things. One is that the teen really wants you to apply consequences to rules. There is no doubt about this. If the teen does test your resolve, it is usually only once. After that there will be a new respect for your authority. Another fact to know is that most teens can survive quite well for three days. They normally have enough sympathetic friends that they can find a place for a few days. Normally they will not be on the streets. After a few days they tend to wear out their welcome and they run out of clothes. Few last longer than a week or two. When they do return, either by phoning and asking or by just showing up, make sure you welcome them and let them know you are glad they are home. Follow this by reminding them that they must live by the rules. Continue this regime until the household situation is again calm. Then you can return to the approach outlined in "Passing the Laws" and "Sentencing the Culprit."

In a minority of cases, the situation is so serious that the teen will not return. Unfortunately this is a chance parents have to take. Remember how you got to this stage. The house was tense and chaotic. You had to do something drastic once all other alternatives had been exhausted. The price of peace for the rest of the family, in a tiny percentage of cases, is that the teen does not return for an extended period of time. **This will usually not happen if the parents make it clear throughout all the stages that the teen is loved and welcome to live in the home if he or she can abide by the rules.** Teens only become street people when they are convinced that they are not wanted at home.

Stage three is indeed a drastic one. It is definitely a scary time for caring parents. If the first two stages are diligently applied, most parents will never get to this point. If they do, then they must not hesitate or the problem will continue for years.

Steps in "Tough Love"

- *Draw up a list of rules that **you** can live with*
- *Meet with the teen to outline the rules*
- *Consistently enforce these rules*
- *If you have to ask the teen to leave, initially set a time limit for his/her return*
- *Always let them know you love them*
- *Reinforce the idea that they are welcome to live at home as long as they can follow the rules*

When Parenting Is Not the Problem

As has been mentioned, out-of-control teens are not always the result of weak parental disciplinary systems or teenage anger over the family situation. There is a percentage of situations where hereditary factors appear to be at work. This is definitely the case when severe emotional problems such as bipolar disorder or schizophrenia are involved. These are dealt with at length in Chapter 6, but suffice it to say here that these disorders can, slowly and steadily, result in teens who are out of their parents' control. Similarly, at least one major study indicates that about four per cent of the population develops into "bad apples" no matter what parenting techniques are applied. These cases are extremely puzzling for parents and professionals alike as they naturally look for environmental factors first. Wise professionals need to be aware of these possibilities and should not adhere slavishly to any one theory of the origin of behavior problems.

Rudeness and Defiance

> *"Rudeness is the weak man's imitation of strength."*
> — Eric Hoffer

Of the changes that take place when a young child starts to exhibit "teenage" behavior, few shock parents more than how rude and how defiant of authority they can be at times. This type of behavior occurs most frequently when their desires are thwarted in some way. Some sample conversations will illustrate this point.

Heather:	Can I go to the mall with Stephanie this afternoon?
Mom:	No. We're all going over to your aunt's this afternoon to see the new baby.
Heather:	I don't care about the baby. I'd rather go to the mall.
Mom:	That's not very nice. She's your new cousin.
Heather:	Who cares? You never let me go with my friends.
Mom:	That's not true. But this afternoon you're going to your aunt's.
Heather:	No I'm not. I'll stay in my room all afternoon if I have to. You can't make me go.

Dad:	Can you please turn that music down a bit?
Tony:	What for? It sounds great this way.
Dad:	Because I don't really like that kind of music and don't want to listen to it.
Tony:	This is great music. I can't help it if you're too dumb to appreciate it.

Both of these conversations show how quickly a perfectly normal situation can turn into an argument, which can then lead to even harsher things being said by both sides. The result is bruised feelings all around and temporary tension in the house. Many parents wonder if the teenage tendency to be rude and defiant is something to worry about, or whether they should just ignore it and let the "stage" pass. The answer is quite clear, this behavior should not only not be ignored, it must be dealt with quickly and effectively. There are several reasons for coming to this conclusion.

The Problem

The first major problem with teenagers who are rude and defiant to their parents is that it can be the beginning of a total breakdown in authority. Parents become uncomfortable when spoken to rudely or when sworn at by their teens. If they are unable to take any action to limit this behavior, they will instead begin to try to avoid saying anything that will upset their adolescent, just to keep away from an unpleasant situation. The result is that the parents will take out the garbage themselves rather than ask their teenager to do what is normally that teen's job. They may stop asking what time the teen will come home to avoid being told that it is none of their business. Gradually their authority will become so eroded that they lose control of their teen, and the next few years will be a horrible experience for everyone.

The situation is compounded when parents defend their child's actions, either in the mistaken belief that they are being supportive to their teen in a time of need, or out of guilt from knowing that they should have been more authoritative at home.

Another concern is the example set for younger children. If youngsters see their older sibling, who they generally look up to, acting in this manner, they too may try it on for size. The problem then spreads to the entire family. Certainly the younger ones can be more easily controlled, but they will be very puzzled as to why there are different standards for children of the same family. When they in their turn start to exhibit teen behavior, they will almost certainly copy the model of the older sibling. This is definitely not a pattern that parents want to develop in their children.

An even greater concern is the danger that this behavior may generalize to other authority figures. If teens believe that speaking rudely to authority figures is acceptable, then this behavior may start to appear in schools, in stores and even to the police. Soon the teen will be getting into trouble wherever authority is met, and the teen becomes a behavior problem. The situation is compounded when parents defend their child's actions, either in the mistaken belief that they are being supportive of their teen in a time of need, or out of guilt from knowing that they should have been more authoritative at home. Teachers in particular are running into this problem more and more. Instead of being supported when they report rude or defiant behavior to parents, they are attacked as being unfair to the child. This does nothing to change the teen's behavior, and more serious problems generally ensue.

There is no doubt that allowing rudeness and defiance in the home, for whatever reason, is poor parenting practice. Almost every teenager will exhibit this type of behavior at some point, and it puzzles parents as to why the child who had been so quiet and polite before the teen years is now so verbally abusive.

The Theory

The reasons that teens start to become rude and defiant are rooted in the very essence of teenage behavior. It often starts as a method of asserting the growing desire to be independent. Being rude or questioning a parental decision feels to them as if they are standing up for themselves. It is a way of showing parents that they can think for themselves and that they are no longer just extensions of their parents. Since teens have very little control over their environment — they have little money of their own and their parents control just about everything in the household — talking back is one of the few areas where they can at least try to assert their independence. Teens believe that they are standing up for themselves and it feels good.

The desire to verbally assert themselves also has another component. This is the emotionality created by the greater amounts of hormones entering their systems. When denied something, teens often become angry almost immediately. When they lose control of their emotions, they are very likely to say things just to hurt their parents. This is something that even adults do when they are angry, but adults tend to reach this stage more slowly. Teens explode very quickly when angry, and lose control of their ability to think rationally. Instead they attack and go for the jugular. The rudeness and bad language tend to follow.

A final reason for their verbal abuses is also a result of the nature of teens. As a result of their insecurities they often use rudeness and defiance as a shock tactic to test their parents' level of caring. Teens are actually testing the limits to see if their parents will do anything.

Deep down they hope they will, although most teens are not conscious of this motivation. If no limits are found teens will test more and more to see where their parents will begin to demonstrate their affection by limiting the verbally aggressive behavior.

Despite the fact that the causes for most teenage rudeness and defiance have natural roots, it cannot be tolerated and requires immediate parental action.

Parental Actions

This problem is more difficult to explain than it is to solve. If they understand the roots of the problem, parents do not need to take rude or defiant behavior personally. This helps to keep parental anger out of the situation so that it can be dealt with effectively. Whenever the teen's verbal expressions are inappropriate the parent should first warn the teen that the language is unacceptable. If this does not bring an instant response, then the teen should be sent to his or her room until able to discuss the situation calmly. If the problem is defiance, the teen must not be allowed to get away with it. The parent should not only not back down, but should insist the teen abide by the parental decision and add consequences if the decision is not complied with immediately. A review of the earlier sample conversations may help to clarify this issue.

Heather: *Can I go to the mall with Stephanie this afternoon?*
Mom: *No. We're all going over to your aunt's this afternoon to see the new baby.*
Heather: *I don't care about the baby. I'd rather go to the mall.*
Mom: *That's not very nice. She's your new cousin.*
Heather: *Who cares? You never let me go with my friends.*
Mom: *That's not true. But this afternoon you're going to your aunt's.*
Heather: *No I'm not. I'll stay in my room all afternoon if I have to. You can't make me go.*

At this point it is vital that Mom not lose control. She should take a long, slow breath and continue.

Mom: *Sorry Heather, but you are going to your aunt's with us. You will not go to your room, because we won't leave until*

130

> *you get in the car. If you persist with this behavior you not*
> *only have to go with us but you will lose your telephone*
> *privileges for a week. Is that clear?*
> Heather: *Why are you so mean?*
> Mom: *It's not meanness — it's just common courtesy. I know you'd*
> *rather be with your friends, but you'll be OK once you see*
> *the baby. Now go and get ready.*

Normally this firmness will end the problem. Both parents have to be working together on this, and no signs of weakness can be shown. Parents often expect some type of physical confrontation, but this is never the case. Just by looking the teen straight in the eye and not budging on the decision, compliance will be forthcoming. If the argument does continue past this point, add the consequences and continue to add them until the defiance ceases. A similar approach should be taken with Tony's rudeness.

> Dad: *Can you please turn that music down a bit?*
> Tony: *What for? It sounds great this way.*
> Dad: *Because I don't really like that kind of music and don't*
> *want to listen to it.*
> Tony: *This is great music. I can't help it if you're too dumb*
> *to appreciate it.*

Again, calmness is required since being called "dumb" is extremely annoying. Since the rudeness has already occurred, then consequences need to be applied immediately.

> Dad: *That language is unacceptable. The music will go off right*
> *now, and you will stay in your room for the rest of the evening.*

That should be all that is necessary. If Tony persists in his rudeness and/or becomes defiant, then consequences need to be added. Again the most effective ones are the loss of telephone, television or video game privileges.

These methods of dealing with name-calling, swearing and defiance work extremely well if applied when the behavior is first noticed. If this behavior is let go for a while, the methods outlined in the

"Out of Control Teens" section may be required. There is never an excuse for teens to act in this manner and parents must deal with it effectively at the outset.

A Personal Tale

Once when the author was a young teen, he discovered a wasp's nest on a tree branch near his house. Deciding that the nest was a hazard, he determined to remove it. Walking back what he thought was a safe distance, he threw a large rock at the nest, hitting it squarely. The wasps were on him instantly, stinging him several times. In pain and frustration he yelled out a mild oath as he ran for home. On reaching his backyard, he not only got no sympathy from his father for his swollen face and neck, he was sternly rebuked for the oath. Two lessons were learned very effectively that day, one about nature, the other about swearing.

The Family Car

"I decided to stop worrying about my teenage daughter's driving
and take advantage of it. I got one of those bumper stickers that say,
'How's my driving?' and put a 900 number on it.
At 50 cents a call, I've been making $48 a week."
— Chris Rade

Allowing teens to use the family automobile brings with it many issues. It is a complex topic that should not be left until the teen is old enough to drive. It should be planned for well in advance due to the large number of issues that surround teenage driving.

The Problems

The problems associated with driving a car are generally quite obvious, but there are so many that parents may not at first realize what a serious issue this is. The main concern is the many responsibilities that driving a care entail. These include the life of your teen, any friends that may be in the car and others on the road. Roads are very crowded in most of the world and the chances of accidents are high. As a parent you want to be assured that your teenage driver thoroughly understands that cars are not toys and is not tempted to let the impetuosity of youth override the responsibilities of driving safely. A mistake could be deadly. Parents also need to make certain that their teenager has the proper skills to safely operate a vehicle in all weather and traffic conditions in order to give their child the best possible chance to avoid accidents.

The financial concerns that arise from driving and maintaining a vehicle are many. Even though modern automobile engines have become very efficient, the high price of gasoline still ensures that driving is expensive. Due to their higher accident rate, insurance costs are extremely high for teens, and rise dramatically should the young driver be at fault in an accident. While these two costs are obvious to most parents, a more subtle expense is routine maintenance such as oil changes, tune-ups and tire wear. They too have to be factored into the costs associated with adding another family driver. The expenditures don't stop there. Even a minor accident that is the teen's fault can cost a lot of money. A recent consumer TV show indicated that backing an SUV into a pole at 5 miles per hour could cost over $2000 in repairs. Tickets and the ensuing fines for speeding and improper parking can also be costly. Teens must have a thorough understanding of all these costs before they ever sit behind the wheel.

A major modern concern involves the potential problems associated with drinking and driving. These have to be thoroughly understood by teenagers. Despite elaborate advertising campaigns designed to reduce drunken driving, thoughtless drivers are still killing themselves and innocent bystanders in large numbers. While this problem is not just associated with teens, if teenage drivers learn to understand the legal and moral implications of drinking and driving, the lessons will more than likely stay with them for the rest of their lives. Our highways will then be much safer places to be for everyone.

A problem of lesser concern, but still of importance to parents, is that of scheduling. That is, who gets which car when? This is especially difficult if more than one child has a driver's license and/or if there is only one family vehicle. To avoid arguments at the last minute, some sort of advance schedule needs to be maintained so that everyone has a fair share of the family jalopy.

There are obviously many issues involved with teenage driving and the use of the family car. Parents need to plan well in advance of their teen's 16th birthday if constant problems are to be avoided.

Parental Actions

Planning for another teenage driver on the highways and byways should start at least six months before the teen reaches driving age. This planning should initially cover two distinct areas. The first is instruction and practice. Once the teen is old enough to get a learner's permit, then driving lessons should be obtained. For a number of reasons, parents should not try to be their teen's main instructor. These include the parental tendency to get emotional when mistakes are made as well as the chance that bad habits may be passed on. Parents also do not have access to the audiovisual materials that driving schools have to reinforce the practical lessons.

There are several sources of driving instruction. One of the best is driver education from local high schools. The only purpose of these programs is to train safe drivers. To this end well-trained instructors, new equipment and a variety of films and videos are available, all at a reasonable price. A major emphasis of these programs is on drinking and driving, which takes much of the onus for these lessons off the parents. If your local school does not have a driver education program, the next best source of lessons is the automobile club. These organizations have all the advantages of driver education programs, but the cost is usually somewhat higher. A final choice would be a commercial driving school. These schools are lower on the priority list as they tend to vary in quality and are almost always more expensive. They are, after all, in business to make money. They also do not tend to emphasize safety to the same degree, and rarely include lessons on drinking and driving. A good such school, however, is still superior to a parent trying to do the job.

In all cases the teens should be expected to pay some portion of the insurance cost and should either have to earn the money to do this, or contribute a portion of their allowance.

A second part of the early planning process should be in the financial area, in particular the insurance costs. Parents need to make their children aware of how much this will be and then decide with the teen what portion of the total bill the teen will be responsible for. They should not make the mistake of simply paying the entire bill. This teaches the adolescents nothing about real life and certainly gives them no appreciation for the cost of the privilege that they are receiving. The teen's portion of the bill should be dependent upon their ability to contribute. In cases where parents cannot afford the yearly cost, then the teen may have to earn the whole amount. In all, teens should be expected to pay some portion of the insurance cost and should either have to earn the money to do this, or contribute a portion of their allowance. Since debt should not be encouraged (another major financial lesson), parents should not advance the money up front and expect the teen to pay them back later. Instead, they should insist that the teen have the money in hand before any use of the family car is permitted.

Once the planning has been done, the driving phase begins. Even though a driving program is doing the bulk of the training, parents are still necessary to help with the practice component. This is an excellent opportunity to not only reinforce the lessons of the driving program and to build skill and confidence, but to spend some time with your teen as well. There are also some cautions involved with these practice drives. *One is that parents must stay calm.* Teens will almost invariably be nervous for the first month or two. Yelling at them or berating them for mistakes will not only add to this nervousness, it will strain your relationship. If you cannot remain calm then let the other parent supervise the practice sessions. Another caution is that the driver training lessons must be reinforced. Try not to undermine their teachings by demonstrating or allowing sloppy driving habits. This is extremely difficult as with confidence comes shortcuts. Adult drivers can often get away with cutting corners because they have done things so many times. For these sessions, be meticulous or you'll find the teen correcting you. This is not only embarrassing but also frustrating, and may lead to arguments.

> *The family car is a resource and a privilege, not a necessity or a right.*

After the teen has obtained a driver's license, then another aspect of the driving phase — control — begins. The parents must now control the use, maintenance and abuse of the family vehicle. It should be viewed by teens as a resource and a privilege — not a necessity or a right. Rules must apply to the use of this resource just as they are to the telephone or the computer. The first should be that the teen asks to use the car well in advance of the event. This is particularly true if there are several drivers in the house, and even more so if there is just one car. Fairness needs to apply and often the parents will be called upon to decide who gets to use it. This can be done either on a "turns" basis (this week is his, next is your turn), or on a priority basis — the prom is more important than a movie. Whatever the system, parents should never let themselves get into a situation where the teen *expects* to be able to use the car whenever he wants or needs it. This is far too important a family resource for it to get out of parents' control.

Several of the control factors are financial. Teens should be made to pay the entire cost of their gasoline as this helps teach them fiscal responsibility. In adult life, automobiles are basically just an expense; they are rarely financial assets. Teens must learn that driving has costs, and paying for gasoline is an easy way to help teach this. This must be done while the car is being used so that it returns with the same amount of gas in the tank that it left with. Again, do not let debt accumulate. How the teens pay for the gas is up to them. They can only use the car when they have saved enough allowance for gas, they can collect from any friends that ride with them or they can get a part-time job (see Part-time Jobs in Chapter 8). The same rules apply to any tickets or fines the teen receives and any damage caused by the teen. While insurance will pay most of the latter, there is always a deductible amount that the teen should be responsible for. Payment plans may have to be set up, but parents should not simply pay the costs and write it off to experience. Teens must learn financial responsibility for such an expensive resource.

A final control factor involves misuse of the resource. Any foolishness that comes to parents' attention should result in immediate consequences, usually loss of the car for a period of time. "Grounding" from use of the car should certainly accompany the receiving of tickets, accidents that were the teens' fault and, above all, drinking and driving. As mentioned above, this offence is so serious that, along with any legal penalties that might result, parents should remove automobile privileges for at least six months. There is one caution to this edict. Always listen to your teen's explanation before handing out the consequences. There might be a plausible reason for the behavior. If there isn't, the car is gone for the required period.

In these days, when an average automobile costs in the $30,000 range, it is vital that teens learn respect and proper use of this resource. Even more important than the finances are the serious consequences that can result from misuse of a vehicle. Lives are now at stake so parents must do all they can to ensure that their child is a safe and courteous driver. There is nothing scarier than handing the car keys to your teen for his first solo outing. The worrying will not be nearly as bad if you know that your teen is well trained and responsible.

Discipline, in all its forms, is a major component of raising a child from an insecure, fearful and irresponsible youngster to a confident and dependable adult. Parents should not let unproven theories and ideas interfere with something that even teens themselves recognize to be a vital component of child-raising. Parents who take a laissez-faire or hands-off approach to discipline give the message to their teens that they don't care about them. If this is the wrong message, then a parental overhaul of the rules and regulations is in order.

Chapter 5

Academic Questions

Parents are often confused as to what their role should be in their teenager's academic life. Some don't know whether to get involved or not so they sit back hoping that teachers will do the right educational things for their students. Others get so involved that they actually interfere with their teen's academic performance. In fact, there is a very real role for parents to play throughout their child's academic career. Unfortunately, this role is difficult because many of the problems experienced by teens in school are too difficult for parents to solve without professional help. Finding the balance between too little and too much involvement requires some knowledge as to how the educational system works and what problems students might encounter throughout their academic careers. This chapter addresses many of the most common problems encountered by today's students and provides some approaches to solving these problems.

Organizing for Academics

One of the advantages of being disorderly is that
one is constantly making exciting discoveries.
— A. A. Milne

One aspect of academic life where parents can be of tremendous help to their teens is that of organizing them for maximum academic performance. Most parents are well aware that good organizational skills can save a tremendous amount of time, and will result in a much better product. For students, this means that they can get their homework done faster and more accurately if they are well organized.

The Problems

There are many factors that can interfere with teenagers' ability to perform up to their potential in school. One of the major factors is rooted in the very nature of teens. This is their basic disorganization. As discussed in Chapter 2, teens do not have the maturity level or the basic skills to get themselves organized. Their attention spans tend to be short and they are highly emotional. They have trouble prioritizing and even more trouble determining the consequences of their actions, or in the case of homework, their inaction, on their future marks. This adds up to a generation that has messy rooms, forgets to do their chores, and can't get their homework done. They tend to leave assignments to the last minute and then forget them in their lockers. Their notebooks look like the family dog has chewed on them and their pens have many of the pieces missing. There are always a few exceptions, usually girls, but generally this description fits most teenage scholars.

Another cause of difficulties in school is the very busy schedule that so many of today's teenagers keep. They have so many activities that they have difficulty fitting their homework in. Their priorities have become confused. Teachers often hear a student say something like, "I couldn't do my homework last night, I had baseball practice." The problem is that the teen really believes that this excuse should be accepted. Even those who do understand that schoolwork should come first have difficulty because they are coming and going too much to get organized. Fatigue also plays a role. After being in school all day, then going to dance, karate, hockey practice or piano lessons, teens are often very tired. If they do their homework at all, it is incomplete or of poor quality.

A poor sense of time management is another aspect of being a teenager. This can cause them to underestimate the amount of time needed to complete an assignment, and they end up starting it too late. This problem not only affects major assignments, but daily homework as well. Teens tend to put off starting the work, assuming they will have plenty of time to complete it. Suddenly the available time is gone and the work is not done.

The following section will concentrate on how parents can help get their teens organized for school and then to ensure that homework, essays and assignments all get done and handed in on time.

Barriers to Teenage Organization

- Teens do not have an innate ability to organize.
- They are highly emotional and distractible.
- Teenagers often have very busy personal schedules.
- Teens are poor time managers.

Parental Actions

"A schedule defends from chaos and whim.
It is a net for catching days, a scaffolding on which a worker
can stand and labor with both hands at sections of time."
— Anne Dillard

The first major role for parents in helping their teens be successful in school is to ensure that their scholars have a quiet place in which to do the assigned work. The best place is in a room of their own, normally their bedroom. If this is not possible, then a spot in a low-traffic area of the house is the next best thing. Kitchens and living rooms should be avoided, as there are too many distractions for most teens. The work area in the room should have a desk or a relatively large flat surface, so the teen can spread out necessary books and reference materials, and it should also have good lighting. A computer is not necessary for each child, but access to one somewhere in the house is strongly recommended (see the "Computer" section of Chapter 4). These should have an electronic encyclopedia and an atlas on CD-ROM. An Internet connection is also an extremely valuable research tool and should be available if possible. There should be a drawer available for writing equipment and this should be well equipped. One excellent way to keep the supplies organized is to use a plastic cutlery tray, such as normally holds knives, forks and spoons, to separate the various implements. These supplies should be replenished each fall when school starts, based on the school recommendations. Do not assume that these will last all year. Check periodically on the number and condition of the supplies, and add where necessary. Paper is also required. Again, check with the school in September to see what is required. Each school and sometimes each teacher has an idea as to how notes should be kept.

Among the supplies purchased at the start of the year should be a daybook or agenda in which the student can keep track of homework and assignments. Many schools supply these with the annual school fees, but if not then parents should definitely purchase one. If the school does not do so, then the parents should instruct the teen in its use. Do not stop there however. A major role for parents is to check on whether homework is being done. If no signs of activity are seen in the evenings, parents should

> *A major role for parents is to check on whether or not homework is being done.*

check the daybook to see if assignments are being written into it. If the book is relatively blank, call the teacher(s) to determine what was supposed to have been done. Start this monitoring in September. Don't wait for the first report card. As a general guideline most junior high school students should have between one half and one hour and a half of homework each evening. Parents can relax considerably if they see that their child is working (on schoolwork) each evening, but should never get to the stage where they are not monitoring the work at all.

In terms of monitoring, one of the key roles of parents is to encourage their teen to get started on their homework. Once again this is necessary due to the relative disorganization of most teens and their poor time management skills. Most do not have an innate ability to set schedules and keep to them. Almost all of them would rather stare at the ceiling than do their homework, so they tend to put off starting it. The most effective method of helping teens get started is to set up a routine time for the work to begin each day. By having this standard start time, students develop a habit that eventually becomes ingrained in their daily routine. The best time to start is right after supper. Teens often need some "winding-down" time after school, so a break between the end of the school day and the start of homework is recommended. This assumes that families have a relatively standard dinnertime. This standard starting time also alerts parents that homework has not yet begun if the time is past but the teen is not in the homework area. Parents can then give a gentle reminder that it is time to begin. Try to keep these reminders light and even humorous to avoid getting an angry response from the teen. Be persistent but don't get angry. Teens who really like to do homework are extremely rare, so the majority cannot be expected to be self-starters, at least in the early teen years.

If there are several activities during the week, it may be necessary to sit down with the teen on Sunday nights and set up a schedule for the next five school days.

One factor that can interfere with the development of a homework routine is the busy schedules that many teens keep. Extra-curricular activities often take place in the late afternoon or early evening, right when homework should be being started. When this happens, another time should be set that gives the teen a break, but gets the work done by a reasonable hour. This should become a routine on those days when the activity happens. For example, if Boy Scout meetings are held every Monday at 7:30, then perhaps homework should be done shortly after school on that day. If there are several activities during the week, it may be necessary to sit down with the teen on Sunday nights and set up a schedule for the next five school days. Since this is much more complex than a set routine, parents will have to actively remind the teen when to start each night. This may go on for several years before the teen begins to function independently, or the teen may get the idea quickly. Do not despair or lose patience if the progress is slow. Just keep smiling and reminding.

One household rule that should be made early in the teenage years is that there should be no telephone calls during the working hours. These hours will vary depending upon the household routine, but the rule should be firm. Friends very quickly learn not to call during these hours, but if someone does call during "telephone timeout," parents should gently inform (or remind) the caller of the rule. There is no need to be rude or peremptory as teens can occasionally forget and new friends may not know the rule. Occasionally outgoing calls may have to be made to obtain information on an assignment, and these should be permitted as long as they are relatively brief. Unless a problem develops, parents should assume that calls made during homework hours are necessary, and not eavesdrop or monitor these calls. Trust is an important part of this process.

Another important guideline for parents is that they should try not to help their teens with the homework. There are several reasons for this. The first is that curricula and teaching methods change. Things may now be taught differently from the way parents learned them. To try to teach a concept to your teens in a different way from that learned in school can be confusing to the student, and can lead to arguments about which methods are best. Parents also rarely have the patience and objectivity a teacher has. They can often become upset when their child does not immediately grasp a concept. Emotions then enter the scenario, and an argument can result. In the early teen years it is definitely acceptable for parents to help their kids to find research materials, magazine pictures for collages and other supplies. It is not a good idea to try to teach concepts they do not understand. Get the teens to ask their teacher or another student how to solve a problem rather than trying to teach it yourself. By the time the teens are in senior high school most parents cannot understand much of the work anyway as they have long since forgotten it. At this point the problem disappears, since they are no longer tempted to try to help.

A final aspect of homework routines is to have a set place to put the materials so they are not forgotten the next day. Parents should ensure that rather than just finishing the assignments and heading directly for the TV or telephone, the students pack up all books and materials needed for the next day and put them into their backpacks or book bags. The bags should then be placed in an obvious position, usually near the exit door, so they are not forgotten in the morning.

Parents have an important role in helping their teens succeed academically, and they should take this role seriously. If done with patience, persistence and humor, the young student cannot but benefit from the interest and attention that their parents are giving them.

The Parental Role in Organizing the Student

- *Each student should have a quiet place to work — preferably their own room.*
- *Ensure that all necessary supplies are available.*
- *Help to set a weekly study schedule around any extracurricular activities.*

- *Gently remind the teen to get started.*
- *No telephone calls during working hours.*
- *Do not try to teach.*
- *Designate a place to put the backpacks or bookbags so they are not forgotten.*

Parent-Teacher Interviews

Generally speaking, parents are trusting people when it comes to the education of their children. They send their children off to school in the morning and the kids return in the late afternoon. Unless they hear otherwise, either through a telephone call from the teacher or from a report card, they assume that all is well academically. Four times a year, via report cards, a progress report is received. These occasionally set off alarm bells, but because teachers usually like to be as positive as possible, they don't always reflect the true progress of the child. Parent-teacher interviews can be enlightening, but due to the lack of time for each interview, and not knowing exactly what to ask, parents don't always get a true picture of their child's progress. On the other hand, if parents prepare well and know what questions to pose, these interviews can give a very accurate picture of how their teens are doing, not only academically, but socially as well.

The Problems

The truth is teachers of junior and senior high school may teach up to 150 students. They may only barely know your child. Unless parents prepare for the interview by reviewing both marks and comments, they may just get a bland and general report on their teen.

Many different factors make it difficult for parents to get a true picture of their child's academic progress during parent-teacher interviews. The first occurs before parents even leave home for the interviews. This involves a lack of preparation. Parents often do not thoroughly review the report card that is usually issued just before the interview time. This means that they are going into the interview not knowing exactly what each teacher said about their child. They may know the mark assigned, but often parents are not even sure of this. If parents have to read the report during the interview, they are wasting precious time and may not be able to formulate specific questions about their child's progress such as why a mark and comments were assigned. In fact, many parents just sit down in front of the teacher and wait, expecting the teacher to launch into a lengthy explanation of their child's progress. This may happen, but do not expect it as teachers have many students and don't necessarily remember each one's progress.

Another factor that can negate the benefits of these interviews is intimidation. Some parents are just a little afraid of teachers, possibly as a result of their own past school experiences. This makes them fearful of asking any questions that may upset the teacher such as those about classroom discipline, methods of marking or possible favoritism or bias towards certain students. This is unfortunate as factors such as these can play a very important role in a student's marks. If teens report problems between themselves and their teacher or difficulties that they are encountering in the class, then it is important for parents to clear the air. If they are afraid of upsetting the teacher, these important questions will not get asked.

Lack of time during the parent-teacher interviews is another major inhibiting factor. There are two main methods of conducting these interviews. One is where the teachers are sitting at tables around a common area, such as a gymnasium or a library. The parents wait in chairs in the middle of this area for their turn. The interviews may be scheduled ahead of time or they may be on a first-come, first-served basis. The other main method is one where the teachers are in their classrooms and the parents wait outside until it is their turn. Again the interviews may have to be scheduled ahead of time or you have to wait until you get your turn. No matter the method, there is usually only a short period allowed for each parent, generally around ten minutes. Often a bell will ring when the time period is up, or an announcement will be made. If a teacher goes overtime with one set of parents, the next ones usually get a shorter time period. Ten minutes is plenty if your child is getting A's in that class, but woefully inadequate if the student is struggling.

All these factors make it difficult for parents to get an accurate picture of how their teen is doing in school. Understanding these factors and planning for them, however, will help parents to make the best possible use of the few minutes per term available for them to meet with their child's teachers.

Parental Actions

Given the inhibiting factors listed above, it seems obvious that parents' first step towards making these interview sessions a success should be to thoroughly review the report card well before the appointed time. The mark is important, but the comments can be even more enlightening. Since marks are usually given at the junior and senior high levels, it is easy for parents to understand their meaning. If the comments are unclear, then they should be explained by the teen. Often these comments are computer generated from a master comment bank, so they may not accurately describe your child's progress. If your teen is either unable or unwilling to explain their meaning, make a note of this so that you can ask the teacher about it.

Having thoroughly reviewed the report card, parents should then list any specific questions they have before they go off to the interviews. The following is a sample list of the types of questions that should be asked:

- *Does this mark seem to be an accurate representation of my child's ability?*
- *How was this mark arrived at? (i.e. What mixture of tests, assignments, etc., was used?)*

If the answers to these questions are satisfactory, then there is little more to ask. If not the following questions might be useful.

- *Is all homework and are all class assignments being done?*
- *Is my student socializing too much or experiencing peer problems?*
- *Are there any specific learning problems such as reading difficulties or problems with mathematics concepts?*
- *Are there behavior problems that interfere with working?*
- *Is the child highly distractible or hyperactive?*

Be sure to take the report card, along with your questions, with you to the interview. The teacher will certainly have the marks, but may not remember what comments he made since there are so many students and a very short time available to teachers to add these remarks to the report cards.

Since time at these interviews is usually very limited, parents need to make the most effective use of what is available. If the interviews have to be scheduled, make sure you book them early. If they are first-come, first-served, then arrive as early as possible so you don't run out of time. This way you will be able to see all the teachers. One important factor to consider is that in order to arrive at these interviews at all, you have to know when they are. Teenagers are notorious for "losing" or forgetting notices. Often the dates for issuing report cards and for the subsequent interviews are published in a newsletter early in the school year. If this is the case, then mark those dates on the calendar. If you do not see any such notices, call the school to check on both sets of dates. Students who are doing poorly often avoid bringing the report cards home until after the interviews, so you can't always count on this cue to alert you to the fact they are imminent.

Another hint to make the best possible use of the time available to you is to clearly identify yourselves and your student to the teacher when you arrive. This will avoid wasting time while the teacher tries to place who you are.

If your child is having serious problems in school, it may be wiser to schedule a meeting with the teachers on another date when there is more time available and when the teachers can focus on your child alone. Do not hesitate to ask for such a session if you don't feel that the regularly scheduled PT interviews have adequately answered your questions.

Finally, the matter of intimidation should be addressed. Parents should not be afraid to ask penetrating questions if they feel that there are problems with their child's education. The teacher is there to help and almost universally wants the best for your child. The secret is to ask any question you feel you need to, calmly. If you are accusatory, then the teacher, being human, will immediately be on the defensive and you may accomplish little. If you are not satisfied with the answers at this interview, don't try to solve the problem there as the time is too limited.

Instead ask for a meeting with the teacher and the principal at a later date to resolve the issues.

If used properly, parent-teacher interviews can be extremely enlightening. With proper preparation and time management, most of the needed information can be elicited at these sessions. Parents should leave these interviews satisfied that their child's education is going well. If not, then be sure to schedule further meetings to clear up any residual issues.

Making the Most of Your Parent/Teacher Interview

- *Read the report card thoroughly before attending the interview*
- *Discuss the marks and comments with your teen*
- *Ensure that you know the dates for the reports to come home and for the interviews*
- *Book your interviews early*
- *If there are serious problems, schedule another interview*

Underachievement

Teenagers are underachieving when their school marks are less than might reasonably be expected of a person with the scholastic ability that they have. A student capable of A's may be getting C's, or a student easily capable of a passing grade may be failing. This does not mean that if the teen has a low Mathematics mark in Term 2 that he is underachieving. There are many reasons why a mark for a particular term might be low. Instead, underachievement is an overall pattern that affects most of the academic marks over several terms and, if not quickly remedied, over a number of years. Parents often notice it first because their child is able to verbalize in an intelligent manner, but cannot get good marks in school. Underachievement may show up as early as kindergarten, or as late as junior high school. It rarely develops any later then Grade 9 but it is possible. The main difficulty for parents and teachers is that there are so many causes of this problem that it is not easy to determine which one applies to which student. Helping the student is thus made very difficult. While the school has a major role in finding a solution, due to the number of students and limited diagnostic and remedial resources available, the onus usually falls on the parents to find the cause and to try to fix it.

The Causes

Let us clear up once and for all what is *not* a cause of underachievement. That is laziness. Eliminate this word from your vocabulary. There is really no such thing. Burn this thought into your cerebral circuits: ALL CHILDREN WANT TO DO WELL IN SCHOOL.

> *Eliminate the word "lazy" from your vocabulary. There is no such thing. There is always a reason for underachievement.*

No child likes to get low marks and be considered "dumb" or "stupid" by his or her peers. It is not pleasant to consistently receive low marks and to go through class after class not understanding the work. While kids may pretend that they don't care about their marks and cover up their lack of achievement with flippancy, inside they hate their situation. They just don't know what to do about it. They feel that the reason they can't perform is that they are just "dumb."

The major problem for parents is that by considering their child to be lazy, they do not look further for the cause. If laziness were in fact the answer, where would it come from? Is it a gene? Could it be caused by a virus? The answer to these questions is an emphatic NO. Unfortunately by

> *Underachievers cover up the problem with defense mechanisms, such as pretending they don't care, becoming the class clown, or by becoming behavior problems.*

believing that laziness is the cause, parents make it worse by putting pressure on the child to do better by working harder. This tends to make the child even more confused because it is impossible to work harder if you don't understand what you are doing. If you cannot read, for example, more reading won't solve the problem. By the time they become teenagers, underachievers often become angry and rebellious. They cover up the problem with defense mechanisms, such as pretending they don't care, becoming the class clown, or becoming behavior problems. There are many possible causes of underachievement but laziness is not one of them.

Having determined what the cause of underachievement is not, let's look at what it might be. The most probable cause is actually a group of problems called learning disabilities. In the past these have been identified as "dyslexia" or "perceptual problems." Learning disabilities are most likely caused by faulty connections in the cerebral cortex that make it difficult for the brain to interpret letters and symbols. These usually first become apparent in the primary grades, but children often learn how to compensate for them at this level. Letter reversals, inability to spell, and extremely messy printing and writing are some of the key signs of this problem. As the work becomes more difficult, particularly at the junior high level, they are no longer able to find ways to compensate and begin to fall behind. The main problem is usually reading, but mathematical disabilities also occur. Naturally if a student can't read well, all other subjects suffer as reading is involved in all of them. Learning disabilities are not related to intelligence. The original definition of a learning-disabled child was someone of at least average intellectual ability but whose achievement was a year or more below his/her actual grade level. This definition has become somewhat blurred of late, but it is still a good guideline to follow.

*"My spelling is Wobbly. It's good spelling
but it Wobbles and the letters get in all the wrong places."*
— *Eeyore in* Winnie-the-Pooh *by A.A. Milne*

Students with low self-esteem feel that they aren't very good at school (or at anything) despite any evidence to the contrary. They don't do their assignments because if they don't try then there is a reason for their not doing well.

Another cause of underachievement is attention deficit disorder. This is such a complex topic that it will be discussed in greater detail in a later section. Again this problem shows up relatively early in a child's school career, but does not always have a major effect on school performance until the later grades. Basically this disorder interferes with a student's ability to concentrate, and even to sit still for an extended period. This not only makes it hard to learn, it makes it almost impossible for the child to control himself (it is far more common in males), and therefore gets the child into disciplinary difficulties as well. The probable cause is a brain chemistry malfunction, but the exact nature of this is not yet known.

Low self-esteem is also a prominent cause of underachievement. Children who do not have confidence in themselves are afraid to try in school. Again this becomes most noticeable in the junior high years when there are so many other issues that depend on self-esteem such as popularity and boy/girl relationships. A child who already has a poor self-concept will generally become even less secure as a result of these issues. Also, at the elementary level children get more attention from their teachers, because there is usually just one teacher for the academic subjects. This often results in the low self-esteem child being able to keep up academically. In junior high students have many teachers, each of whom sees up to 150 students a day. Children with low levels of confidence in themselves get lost in the shuffle and begin to fall behind academically. They feel that they aren't very good at school (or at anything) despite any evidence to the contrary. They don't do their assignments because if they don't try then there is a reason for their not doing well. They are, in fact, afraid to try. They think that if they hand something in, they may get a poor mark and that will confirm their fear that they are "stupid." This type of student will often complete assignments, but not hand them in. Instead they leave them in their locker or "lose" them. This problem is not just seen in school, it can also be found in sports. The low self-esteem child will usually not try out for teams or other extracurricular activities, even when they show ability in class. Some have tremendous ability and get coerced to try out for teams. If they make the team, they often don't give 100% for the same reason that they don't try in school (i.e., What if they try hard and really aren't that good?). This can be very puzzling and frustrating for coaches.

Teenagers almost universally hate having their parents split up, and may try to get back at their parents by not working at school.

Anger is yet another cause that has to be considered when looking for the source of underachievement. When children are angry with their parents, they often deliberately do poorly in school just to get their parent's attention. Very little grabs parents' attention faster than poor school performance. The anger may stem from several sources. The major one is family breakup. Teens often become angry with the parent that leaves the home, blaming him or her for the destruction of their family. Teenagers almost universally hate having their parents split up, and may try to get back at their parents by not working at school. If the breakup itself does not generate an angry response, the moving in of a parent's new boyfriend or girlfriend certainly can. As will be discussed in greater detail in a later chapter, teens almost unanimously dislike having a stranger move into their home. They see this person as trying to replace their natural parent, and they don't like it. One form of expressing this anger might be to do poorly in school.

Lack of attention is another source of this anger. Teenagers, despite their apparent indifference, need a considerable amount of parental attention. If they don't get it, they may use school as a weapon to regain their parent's notice. While this can happen in any busy family — generally when both parents work — it tends to occur more often in split families where teens usually have contact with just one natural parent.

Other factors may also come into play when anger is rooted in a lack of attention. For example in multi-child families, one sibling may get more attention than another does. This can result from one having more natural talent than the other. A boy who is good in football may get more attention from a sports-minded father than a brother who likes chess. It can also be a consequence of something as simple as a child's sex. If the parents really wanted a girl, and instead got a boy, a later-born girl might get more attention than the boy gets. The middle-child syndrome is also well known, with the older child and the baby of the family having a greater share of the parents' time and attention.

Finally, depression can also be a cause of poor marks in school. While most teenagers experience periodic bouts of being down due to social events in their lives, some experience a much more serious form. This clinical depression can last from a few weeks to several months, and may recur throughout the teen years and into adulthood. It is not necessarily related to events in the teen's life, but instead is the result of a brain chemistry disorder. While this is relatively rare compared to the other causes, it does occur and parents should be alert to this possibility. A more detailed explanation of this illness will be presented in the "Family Problems" section of this book.

It should be clear, at this point, that underachievement is a complex phenomenon that has many possible explanations, none of which includes laziness. It is vital that the correct explanation be found if the problem is to be solved before the teen gets so far behind academically that it is difficult to catch up.

The Mechanism

In reading the causes of underachievement listed above, parents may get the idea that, in the cases of anger and low self-esteem, their teens are consciously doing poorly in school. This is not the case. Teens do not lay awake late at night planning ways to get back at their parents or draw attention to themselves. Instead the pattern develops virtually subconsciously. Teens themselves do not know the reason for their underachievement. It slowly becomes a habit because it feels better to for them to underachieve than it does to try. While they usually do not like getting poor marks, it is the only way they know to make themselves feel better.

The problem with underachievement seems obvious. Your child is capable of doing well in school, but isn't. This is indeed the main problem. However, the situation often becomes compounded when parents either do nothing about underachievement, or worse, they pressure the teen to do better on his own. Doing nothing means the problem will drag on, possibly for years, so that the student gets further and further behind academically. This can result in the teen being forced to take a lower level high school program than she is capable of, which brings about the risks of boredom and dropping out. Even if the teen persists, she will more than likely have to settle for a career in a lower paying and less skilled area than she is capable of.

Pressuring the teen through lecturing and levying consequences, such as grounding for a poor report card, will usually result in rebellion. Arguments and defiance will follow, and possibly dropping out of school. At the very least the school years will be filled with tension, and marks will not improve because the teen doesn't really know the cause of the underachievement. It is up to the parents and the educational professionals to find the cause and a possible cure for the problem, not the teen. Pressure tactics only make the situation worse.

Parents definitely need to take action when they realize that their teen has ability but is not achieving to that level. However, this action should not involve nagging, lecturing, threats or punishments. There are far more effective ways to deal with this problem.

Possible Causes of Underachievement

- *Learning disabilities*
- *Attention deficit disorder*
- *Low self-esteem*
- *Anger*
- *Lack of parental attention*
- *Depression*

Parental Actions

Underachievement may come to a parent's attention in two distinct ways. The first occurs early in the child's school career when school performance is poor, but the child seems to be intelligent enough at home. This can often go unresolved for many years because parents may "feel" that their child is reasonably intelligent, but are not sure. There is little concrete evidence for them to base their feeling on except the child's verbal skills. Underachievement can also appear more suddenly in later grades. The student may have been doing very well for several years then, term by term, the marks keep dropping. In this case there is more to alarm the parents because there has been a previous history of good academic performance. Whether parents just suspect that something is wrong, or whether they are reasonably sure that their child is underachieving, they have to act as quickly as possible so that their student does not fall too far behind.

The first step is to get an academic assessment done by a psychologist. This assessment should start with an intelligence test, usually the Wechsler Intelligence Test for Children–Version 3 (WISC III). This will give a clear picture of your child's academic ability so that you can gauge whether he or she really is underachieving, or if the work actually is too hard. If the intelligence test indicates that your student has adequate ability to handle the workload of the present grade, then the psychologist will usually proceed to test for learning disabilities. Since these tests require concentration for relatively long periods of time, the psychologist can also get an indication during the session if attention deficit disorder is a possibility.

Most school districts have psychologists attached to them for this very purpose, and this should be your primary resource as not only do they do the testing, they can also expedite entry into special classes. Unfortunately school psychologists are often over-tasked, and if your child does not have any other difficulties, such as behavior problems, it may be difficult to arrange for testing. In this case parents should ask either the school counselor or their family physician for a recommendation to either the local children's hospital, a provincial/state clinic or a psychologist in private practice who specializes in educational assessment.

If the assessment finds that the child has adequate intellectual ability and does not find any learning problems, then parents need to look at the emotional health of the child. Again a psychologist or a counselor may be helpful in this process, as they are neutral and will not let emotion interfere with the facts. Many parents do not want to hear that they may be the cause, however unwittingly, of their child's poor academic performance, often preferring to blame the child rather than face the facts. The professional will objectively look for signs of anger, insecurity or a need for attention, all of which can be major contributors to underachievement. If a cause is found, it is up to the parents to face the facts and carry out the recommendations suggested by the professional. This seems straightforward, but it is amazing how often parents ignore professional suggestions because the answers are not what they want to hear. This is unfortunate because no professional points fingers at parents and blames them for problems. They understand that most people try to do the best they can for their children, but sometimes life conspires against them. It is vital that parents listen to the professional opinion and then try to carry out the recommendations in order that the problem can be solved.

> ### Famous Underachievers
>
> *Thomas Edison, Albert Einstein and Winston Churchill are all examples of people who did poorly in school at an early age.*

Since there are so many different causes of underachievement, there are also many possible recommendations that might be made. Some might be relatively straightforward, but many will involve a combination of parental actions. For example, if the problem is a learning disability, or attention deficit disorder, the best possible answer is for the parents to hire a tutor for their child. Many school districts do have resources for children with these problems, but these are usually woefully inadequate. Classes for these children range in size from 12 to 20, which is too large for a single teacher. Parents should definitely consider these classes if a placement is offered because they are superior to a regular classroom, but should not feel that this is the complete answer.

Parents should shop carefully for a tutor, just as they would for a doctor or lawyer.

A private tutor, either alone or along with a special class, has several advantages. The first is that the one-to-one instruction allows the child to catch up far faster than would happen in any classroom setting. Another is that a good tutor also helps to rebuild an underachiever's shattered confidence. For this to happen it is vital that a good rapport be established between tutor and pupil. When this takes place, the student begins to enjoy learning, possibly for the first time. To be able to understand the work and enjoy it as well is a fantastic experience, one that the child may never have had. Parents should shop carefully for a tutor, just as they would for a doctor or lawyer. If the underachiever does not like the tutor, it is unlikely that much progress will be made. Knowledge of the subject is important, but the ability to connect with the child is even more so. The results obtained more than justify the expense.

A good tutor is a key ingredient in solving underachievement problems. This helps the child to catch up much faster than any other method. However, if the underlying cause of the educational problems is emotional, then family counseling will also be required. Note the word "family" in front of counseling. If a child of any age is under-achieving due to anger, depression or a need for attention, counseling for the entire family will be necessary, as all family members are a part of the problem as well as a part of the solution. Parents are actually even more important in the counseling process than the child, as they are the mature ones. They are capable of understanding the genesis of the problem and helping the child to follow through to a solution. The immature, emotional children are rarely capable of doing this on their own. Furthermore if the problem is anger or a need for attention, then parents are directly involved, and will need to make changes in their behavior for the problem to be solved. Parents must involve themselves deeply in any underachieving problem, but most of all in those that have emotional causes.

As soon as parents suspect that their child is underachieving, they need to act. Once the problem has been diagnosed, and a solution suggested, then parents, teachers (including a tutor) and the child need to work together until the difficulties are gone. This may take anywhere from 6 months to several years, but the expense and effort of helping to ensure that your child has a bright future is definitely well worth it.

A Tale of Tutoring

Kayla was in Grade 7 when she first appeared at her tutor's door. She had spent all of her elementary school years in special programs and resource rooms due to a severe learning disability. The relative lack of facilities at her junior high school, due to the popular philosophy of "inclusion," meant that she got little or no extra help in her academic classes. Her parents, both teachers, realized that Kayla could not cope under these circumstances and decided to hire a tutor. The tutor was a former elementary teacher who had left the profession to raise her children and who saw a few students a week for extra help.

For the next three years, Kayla was tutored twice a week throughout the school year. She barely passed each year, with most of her academic marks being in the 50s. As teenage hormones started flowing, many of the sessions were as much devoted to listening to her problems and counseling as they were to academics. Her parents were usually too tired or too busy with household duties and driving their son to swimming practices and meets to deal with Kayla's normal teenage worries. By the time high school registration came along, her marks were just enough to qualify for the lower or "general" level of courses.

Throughout high school Kayla continued to see her tutor, but on a reduced basis. At first it was once a week, but by Grade 12 it was on a demand basis whenever there was a particularly difficult unit or assignment. Again many of the sessions were of a counseling nature, as often the work was almost overwhelming and normal teenage problems continued. With this help and encouragement, Kayla not only finished high school, but also upgraded several of her core subjects to the "academic" level. To accomplish this she needed one extra semester and special permission to get extra time on her exams and to be able to use a computer to spell-check her work.

From high school she went on to college, completed a diploma program in Drama, and was one of only seven successful candidates out of several hundred to be accepted into a famous theatre company. Not bad for a child who needed special help right from the start of school. While Kayla's hard work and determination were the key ingredient, the academic instruction and counseling support provided by the tutor were vital to her eventual success.

Skipping Classes

Every normal teenager skips a class once in a while. The thrill of doing something forbidden or just plain boredom tempts most teens to miss the odd classroom period. The credit system, in which most high schools operate, facilitates skipping by not having a class move together from subject to subject as they do in junior high school. Each class is composed of different students so it is up to each teacher to keep records of which students are absent each day and report these absences to the office. Unfortunately not all teachers are good at record keeping. Worse, school offices are often understaffed and do not have the resources to phone parents or send them a letter even when the teacher does report that the teen has missed their class. Students quickly catch on to these flaws in the system and exploit them whenever possible. This is normal teenage behavior and, while it should be unacceptable to parents, it is usually relatively harmless.

However, when the skipping becomes frequent or habitual, parents must find both the cause and the solution to the problem before the teen gets too far behind. Time is of the essence as the school may not be able to inform the parents until between 10 and 20 classes have been missed. Habitual skipping, though, has many possible causes and parents may need the help of a counselor or a psychologist in order to find a solution.

The Problems

As with most school problems there is rarely a simple answer as to why a teen begins to miss classes, or entire school days. One straightforward explanation is that a teen skips a few classes as a lark or because a friend has talked her into it, then becomes afraid to return. This fear can either be a result of the questions that might be asked when the teen suddenly begins attending class again, or it may be a fear of trying to catch up on the missed work. The more classes the youngster misses, the harder it is to go back, so what started out as teenage risk-taking ends up as an educational problem.

Like underachievement, skipping school can also be a sign that the teen is angry and is using skipping to bring this anger to the parents' attention. The anger usually results from family disharmony, and again the most frequent causes are family breakups, new spouses or live-ins. Other causes of this anger are sibling rivalries or relatives living in the same house. Usually the teen is only vaguely aware of what the real cause of skipping class is. Like so much of teen motivation, it is often subconscious and only comes out in counseling. When first confronted teens will often come up with a more benign cause such as the class is boring or the teacher does not like them. It is only with patient probing that the true cause eventually emerges.

A need for attention or for signs that their parents care about them can precipitate skipping class. This tends to occur when parents are rarely home or if they pay little attention to their teens when they are home. Skipping school is one way teens can get their parents' attention, as most parents want their kids to do well in school, and all parents hate the school calling them with problems. If the true cause goes unrecognized, parents may simply react with anger and severe discipline. This can result in rebellion and the problem could escalate rather than being solved.

Social rejection is a devastating experience for a teenager that can eventually result in skipping school if the teen's problems are not recognized and no help is obtained. This situation often happens when a teen is new to a school or has difficulty relating to peers. The great majority of teens hate changing schools because it means that they have to leave friends they may have had for years, and because they are afraid of having to make new friends. The more outgoing teens tend to make friends easily in a new situation, but the quiet or shy ones have more difficulty. If the difficulty persists, school then becomes an unpleasant place to be and teens begin to try to avoid it. They may either start to complain of illness frequently so that they can stay home, or they may simply start to skip classes. There may also be a combination where the teen tries to stay home and the parents, recognizing that the youngster is not actually ill, try to solve the problem by insisting that the teen attend school. The only option that the teen then sees is to skip classes. Again there is little conscious planning that goes into this; it occurs just because it is so unpleasant to attend classes.

Matthew the Angry Skipper

Matthew, a fourteen-year-old Grade 9 student, was brought to the psychologist by his parents at the recommendation of the school counselor for his persistent skipping of classes. In the first interview, Matt had all the usual excuses for missing these classes, particularly the one about the teacher not liking him. The parents had bought into this and had frequent interviews with both the teacher and the principal, but the skipping continued. When the psychologist saw Matt without his parents, a different story slowly emerged.

Matt's 20-year-old sister had recently moved back into their house, bringing her boyfriend to live there too. The sister had been a problem for their parents for years. She had been in and out of school and in and out of the home several times. The parents had even purchased a town home for her as an inducement to go to school, but she had dropped out again anyway. Without a job or any source of income, she and her equally unemployed boyfriend had been allowed to move back into the house. They paid no rent, assumed no responsibilities and generally made nuisances of themselves all day long.

Matt resented the time and attention his parents gave his sister. He also resented how she and the boyfriend ate all the food, monopolized the TV set and even borrowed his clothes without asking. Interestingly, it was right after the sister moved back in that the skipping started.

Matt's parents were advised to take a strong stand with his sister by giving her a deadline by which she must have a job then, after she had a source of income, a further deadline by which she must find a place of her own. The parents had some difficulty being this tough with their daughter but, after several sessions with the psychologist, were finally able to comply. Shortly after the sister and boyfriend moved out Matt's skipping stopped and has never resumed. A problem with an apparently simple cause was actually a complex one, fuelled by anger with the parents over their lack of control of their daughter.

Teenagers who have difficulty relating to peers or who are clearly rejected by students in their grade also can become frequent class skippers. These are usually students who are different in some way from their contemporaries, and who are also shy and somewhat withdrawn. These differences include being overweight, shorter than average, or having a stuttering problem. If these children are also relatively shy, they may be the objects of teasing or even bullying by their more aggressive peers. The problem may not appear in elementary school as friends and peer relationships are not nearly as vital as they become in junior high and high school. Suddenly these children realize that they are social isolates, and naturally this bothers them. Again they may try to feign sickness or, as often happens, they may really feel sick to their stomachs as a result of the tension they experience at the thought of going to school. If not allowed to stay at home they may feel compelled to skip classes as relief from the teasing and rejection that they are subject to on a daily basis.

Of all the reasons that teens skip school, the most easily understood by parents and teachers alike are those that involve academic problems. For teenagers who have difficulty doing the work, school is as unpleasant a place to be as for those with social problems. While they may cover up their frustration by developing an "I don't care" attitude or becoming a class clown, inside these teens feel badly about their scholastic deficiencies. They feel "dumb" or "stupid." If the problems are occurring in one particular class, such as Mathematics, then this may be the class that is constantly being skipped. If the problems are more general, then any or all of the classes may be missed. The struggles can start just because the work has gradually become more difficult so that, by Grade 11 for example, either a single subject could become too complex for the student or the entire curriculum could be an academic roadblock. The problems can also start suddenly with a particular unit that is incomprehensible to the teen. In this case, one flunked mid-term could lead to skipping that class. If the work is too hard, the classroom is an uncomfortable place to be. Avoiding it postpones the penalties, which is enough for teenagers as they have a hard time looking ahead to the potential consequences of their actions.

If students who skip class are not caught and the causes are not dealt with at a relatively early stage, then the problems that started the skipping may become compounded by the amount of school work that is missed. The further these students feel themselves getting behind, the harder it becomes to return. This fear of the academic workload at best results in skipping becoming chronic, and at worst can lead to the student dropping out of school entirely. Amazingly, many parents allow the problems to get to this stage without taking any action. This does not need to occur as teens would much rather be in school with friends than be skipping, usually by themselves. If the causes of skipping are determined and a solution found, the teens will not only be happier, they will ensure a brighter future for themselves.

Possible Causes for Skipping Classes

- *Starts as a lark, then student afraid to return*
- *Anger, usually as a result of a family situation*
- *Need for attention*
- *Social rejection due to a new school or teasing/bullying*
- *Academic problems*

Parental Actions

The most important action a parent can take when it comes to their teenagers skipping classes is to prevent this in the first place. This is done in two ways. First parents should be in close touch with how their teenagers are doing in school, both academically and socially. Teachers always know the academic side of the picture, and they usually are aware of the social aspects of the teenagers' situation as well. Attending "meet the teacher" nights and parent-teacher interviews regularly (see the section on PT interviews in this chapter) will head off most problems before they become serious. When parents become aware of developing academic or social problems they should immediately meet with principal, teachers and counselor or resource teacher to find possible solutions to the problem. Parents then need to carefully follow and support the program that results from these meetings.

The other aspect of prevention is to pay careful attention to your teen's behavior, both in school and socially. Even if the school has not called, teens give many clues that all is not well in their world. Never having any homework at night, no friends calling, vague and evasive answers when questioned about school progress and depression are all signs that something is wrong. Parents who see any of these symptoms should immediately check with teachers to see how things are going. Skipping will then quickly come to light, as will the problems that are causing it.

When problems are discovered, then parents must act immediately to find a solution, before the problem becomes chronic. If the problems are purely academic, then a special class, tutoring or a combination of both may be required (refer to the section on "Underachievement" for more details on these problems). While there are no "quick fixes" for children who struggle academically, just the extra effort by parents and teachers to solve the problems will make the teen feel cared about and will prompt him to make a greater effort in school.

Problems caused by anger or social rejection are far more difficult. The first step is to find the source of the problem. This is not easy, as teenagers are rarely able to communicate the problem to their parents in a normal manner. If they could, they would not have to go so far as to start skipping school to bring attention to their problems. Even when parents have a relatively close relationship with their teens, the youngsters often find it difficult to discuss sensitive issues. They are afraid of upsetting their parents. When parents do become aware of problems with skipped classes, the teens will often make superficial excuses, such as "the teacher doesn't like me," rather than broach the true cause of the problem.

In families where the relationship is not close, then teens will not discuss the problems for a different reason. In this case they believe that they would not be listened to anyway, so they don't bother to try. Unfortunately this is the situation in the majority of cases where skipping becomes a serious problem.

No matter the relationship, when skipping school is first discovered, parents should sit down with their teen and *calmly* try to sort out the reasons. If the difficulty is that the student is angry, parents must attempt to eliminate the cause from the teen's environment. This is not always easy. A recent divorce, for example, cannot be undone. In this case the divorced parents must work together with a counselor to help the teen accept and cope with the situation. Whatever the source of the anger, it is up to the parents to try to either remove it or help the teen understand the situation more clearly. If discussing the situation does not reveal the source of the problem, then professional help should be sought.

If social problems are at the root of the skipping, then immediate steps must be taken to eliminate the rejection. Again this can be a complex task. It will more than likely be necessary to work closely with the school principal and counselor to eliminate the problems, and even then they may not go away. Consider the following example:

Rosemary was a Grade 7 student at a relatively academic junior high school. She had come from a different elementary school than most of her peers, but she was relatively outgoing and quickly had a large circle of friends. These girls were good students, popular and were a delight to have in the school. A few months into the school year a rift began to develop between Rosemary and her friends. Her friends complained both to each other and to the school counselor that Rosemary was a habitual liar. She made up non-existent boyfriends, exaggerated her social life away from these friends and spread rumors about them. Eventually the girls caught on and began to make excuses to not be with Rosemary.

> *As soon as she began to perceive this rejection, Rosemary told her mother about it. The mother and father were going through a divorce at the time, and the mother was feeling extremely protective of her daughter. She blamed the other girls for the rejection and would listen to no arguments to the contrary from either the principal of the school or the counselor. Rather than face the problem and try to eliminate the lying, the mother chose to move Rosemary to another school where the problems probably continued.*

In this case the social problems could have been solved with little difficulty. Rosemary needed attention and was getting it through her exaggerations. She probably felt that her parents were so tied up in their own problems that they had no time for her, so she turned to her friends for the attention she craved. Most of the social problems experienced by teens can be solved if the parents and the school work together, but parents have to be willing to accept that their child might be at least partly to blame for the difficulties if a solution is to be found.

There are many ways the parents and school officials can work together to solve social problems. Usually this involves counseling to teach the child how to deal with teasing and to bolster the student's self-image. For example, counseling may help the teen to lose weight sensibly, if this is the cause of the social rejection. It might also help to make cosmetic changes, such as wearing clothing more like the bulk of the student population wears or exchanging glasses for contact lenses if the teasing and rejection comes from these sources. If the parents are kept informed of what the school or a psychologist is trying to do, and they reinforce it, then the problems should disappear fairly quickly.

Once the reason has been found and a solution put into practice, parents will need to closely monitor school attendance for the next few months. Parents should be up front with their teen about this. The teen has lost some trust here, albeit often for understandable reasons. The parents need to explain to their teen that they will be checking with teachers weekly for a while, and they should make it clear that this is to ensure that no problems reoccur. They should

One very effective technique is to tell the teen that the very next time she skips so much as a class, you will go to her school the next day and attend each class with her.

adopt a supportive role rather than a policing one. Generally consequences for the skipping are not necessary, as missing school was a symptom of difficulties, rather than a problem in itself.

On the other hand, if the skipping started as a lark, then got out of hand, consequences need to be applied. One very effective technique is to tell the teen that the very next time she skips so much as a class, you will go to her school the next day and attend each class with her. If a parent follows through with this (teens usually don't believe that they will) there is rarely a reoccurrence of the problem. This should also be followed with a period of at least a month of checking weekly with teachers for attendance and progress. The checking up should still be supportive, as the teen has made a mistake caused by impulsiveness and immaturity. In other words it should not be done punitively as in "Obviously you can't be trusted to attend school so I will have to check up on you." Instead it should be, "You have made some mistakes so, to help you to not make them again in a moment of weakness, I'll be checking on you for a while." Once these consequences have been applied the incident is closed as long as there are no future skipping episodes.

Dealing with a Class Skipper

- *Keep closely in touch with your teen's academic progress*
- *Pay attention to any behavior changes*
- *Calmly discuss the situation with the teen to ascertain the cause*
- *Get counseling help if necessary*
- *Attend classes with your teen if the skipping continues*

School Refusal

This is a special form of skipping school where, instead of heading out the door in the morning pretending to go to school, the teen blatantly refuses to go at all. It used to be called "school phobia." Missing school might start with apparent sickness so that the parents let the teen stay at home for a few days. The adolescent may actually feel sick to the stomach at the thought of going to school, or it may be feigned. In any case, after anywhere from a few days to a week, the parents usually start to catch on that there is no real illness and try to get the teen to go to school. In cases of school refusal, teens either stubbornly will not go, or they beg and plead with the parents until the parents give up trying and go to work.

Amazingly, in many cases teens get away with this behavior, usually because parents just don't know what to do. They feel that they can't pick up the teen and bodily carry the kid to school, so they do nothing. In some cases these parents even write notes of sickness to the school rather than admit that they have a problem.

Eventually either the parents contact the school or the school begins to call the home and the situation becomes known to all. In the most difficult cases the teen either still does not attend school, or goes for a day or so then stays home again. The school principal or counselor may try to help the teenager, but rarely with any success unless they have the full cooperation of the parents. The teen is refusing to go to school for a reason, and this reason may not be connected with the school at all.

The reasons for school refusal are usually very similar to those of severe skipping. Anger at the parents for some reason, weak academic skills and social rejection or fear of bullying can all be the root of the problem. Like skipping, the first step is to find the cause. Parents can occasionally do this but usually they can not because, again, if communication in the family were good, the teenager would not have to resort to refusing to go to school to make the point. Instead it is usually necessary to either make use of the school counselor or employ a psychologist to discover the root of the problem.

Finding the cause of the school refusal is not enough by itself. The problem has to be eliminated if possible or the teen will require counseling to help him accept the situation. Parents also have to insist that the child begin attending school immediately. This requires parents to be absolutely unbending in their insistence. No exceptions can be allowed unless there are physical signs of illness. The adults must not leave the house until the child has left for school. In fact, parents should be escorting their teen to school for the first week or so just to let the child know that they are adamant about school attendance. After that, daily calls to the school for a further week. All the while parents and counselor or psychologist are working together with the teen to eliminate the cause of the refusal to attend school. There must be compromise from both sides for the process to work.

Megan's Story

Megan was in Grade 7 when her attendance problems were first noticed. Initially she would be sick for 3 or 4 days at a time, but after a few weeks of this she stopped attending school at all. After about three weeks of non-attendance, Megan's mother called the school counselor for help. By this time Megan was not even pretending to be sick, she just wouldn't go. Her mother had to be at work by 8 AM so if Megan wasn't out of the house by 7:30, mom just left. The counselor requested that the mother take a morning off work and insist that Megan come with her to the school. She was instructed to stand by the bed and keep insisting until the youngster gave up and came along. It worked.

Megan's mother took her to school and, amazingly, not only was she immediately willing to discuss the problem, she even knew exactly why she was not going to school.

It turned out that her parents had broken up just a few months before and she was angry with them for doing so. She readily admitted this anger, stating that she wasn't going to school because she wanted her parents back together again. After several weeks of counseling, during which attendance was sporadic, Megan began to attend regularly again.

Suddenly, after just over a month of regular attendance, she began to refuse again. The same process was followed and Megan was once again brought into the counselor's office. Again she knew exactly what was wrong and was more than willing to talk about it. This time the problem was her father. He had found a girlfriend and moved her into his place. Megan was furious because it was now clear that her parents would never get back together again. Naturally she hated the girlfriend and was refusing to go to her father's place at all.

Unfortunately, the father was somewhat less than understanding. His position was that this was his life and if Megan didn't like it that was too bad. Her stubbornness was admirable. She continued to refuse to go to school for most of the school year and her mother was not willing to take time off work for a few days to insist she attend. Finally towards the end of the school year Megan relented and began to attend. This gave the counselor a chance to work with her towards understanding that the situation was final, and hurting herself by not attending school would not change anything.

Megan now attends regularly, but still misses more days than she should. She is behind in school due to missing most of a year's work. If her parents had worked together to solve the problem, Megan would have missed only a few weeks. Their stubbornness in not admitting that they were the source of the school refusal was matched only by Megan's adamancy in refusing to attend. It took no time at all to find out what the problem was, but many, many months to solve it.

Attention Deficit Disorder

"My ADD gives me mood swings and makes me want to fight all the time. If I don't take my Ritalin I'll have 10 fights a week."
— Cory

Attention deficit disorder (ADD), and its more severe cousin attention deficit hyperactivity disorder (ADHD), have become among the most common childhood disorders of today. The symptoms vary widely from a relatively simple inability to concentrate for more than a very short period of time, to aggressiveness, disruptive behavior and impulsiveness. The causes of ADD and ADHD are not yet known, except that they originate in the brain. There may not, in fact, be just one cause, but these disorders may be a result of one or more of genetic abnormalities, birth injuries, brain chemistry abnormalities, hormonal disturbances, toxins or enzyme defects.

A child is considered to have ADD or ADHD:

- *when there are clear signs of inattention or hyperactivity/impulsiveness before the age of 7 years*
- *when the symptoms have been present for more than 6 months*
- *when the symptoms are present in two or more settings (usually the home and school for young children).*

There is no one specific and conclusive diagnostic test. Instead, the diagnostic process includes interviews and observations of the parents and child, behavior rating scales, physical and neurological examinations, cognitive testing and hearing and vision screening. A medical doctor must make the official diagnosis, although the symptoms are often so clear that the presence of ADD/ADHD can be suggested by parents, teachers and psychologists.

While the symptoms of ADD/ADHD are usually seen before the age of 7, parents often miss them as they may not be particularly severe, or the symptoms may be dismissed as those of an "active" child. They will almost certainly slow school progress but again, this may be mistaken for a learning disability or as the child just not liking school. The fact that the child usually has just one teacher may also help him progress better than might be expected of an ADD child.

However, by the time the child is in junior high school, the symptoms can no longer be hidden. The youngster now has several teachers in many different locations. This constant moving around plays havoc with an already distractible or hyperactive child and the symptoms stand out clearly. For this reason this section is being included in this book about teenagers.

The Problems

The diagnosis of ADD (attention deficit disorder), or its more severe cousin ADHD (attention deficit hyperactivity disorder), applied to a youngster has become a controversial one. Attaching a label to a set of symptoms usually helps to solve the problem by suggesting a method of treatment. For example, once it is discovered that a child has pneumonia, the proper antibiotics can be prescribed, and the illness is usually cured. Pneumonia has a relatively clear set of symptoms that suggest the disease, and the suggestion can be confirmed using laboratory tests. ADD is not like this.

Instead, ADD/ADHD is a loose set of behaviors that include hyperactivity, distractibility and impulsivity. There is as yet no objective diagnostic test, such as a lab test, that can give a definitive diagnosis. Instead, the disorder is usually diagnosed either by an anecdotal description of the symptoms to a medical doctor, or by use of a rating scale given to parents and teachers. This scale lists a wide range of behaviors and asks that the severity of the behavior be rated on a scale of 1 to 5. There are two problems with this method of diagnosis. The first is that the ratings can be highly subjective. Attitudes towards the child can color the score given, as can a lack of experience with children in general. A teacher, for example, who has had little experience with children with behavioral problems may rate the behavior much higher than another teacher who works with difficult children frequently.

The second problem with diagnosis is much more fundamental. The behaviors that are being rated can be attributable to many other causes than ADD/ADHD. The case described below provides a clear example.

It's Not Always ADD

A 10-year-old was referred to a psychologist for anger outbursts. He had been diagnosed as ADHD and placed on Ritalin, but there had been little change in his behavior. After looking into the problem it seemed more likely to the psychologist that his behaviors were the result of boredom caused by a very high intelligence level. IQ testing confirmed this diagnosis. Changes were made to the school program by adding enrichment activities. The parents also began to provide extracurricular enrichment opportunities such as trips to the planetarium, enrolling him in a chess club and providing him with a computer. The anger problems quickly disappeared.

This case is typical of the problem. Boredom, depression, allergies, high stress levels, and a lack of discipline in the home can all cause ADD/ADHD behaviors. Trying to determine the true cause of the behavior pattern requires a more complex response than the mere administration of a rating scale. It requires a thorough look at the child's lifestyle and considerable experience with children.

According to the recent writings of Dr. Thomas Armstrong, a highly respected educator and psychologist, ADD/ADHD has become a popular diagnosis in the 90s because it has become an explanation for behaviors caused by the complexities of modern life. It helps to rationalize actions that are in fact caused by the erosion of the traditional family structure, the lack of respect for authority, the short attention spans created by the mass media, particularly television, and the high stress levels present in the modern world. By using drugs such as Ritalin and Dexedrine to control these behaviors, Dr. Armstrong feels we are not addressing the causes of the problems, but merely masking them.

Whether or not to medicate is a major decision for parents to make. If they decide not to use these drugs, it is possible to cope, but it will be much more difficult than it would be with effective medication.

If a reasonably clear-cut diagnosis of ADD/ADHD can be made, parents have a difficult decision to make. This involves whether or not to medicate the youngster. Many parents have a strong bias against "doping up" their child, but the reality of the situation is that medication is still the only form of treatment with any chance of success. Drugs shown to be effective against ADD and ADHD are those known as psychostimulants. These include Ritalin, Dexedrine and Cylert. Antidepressants may also be used, but rarely as the primary medication. The problem is determining which medication should be used and at what dosage, since each child is very different in their response to these drugs. Where one child might respond immediately and dramatically to the initial dosage of Ritalin, for example, it may takes months of painstaking experimentation before it is discovered that a totally different dosage of Dexedrine is effective for another child with similar symptoms. Approximately 20% of ADD and ADHD sufferers may not respond to medication at all. Whether or not to medicate is a major decision for parents to make. If they decide not to use these drugs, it is possible to cope, but it will be much more difficult than it would be with effective medication.

The place where ADD/ADHD becomes the biggest problem is in school. Classes require concentration and self-discipline, which are almost impossible for these children. Teachers are aware that these are symptoms of the syndrome, but cannot cope with them in a regular classroom. They can be sympathetic, but can rarely teach these children if they are not medicated or if the medication is not fully effective. The parents hear the same litany of offences over and over again. Parents and teachers alike become extremely frustrated.

School is where the symptoms of ADD/ADHD show up most clearly, but the problems caused by this disorder are not confined here. They are also present in the home. It would be nice if home was a calm and relaxed place for ADD children after a hectic and frustrating day at school, but this is rarely so. These children require more structure and discipline than do the majority of children, and this becomes exhausting for parents. If parents have had a hard day at work or feel sick, the patience needed to administer the structure and discipline their child requires may not be there. Also, as ADD/ADHD children reach their teens, normal teenage challenges, such as argumentativeness and rebelliousness are added to the mixture, and the teens become even more difficult to parent. Worse, if there is only one parent in the household, or if there is a stepparent who does not understand the problem, then the conflicts can be even greater. The short attention spans, impulsiveness and aggressiveness towards friends and siblings wear away the patience of families with two natural parents fast enough. Just one parent or a non-comprehending stepparent can lose it far faster.

By now it is obvious that ADD/ADHD is a very challenging syndrome for parents to deal with. While it is a long and often frustrating road to follow, parents who are patient and prepared can learn to cope effectively with the symptoms.

Parental Actions

To get an unequivocal diagnosis of ADD/ADHD is difficult but possible if sources experienced with the syndrome are consulted. Parents should either try to find a medical doctor who specializes in this area or get a referral to the local children's hospital for assessment. Getting a second or even third opinion is a wise course of action due to the lack of any medical tests for the syndrome. There are too many other possible causes of this behavior to settle for the hurried diagnosis of the family physician.

Once a reasonably certain diagnosis has been made, parents should seriously consider medication. As discussed above, it may take some time to find the right drug at the most effective dosage, but medication is still the only method of control for this problem. If effective, the changes in the child are dramatic. If not effective, either the problem is not ADD/ADHD, or your child is a non-responder. Do not be hesitant about asking your doctor to change the dosage or the drug itself if you do not initially notice an improvement in attention and behavior. Doctors are busy people and will not usually follow up to check on the effectiveness of their prescriptions. Keep pestering until you are satisfied either that the medication is working or that your child is one of those who do not respond to psychostimulants.

If possible, a special class is the most effective academic approach. This will be one where the pupil-teacher ratio is significantly lower than the average class, and where the teacher is experienced in working with ADD/ADHD children.

If medication either does not work for the child, or is only partially successful, then parents have to shoulder the burden of dealing with the problem. One of the first things to do is to meet with the school authorities to develop a program for the ADD child. If possible, a special class is the most effective academic approach. This will be one where the pupil-teacher ratio is significantly lower than the average class, and where the teacher is experienced in working with ADD/ADHD children. Even with this support, school can still be a struggle for these children, and parents need to be prepared either to hire a tutor if their child is falling behind, or to work closely with them on homework and assignments.

For parents, helping their ADD children with schoolwork is a tremendous challenge. It requires patience and structure well beyond that necessary for children without this disorder. After a day's work, parents often do not have the energy or patience that this job requires. Unfortunately the kids need this help, so parents need to be prepared to stay calm and to be methodical. That's why it is much better to have two parents, so that they can take turns helping with the homework. Parents also need to keep in close touch with the teachers, so that they understand what needs to be done, and, sometimes, how to do it.

Parents also need to teach their ADD/ADHD child organizational skills. Most teenagers have trouble in this area, but children with this disorder are even more disorganized. Parents need to be constantly helping youngsters to organize their notes, replenish their school supplies, and keep track of their homework and assignments. This is a long, slow job. Because of the disability, these children will not learn the first time they are taught. They need constant reminders and encouragement over a period of *several years*. Huge amounts of patience are required. Reminding and encouraging, rather than nagging, require a very special touch. The use of humor in this process is encouraged to lighten the effects of the reminders. Parents must stay relaxed and positive to avoid emotional confrontations with the frustrated youngster. Use lines like the following:

Instead of this:	*Say this:*
"Get going on your homework!"	*"I hear your homework calling you. Time to get at it."*
"Your notebook is a mess."	*"Somebody messed up your notebook again. Let's fix it up."*
"This work is all wrong."	*"That's a good try, but I see some problems. Let's try these ones again."*
"What do you mean you lost your pens again?"	*"So the pen fairy struck again and took all your pens. Let's see if we can't find a way to fool her next time."*
"How many times have I told you to write down all your assignments?"	*"It's really important that you keep track of all your assignments. Let's call Erica and see if she knows what you have to do tonight."*

Besides schoolwork, parents of ADD/ADHD children need to have a very effective disciplinary structure in place. These children tend to be more aggressive, more defiant, more frustrated and often ruder than children without these problems. It is vital that parents deal with these outbursts in a calm, effective manner. Excusing the behavior by saying, "It's because of the ADD," does nothing to help the teen to succeed in society. Getting angry with them is even worse. The ideal is to develop clear rules with immediate consequences for unacceptable behavior. Again, parents need to understand that it will take longer than usual for these children to develop self-discipline, but with patience and persistence, it will happen. For a more detailed explanation of discipline, see Chapter 4.

There is no question that parents of ADD/ADHD children will have to work harder with them than with children without the disorder. Hard work in the early years will make the job much easier by the time the children are in their teens. The good news is that this hard work will pay off and by the late teens adolescents will take over the responsibility for their behavior and schoolwork, and parents can relax a little.

Chapter 6

Family Issues

While many things a teenager does often involves at least part of the family in some way, there are some issues that involve the entire family. This is most often the case either because the issue actually does involve all family members equally, or because one teenager's problem is so serious it affects the entire family in some way. In most of these situations the onus falls on the parents to find a solution that is acceptable to all family members. This often requires the negotiating skills of a career diplomat.

Family Dinners

This is a family problem of omission rather than commission. The lack of family dinners in this hurry-up world is depriving teenagers of a vital family activity. Dinnertime is the best time of the day for family members to catch up on each other's activities. If a teenager is having a problem, it is often noticeable at dinnertime, either from what is said, or from the ominous silence. This is when teens have the opportunity to vent their frustrations with school and their friends. It is also where parents find out what is happening in their teen's lives, so they can monitor these activities.

It is a chance for family communication in a non-threatening situation. By the time dinner is on the table, everyone has started to relax a little from the tensions of the day. Sensible discussions can take place on all topics and ideas can be exchanged. Since eating food requires little concentration, family members can pay attention to what each person is saying, and actually "hear" the content of the discussion. Family dinners help keep the family together and are usually positive experiences for everyone.

The Problems

The concept of family dinners seems so simple and the reasons for having them so compelling that many may wonder why this is a problem. The answer is that our busy society is interfering. To start with, in most families both parents work. Often their workdays go to at least 5:00 PM, and then they have to try to get home. This often means commuting through rush hour traffic, so that an extra hour or more is added to the workday. By the time the parents get home, they are exhausted, and no one wants to cook supper. By then the teens have been home for at least 2 hours and they are hungry. If no supper is immediately forthcoming, they will scrounge for themselves. Eventually this becomes the norm, and everyone ends up fending for him or herself.

Teen schedules can also be part of the family dinner problem. Lessons and practices after school can run right into the supper hour, causing that member to miss dinner. Often teens need a ride to and from the activity, which means that a parent too might either be late, or miss dinner entirely. When there are two or more active youngsters in the family, the schedule can get so hectic that not only does the family not have dinner together, the members hardly see each other at all.

There is also another problem that develops from the lack of family dinners. When no adult is in control of the dinner menu, teens tend to grab something quick and sit in front of the TV set to eat it. A recent study by researchers at Tufts University School of Nutrition in Boston found that teens who watch TV while eating tend to eat more pizza and potato chips and drink more soda than peers who sit at the dinner table for their meal. These poor diets lead to obesity, a growing problem in most Western countries, and to poor health among our teenage population. Teens just do not have the knowledge or the patience to cook wholesome, nutritional meals.

This situation rarely develops by design. Most parents would agree, if asked, that family dinners are important. Instead the situation usually develops gradually as parents get more and more responsibility in their jobs, and as teens get increasingly active. Also, when children are young and dependent, parents make the effort to ensure the meals are made for them. As the kids grow older and begin to be

> *One of the most important actions parents can take to maintain communication and cohesiveness in the family is to insist that the family eat dinner together every night.*

more independent, then parents begin to let them cope for themselves more. Parents often do not feel the obligation to look after their teens as they would younger children. In fact they may often feel that they are doing them a favor by fostering their independence. Fortunately there are ways to support this independence without giving up family dinners.

Parental Actions

One of the most important actions parents can take to maintain communication and cohesiveness in the family is to insist that the family eat dinner together every night. To do this parents may have to be extremely well organized and may have to make some sacrifices — but it can be done.

If parental jobs are a major part of the problem, then parents need to organize well and mobilize their teens to help. One effective method is to set up the weekly menu on Sunday night. This can even be made into a family activity. Dinner menus for each day can be discussed so that each family member has some input into what will be eaten. Once this is done, then the ingredients need to be organized. Some main courses might need to be made in advance and then frozen. In other cases the ingredients may need to be measured out ready to be mixed together and cooked. If most of the preparation is done ahead of time, then the actual cooking may take only a few minutes.

> *"It's bizarre that the produce manager is more important to my children's health than the pediatrician."*
> — Meryl Streep

For more complicated meals, if the ingredients are ready, and instructions left, then the teens themselves can look after the cooking. This can be very good training for them if they ever leave home (the average age of leaving home permanently is now up to 28). Hopefully they will even enjoy the process. It definitely works best if all the instructions are left along with the measured ingredients. Teens are usually too disorganized to decide what to eat, gather the fixings, then do the cooking as well.

If extracurricular activities are the culprit, then new arrangements need to be made. It is one thing for a family member to miss an occasional meal, it is another for that person to regularly miss meals. Parents need to select their children's activities so that, if at all possible, they do not interfere with family dinnertime. This can be done simply by saying "NO" to activities that would regularly impinge on the dinner hour. Or, if after-school games or practices cut into this time, it may be necessary to set the regular dinnertime back a half-hour or so during that particular season. Parents must guard against their children being too busy for family activities through organization and flexibility. If they don't, what starts out as merely interference can become the death knell of one of the most important aspects of family life.

Moving House

While moving can be good for an adult's career, it is devastating for teenagers.

One of the salient features of modern society is its mobile nature. Where once people lived their entire lives in their hometowns, now it is commonplace to move many times over the course of a career. Modern transportation has made moving fast and relatively inexpensive. Advanced communications, especially television and cheap long-distance rates, have made familiar all parts of the country, and indeed much of the world. Moving to another part of the country no longer entails a leap into the unknown, since most people have already seen their destination on TV. Once a move has taken place, it is much easier than ever before to keep in touch with friends and relatives back home. The result is that when a better job is offered in another city, parents rarely hesitate to take it.

While moving can be good for an adult's career, it is devastating for teenagers. Unfortunately, few parents realize how hard it can be on their teens, and rarely take their children's concerns into consideration when deciding whether or not to make a major move.

The Problems

No matter how many positive things parents can say about the move to a new location — bigger house, better climate, etc. — teenagers will still not want to leave. The problems center on their insecurity. As has been said many times in this book, the teen years are the most insecure of a person's life. At this time a youngster needs both stability and friends to help them feel secure and to develop confidence in themselves. Their stability comes from familiar surroundings, including the house they are living in, their neighborhood, their school and the shopping malls. Despite the many features the new location has, it is not home and represents a huge unknown to a teenager. Few arguments can overcome the sense of permanence and belonging that they get from a well-known environment.

Even worse for a teen is having to leave their friends. As will be discussed in detail in Chapter 8, few things play a more vital role in a teenager's life than their friends. Again it has to do with security. In trying to find out who they are and become independent from their parents, teens rely tremendously on their friends for support. They still need their parents much more than most adults realize, but their friends assume a more prominent role in their lives than they ever have before and probably ever will again. They try to spend so much time with their friends, both in person and on the telephone, that parents often get very frustrated with teens. Friends are so important to teenagers that the thought of leaving them to go to a place where they don't know anyone is frightening for them. Even having relatives in the new area is not enough to overcome the terror induced by the thought of moving.

As a result, teens will not only be upset with the idea of moving, they will often show their displeasure in many different ways. They may become depressed and withdraw inwards as moving day becomes imminent. At the opposite end of the spectrum, teenagers may become behavior problems, arguing every little point and throwing tantrums at the slightest provocation. Neither is a planned behavior. The teens are truly upset about the possibility of a move, and don't know any other way to show their displeasure. They react in ways that feel best to them.

Their insecurity not only makes them crave stability and want to stay with their friends, it causes them to be terrified at the thought of having to make new friends in the future location. Teens generally have very little confidence in themselves, and they honestly believe that they will never be able to replace their old friends. They agonize at the thought of having to walk into an unknown school and sit in a classroom where they don't know a soul. Having adults assure them that they will soon make new friends, although generally true, has little effect on them as they do not have the experience that an adult has and cannot conceive that it is possible to make new friends after so many years with the old ones.

With insecurity and lack of self-confidence at the root of teenage dislike of moving, it is almost impossible for parents to persuade their teens to approve of the shuffle. However, there are ways to at least make the change of address a little bit easier for them.

Reasons Teens Don't Like to Move

- *They don't want to leave their friends*
- *They fear the unknown*
- *Home provides stability and security for them*
- *They still don't want to leave their friends*

Parental Actions

It is vital that parents understand the roots of their teenagers' concerns about an upcoming move. To put down their concerns as either trivial or selfish will only make the problem worse. Instead parents need to realize just how terrifying the thought of moving is to teens and to do their best to minimize the impact.

The first thing to do is to ensure that this move really has to be made. It is best that there be as much stability as possible during the teen years. If a major move can be avoided, it should be. If this means turning down a promotion, that should be considered for the sake of the teens. This may seem like a radical thought, to sacrifice for your kids, but it will pay huge dividends in future years.

If the offer is just too good to refuse, or if it is an economic necessity, then everything possible should be done to smooth the way for the teens. Start by keeping the teens fully informed from the very start of the process. Don't spring it on them as a fait accompli. The more time they have to get used to the idea the better they will be able to accept it. Call a family meeting to let them know the reasons behind the move and all its advantages. Let them voice their concerns and try to address them as best as you can.

Once the plans are becoming finalized, involve them in the house-hunting process right from the real estate brochure stage. Get a map of the new location and let them help decide where the best place to live might be. Let the youngsters come on the house-hunting trip with you, and allow them input into which house to buy. Help them to understand the various factors to consider such as neighborhood, mortgage rates, transportation and schools. Once a house is decided on, get a floor plan and let them pick out their rooms and start planning the decor.

Try to plan the move for the late summer if at all possible. This will allow the teens to start school at the beginning of the year, when there will be many other newcomers to the school. Walking into a school part way through the year, when everyone knows where everything is and when friendships have already started to solidify, is much harder than coming in at the beginning. Take the teens on a tour of the school if possible. Schools are usually open a few days before the term actually starts, and the teachers and staff will be present. This will allow the teens to become familiar with where they will have to go on the first day, which will also help to reduce the fear of the unknown.

Finally, if possible, try to find some neighbors who have teens in about the same age group. Ask if these kids will take yours with them on the first day to show them the ropes and to help reduce their fears. Anything parents can do to ease the transition pains will usually be greatly appreciated by the reluctant teens.

Parents need to take their teens' concerns seriously and to involve them right from the start in all aspects of the future move. This involvement combined with taking steps in the new location to familiarize the teens with the new neighborhood and school will make the best of a difficult situation for them. While nothing will make them happy to move, at least it can be as painless as possible.

Allowances

*"I think a weekly allowance is good for teaching money management.
An allowance is like a budget and by staying within that amount
you are learning an essential life skill."*
— *Shawn*

An important aspect of parenting teenagers is teaching them to be responsible. Teens should have chores not only to help out around the house but also to teach them that in the adult world, responsibilities need to be carried out. Teens have to learn to do their homework so that, as adults, they will have the self-discipline to take work home from the office if it needs to be finished immediately. Teens also need to learn to be responsible with money. Adults who cannot manage their money end up bankrupt. With the prevalence of credit cards today, this is very easy to do.

The two key components of money management are budgeting and saving. Budgeting teaches teens how to manage a limited amount of money, very much like adults have to do with their salaries. Saving teaches them to put away small amounts of money in order to make major purchases at a later date. Both of these skills are invaluable to adults, and teens who learn them well will find that they have far fewer pressures as adults. After all, the main cause of marriage breakups is money problems.

*"We need an allowance so we can learn how to spend our money wisely.
We can learn from our mistakes so you don't make big mistakes
when you are older."*
— *Amanda*

The Problems

Few parents would argue that their teenagers need some pocket money. Entertainment, for example, is a major expense for most teens. Whether they go to a movie on Saturday night and pay for both the movie and the accompanying snacks that are almost mandatory, or whether they just go to the mall and hang out around the food fair, money is required. Then there is transportation, by bus for the younger ones or by car for the older teens. That requires money too. Music is an essential for all teens and popular CDs are extremely expensive. Grooming products, snacks, more snacks and non-essential clothing (the things that parents won't buy) also are a drain on teenage finances. In fact, a large segment of the consumer world is directed right at teenagers. Music, clothing and electronic products are all promoted to teenagers because the manufacturers know that this is a huge market. The problem is, with all the legitimate expenses they have, and with all the temptations paraded in front of them by the advertising world, there are more things to spend money on than there are financial resources. For teenagers there is never enough money to go around, so they often end up pestering their parents for more.

One major problem area regarding money is rooted in the nature of teens. As they are not yet adults, they still retain many immature characteristics. One of these is impulsiveness. If they see something they want, and if they have the money, they buy it. Often they regret these impulse purchases later, but they continue to do it throughout the teen years anyway. Shalina is a clear example of this trend.

One morning Shalina came into school sucking on a large Slurpee, with a bag of candy in one hand and a chocolate bar in the other. Knowing that she came from a very poor family, her teacher asked her where she got the goodies. She replied that she had babysat the night before and earned $20. She went on to state that she still had $15 left, so she was going to buy lunch that day for herself and a friend. When the teacher suggested that she save some, Shalina replied that it was OK because she was going to babysit again the next week.

Despite coming from a home that was in constant need of money, Shalina had no thoughts of saving her money for something significant. She had money; she wanted sweets, so she bought them. This is a typical teenage spending pattern.

Another immature characteristic of teens is vulnerability to fads and advertising. If pop or young movie stars wear it, then they want it. If popular peers have one, they want one too. Marketing agencies know this and trade on these vulnerabilities. Cost is not a factor to young teens because they want to be "one of the crowd" or "popular" and they feel that to do this they need the right consumer goods, be it clothing, music or toys. The problem occurs when they do not have enough money for these things. They want them anyway, so they often put pressure on their parents to buy them.

A third teenage characteristic that creates money problems is their inability to look ahead. It takes years of experience before youngsters learn that just because you have some money at this moment, this may not always be the case. This results in binge spending, not just because teens are impulsive, but also because they can't see that there may be leaner times ahead. The old expression that money "burned a hole in their pocket" must have been coined for teenagers. If they have it now, they need to spend it now, and tomorrow will look after itself.

Many parents believe that their teenagers should not have to worry about money, so they give it to them whenever they ask for it.

The nature of teenagers is not the only factor in creating money difficulties for them. Adults also often contribute to the problem. As a result of today's relatively affluent society, parents can afford to give their teens money. Historically this has not always been the case. In previous generations, money was often hard to come by and parents were often unable to spare money for teenage purchases. This is not so today. Many parents believe that their teenagers should not have to worry about money, so they give it to them whenever they ask for it. They believe that this removes a burden from their children so that they can relax and enjoy life. Unfortunately this teaches teenagers nothing about handling money. They learn that if they need money, they get it. Life unfortunately does not work like this. Teenagers need to learn how to budget money and how to save for expensive items. By giving them money whenever they ask, parents are creating a problem rather than solving one.

With their nature against them when it comes to handling money, it is up to parents to create an atmosphere that teaches the value of money, how to budget resources and how to save for future purchases. If parents fail in this duty, they may be setting their children up for financial failure in the future, especially with credit as easy as it is to obtain.

Parental Actions

"I think I should get an allowance because money is good to have and I could use the money to buy myself stuff instead of bugging my parents all the time."
— Nicole

For the reasons stated above, it should now be clear that all children need an allowance. From the time they are old enough to understand the value of money, they should get a small amount of money on a regular basis so that they can learn to use it responsibly. For teenagers, a "regular basis" usually means weekly. Longer periods make it almost impossible for the impulsive teens to stretch their allowances out over the entire interval. Parents often like to tie this interval to their own pay periods, but if these are longer than a week, then only the most well-organized teens will be able to make it last until the next payment. These teens will probably grow up to be accountants. The rest will be pestering their parents for money days before their next allowance is due. To avoid this unpleasant situation, it is best for parents to dole out the stipend weekly. The next step is to decide on the weekly amount.

In order to decide what a fair amount for a teenager is, some research needs to be done. Each year parents should sit down with their teens to review the allowance situation. This can be done in conjunction with the yearly rules review (see "Passing the Laws" in Chapter 4). The first factor to be taken into account is what expenses teens regularly have. Whether these expenses are rolled into the allowance needs to be decided at the outset. In other words, should the allowance be just for entertainment and treats, or should it also be for routine expenses? To avoid being constantly asked for bus fares or lunch money, it is usually best for these expenses to be included as part of the overall allowance. This way it also teaches more about budgeting since if they blow the entire amount on a movie and snacks on the first weekend, they won't be able to take the bus anywhere for the rest of the week. In the meeting parents should add up the cost of taking the bus, possible lunch costs, and any other expenses that occur on a regular basis. This will determine the base amount.

Once the expenses are totaled, the remainder of the allowance needs to be established. To do this, the cost of non-essentials needs to be taken into account. How much do movies cost? How much is an occasional Slurpee or chocolate bar? In the later teen years the cost of a date may need to be factored in. By checking on these costs and adding them up, the non-essential part of the allowance can then be determined. When a small amount for potential saving is added in to the expense amount and the non-essential amount, the full allowance figure can be settled.

To be safe, parents should also check with other parents to see what the *average* allowance amount is. While the final decision is yours, if your amount differs radically from that of other parents, then either your teen will be complaining, or other teens will be constantly borrowing from yours. It should be noted that the allowance amount should be a guideline and not an absolute. In other words, if a major event occurs, like a graduation, Christmas, the local fair or even a school dance, then extra amounts can be given. These amounts are not rights, though. They should be contingent upon good behavior, and they should be reserved only for emergencies and extraordinary events.

Along with the amounts for expenses and entertainment, a small sum should be included to encourage saving. From the time children start receiving an allowance, which should be as soon as they understand the concept of money, they should be encouraged to save a portion of their allowance. Parents should ensure that their children have a bank account at the same time that they start an allowance. They should then "strongly encourage" a savings program. By the time the children are in their teens, they should understand that by saving small amounts regularly, they would have the cash at a later date for major purchases. Examples of major purchases might be designer clothing that their parents are not willing to buy, gifts for friends and relatives and electronic goods such as computer games, CDs, or MP3 players. The majority of the money from babysitting or part-time jobs should also go into this account along with the cash Christmas and birthday presents that most teens receive.

If parents discover that their teenager is not putting any into savings, this extra amount can always be withdrawn. Parents need not try to force a savings program with teenagers because the natural consequences of not saving are never having the money for the purchases described above. On the other hand, they should not reinforce this poor money management by giving their teens the cash for luxury items when the teens themselves have not saved any. Instead they should seize the opportunity presented when their teenager whines for more money by giving a *short* lecture on the value of saving.

> *"Getting a weekly allowance is good because*
> *if kids don't get one they will try other methods to get*
> *money, such as stealing or borrowing from friends.*
> *All teens need money for something."*
> — *Lindsay*

One of the things about allowances that puzzles many parents is whether the weekly amount should be tied in with doing chores. There is good reason for parents to be puzzled, because even the experts are divided on this topic. There are basically two schools of thought. The one side feels that allowance should be totally separate from chores. The reasoning is that teens should not be paid for household duties. According to this side, chores are assigned to help teach youngsters responsibility. They are members of the household and therefore should be taught to pitch in and help with the endless tasks that owning a home generates. These pundits reason that since teens reap the benefits of having a roof over their heads and having food on the table, they should be able to help with the chores that result without the expectation of compensation. There is sound logic to this position.

The other group of parenting authorities believes that it is good training for life to receive recompense for work done. After all, that is what happens with jobs in the real world. Interestingly, most teens also feel this way. Here is a sampling of teen opinions:

"We should get an allowance because we do work around the house. Our parents get paid for their work, so we should too."
— Nicole

"I think we should get a weekly allowance because we try in school and we do chores when we get home — so we also work very hard."
— Corrinna

"Personally I don't get an allowance but I guess that's because I don't really do any work. But still, every kid needs to get a weekly allowance. This way it gives us some cash to go catch a movie or buy some food."
— Lindsay

The majority of teenagers feel this way, but in some ways the thinking is naïve. They generally do not realize the role of chores in teaching responsibility. This method also sets up an expectation that teens should be paid for anything they do, something that does not always happen in the working world. It does have the advantage of giving a natural consequence for failure to complete assigned duties. A portion of the allowance can be withheld until the job gets done, or permanently if it is never completed.

Probably the most effective allowance method is to divorce the weekly stipend from routine chores. These should be considered part of the teen's contribution to the household. However, for unusual or particularly difficult chores, such as shoveling the sidewalk after a very heavy snowfall, an extra amount can be given.

One note of caution needs to be sounded with regard to allowances. School grades should not be tied to the allowance in any way. This is a completely separate matter (see the section on "Underachievement" in Chapter 5). No matter what the marks are like, the allowance should continue. If the report card is poor, there is a reason that needs to be addressed. Punishing the teen by withholding the allowance will not fix the problem.

> ### *Setting the Allowance Amount*
>
> - *Decide whether regular expenses, such as bus fares and lunches, should be rolled into the allowance*
> - *Check the cost of movies and snacks and decide what is a reasonable number of these per week*
> - *Check with other parents to determine the average*
> - *Add a small amount for enforced saving*
> - *Do not tie the allowance to grades*

Sibling Rivalry

Competition between children in a family is a common phenomenon that has many causes. It is probably fair to say that there are more siblings who compete with each other than there are those that are the best of friends. Even the latter will fight on occasion, especially when they become teenagers. Issues such as telephone and family car usage can ignite a small war in seconds. If the rivalry is severe among teens, the entire household atmosphere can be poisoned, making it uncomfortable for parents and teens alike.

Sibling rivalry rarely starts when the children become teenagers; it usually has its beginnings much earlier. However, the added influence of hormones can take the competition between children to dangerous levels, so that the entire family suffers. Teenage emotionality makes them explode far more easily when they are frustrated. For example, if one sibling appears to be monopolizing the telephone, the other will start screaming or will keep picking up the extension and interrupting. Smaller children will not usually be so aggressive. Similarly teenagers are impatient and easily spot unfairness on the part of their parents. All of these traits will often exacerbate existing sibling rivalry.

This competition between children is not always negative. It has its positive side in giving parents opportunities to teach sharing, respect for each other, and respect for property and of space. If handled effectively, these natural rivalries can turn into lifelong friendships. On the opposite side, if dealt with poorly, sibling rivalry can result in badly divided families.

The Causes

There are many reasons why sibling rivalry develops in a family. A common beginning is the arrival of a new baby. If not properly prepared, young children, especially those under the age of five, can become jealous of the attention the newborn is getting. They see it as attention being taken from them and often interpret it as a loss of affection from their parents. This rivalry shows itself in the older child doing such things as poking the baby to make it cry, taking its bottle away or pulling out the baby's soother. Generally, the closer in age the siblings are, the more chance there is for this antagonism to develop.

Another way in which sibling rivalry can arise is when one child obviously has more talent than the other. No matter whether this ability is in athletics, music or academics, the less talented child is apt to be jealous of the extra attention that the more talented sibling draws from parents and relatives. As the children become older and more aware, it is not even necessary that the parents give the more talented child extra attention. The less talented one will automatically compare his or her abilities to those of the siblings and develop insecurities and jealousies unless the parents are very aware of this problem and take steps to head it off.

A factor as simple as sex differences can result in one child being treated differently than another, resulting in feelings of jealousy and rivalry. An example would be a father who loves sports and wants a son to follow in his footsteps, but gets a girl instead. If the second child is the boy he always wanted, the father may tend to spend more time with and pay more attention to the son. Similarly a mother who feels more comfortable with girls may lavish attention on her daughter to the detriment of her son. As the children get older they begin to notice the different treatment their brother or sister gets and start to resent it. The resentment can emerge as fights and arguments with the "preferred" sibling.

Another factor that can result in increased attention to one sibling over another is rooted in the basic personalities of children. There are some factors of the personality that are genetic, and appear from day one. Aggressiveness is one of these traits. While aggressive behavior can certainly be modeled for young children by belligerent parents and then become a learned behavior in the child, some children are simply born more aggressive than others. These children are more demanding from their earliest days. They are the ones who do not simply stop asking when told "no." Instead they need to be told several times before they cease their demands. They are frequently seen throwing tantrums in the supermarket until they get what they want. Many parents tend to give in rather than expend the energy that is constantly required to discipline these children. This baffles their more compliant siblings, and eventually results in frustration and jealousy on their part. Their thinking is, "Why should I follow the rules when my sister doesn't have to?" This is especially true in the teen years, when the children become more aware of the concepts of "fair" and "unfair." The awakened social consciences that are common to teenagers cry foul when their parents display signs of differential treatment of their children. Generally the parents too are aware of the situation; they just don't know what to do about it. The result is resentment from the less aggressive teen.

A similar situation occurs with extremely shy children. There is now considerable evidence to indicate that extreme shyness is a genetic condition. Many parents tend to overprotect these children, allowing them more lenience because of their social awkwardness. Once again their siblings tend to resent this protection when it is not afforded to them. Cheryl's story is typical.

Cheryl was different from her older brother right from the start. She was extremely quiet and complacent as a baby, which her parents took as a blessing. However, as she became older she exhibited extreme shyness in the presence of other children or strange adults. In her first year of school her kindergarten teacher wanted to hold her back due to her poor social skills, despite the fact that she could read fluently at home. The same situation occurred in Grade 1. This time the teacher and principal were adamant that Cheryl not go on to the next grade, no matter what her academic performance was. Cheryl's mother spent hours at both the school and the superintendent's office ensuring that her daughter was promoted to Grade 2.

After this Cheryl's mother became extremely protective of her, spending many hours with her trying to boost her self-confidence. Everything pos-

sible was lavished with praise, while more negative actions were ignored. Her older brother was not actually ignored, but the attention he received was nowhere near as much as that received by Cheryl, even though he was a good student and a natural athlete. By the time the brother was in junior high he had become a serious behavior problem at school, and he was constantly fighting with Cheryl. It took several visits to a psychologist before the parents realized what was happening and adjusted their overprotective behavior towards Cheryl.

Yet another cause of sibling rivalry can be differential treatment due to the age of the children. Older children may be constantly blamed for starting fights with their younger siblings, even when the problem was actually caused by the younger child. The usual refrain is, "You're older, so you should know better." Older children are also often expected to do a larger share of the household chores than are their younger siblings. Both of these situations can lead to the jealousies and resentment that typify sibling competition. The other side of the coin is seen when older teens receive more privileges than do the younger ones. While this is expected, it becomes a problem when parents do not adjust the privileges as the younger one gets older. For example, if the older child's weekend curfew was 12:00 AM when he was 15, then the younger child should reasonably expect to have the same curfew when he reaches that age. If this does not happen, then resentment flourishes. Kristina's complaint is typical of this situation.

> *"I have an older sister and my parents let her get away with more things than me. If she does something like telling my parents off, they won't do anything, but if I do the same thing, they'll start yelling at me and nagging me."*

Finally, resentment can build when one child has special needs. Children with physical deformities as well as those who are mentally challenged fall into this category. These children require so much extra care that parents have no choice but to give them the lion's share of their attention. Even though other siblings can understand the problem, it is still resented. This is one of the most difficult forms of sibling rivalry for parents to handle, as the amount of attention given to the child with special needs is hard to change.

The Problems

> *"My parents pay more attention to my older sister.*
> *They even do her homework for her.*
> *I think we should be treated equally, not as #1 and #2."*
> — *Erin*

Sibling rivalry is generally upsetting to parents because most have the idea that in an ideal family children do not fight with each other. Instead they should support and encourage one another at all times. Perhaps this idea comes from such TV shows as *The Waltons* or *Little House on the Prairie*. In fact, this is not always the case. A certain amount of competition between children can give parents opportunities to teach them to share, respect each other and show consideration for each other's space and property. Since it is virtually inevitable that children who live together in the same house and who compete for the affections of the same parents will fight on occasion, parents might as well make use of these situations to teach important lessons.

Unfortunately, when the rivalry between siblings becomes too intense and too frequent, the emphasis shifts from teaching lessons to just trying to keep peace in the family. At this stage family life becomes miserable. At home the children fight over everything from which TV channel to watch to how long each is on the telephone. They try to sabotage each other's relationships with their friends by listening in on phone conversations, spreading gossip about the sibling or reading their diaries. If there are no actual issues, verbal and physical fights can still break out over a relatively harmless comment made by one or the other. Family holidays, no matter how exotic the location, become constant battlegrounds so that no one gets to relax throughout the vacation period. While most of the battles are verbal, many deteriorate into physical fights, which tend to be extremely upsetting for parents. This amount of sibling rivalry is certainly not healthy and needs to be remedied as soon as possible.

Parental Actions

*"My brothers and sister do worse stuff than what I did when
I was their age, but my parents never say anything to them."*
— Monica

The first step in dealing with sibling rivalry has to be awareness. Parents need to have a clear understanding of the strengths and weaknesses of each child, so that they can avoid treating them differently. Parents of high-needs children, for example, have to be aware of the effect that lavishing attention on the needy child can have on the more normal one, and then must make a conscious effort to spend as much time as possible with the other child. While this can be difficult, this extra effort will pay off in developing a child who will help with the needs of the less fortunate one, rather than creating an enemy who tries to sabotage the parents' efforts. Parents also need to be aware of their own preferences and biases so that they do not inadvertently appear to favor one child over another. The father who loves sports needs to be cognizant of the effect this attitude might have on a non-athletic child. This is especially true if one child in the family does turn out to be athletic. It is vital that parents understand the effects the differences in their children have on them so that they can try to treat them as equally as possible.

> *Parents need to have a clear understanding of the strengths and weaknesses of each child, so that they can avoid treating them differently.*

Along with this awareness, there are several other actions parents need to take to avoid making natural sibling rivalries any worse. One such action involves keeping household chores as equal as possible. All children in the family should be assigned chores at their own level of competence, and parents need to ensure that everyone completes these tasks. In many families the burden of the work either falls on the eldest or on the female. Unfair distribution of chores, or insisting that older children complete their tasks while excusing younger ones on the basis of their age tends to breed resentment of the "favored" siblings as much as it breeds anger towards the parents.

Another preventative action involves keeping family limits consistent. This means that rules for one child at a particular age should be similar for the next child when he or she reaches the same age. Many parents tend to have stricter rules for girls than they do for their sons. While girls certainly can be more vulnerable than boys, different sets of rules only breed resentment between the siblings. If parents are concerned about the extra vulnerability of their female child, they need not keep the rules tighter for her. Instead they should have the same limits, but ensure that the girls always have a ride to and from their destination.

Any differential treatment of siblings should always be explained to them. If parents have clear reasons, then there will be much less resentment. For example, if one teen in a family has proven to be less trustworthy than another, then the rules do need to be different. Just make sure the reasons are clearly outlined, and that the teen eventually gets a chance to redeem the trust.

Along with preventative actions, there are also steps parents can take to minimize sibling rivalry when the teens are in the act of a disagreement. The first step is to intervene only when necessary. Try to stay as neutral as possible and let the teens work it out themselves. Many parents attempt to halt the disagreement as soon as possible by trying to assign blame, then punishing the guilty party. The problem with this is it is very difficult to discover what actually happened. Both parties portray their part in the altercation in as positive a light as possible. In a word, they lie. At best they tend to leave out a few details. Rather than get sucked into this kind of mess, parents should stay neutral and uninvolved as long as possible. Just close the door or turn up the TV so that you can't hear the discussion.

The exception to this is when the disturbance becomes physical. This should never be allowed. If this happens parents need to step in immediately, but not with the idea of assigning blame. Assume both sides are equally responsible and send them both to their rooms for the same length of time. The tendency is often to blame the older teen on the grounds that he or she is "more mature" and should "know better." Unfortunately younger siblings can be very creative in their ability to antagonize — to the point where the older brother or sister can no longer tolerate it. It is best for parents to pretend they are from Switzerland and remain neutral at all times.

Rivalry among siblings is a natural process that exists in most families. Parents who are aware of the reasons it happens and who know how to treat their children fairly will have fewer problems with sibling rivalry than will their unaware counterparts.

Family Holidays

A frightening phenomenon often appears to parents of teenagers — their kids start complaining about family holidays and vacations. Suddenly it appears that their children don't want to be with them any more. To a family that has had nothing but good times on vacations with their young children, this phenomenon comes as a distinct shock. Many parents take this behavior as a rejection of themselves and their parenting and are very hurt. As it turns out this is a natural phenomenon brought about by the nature of teenagers. Fortunately it is preventable if parents take the time to understand why their teens are complaining and take these factors into account when planning these family holidays.

The Problems

The problems with family holidays usually show up when teens start to complain about *having* to go on them. Where once they looked forward to going on weekend outings and summer vacations, teenagers now whine and snivel at the idea of going anywhere with the family. This results in one of the most common misconceptions that parents of teenagers have — that their children no longer want to spend time with them. It certainly seems like a natural conclusion based on their teens' behavior whenever a holiday is mentioned.

This misconception stems partially from the rising importance of friends for teenagers. As children enter the teen years, their friends take on a much more prominent role. Their natural insecurities, which result from trying to develop separate identities from their parents, make their friends an important support mechanism. They spend so much more time with their friends as teenagers than they did in earlier years, that parents begin to think that they would rather be with their friends than with them. Thus begins parents' erroneous belief that their teenagers do not want to spend time with them.

It is vital that parents banish this misconception forever. Teens not only want to spend time with their parents, they become angry and frustrated when they can't. The teenage years are the most insecure that children experience. They badly need the presence of their parents, both as company and as mentors. BUT — there is a difference. Now that the kids are older, and as they are beginning to develop an identity of their own, they no longer accept their parents' bidding unquestioningly. They don't like to be told where they are going and when, they want to have some input. They want the outing to be at least partially their idea. This is where the complaining often comes from. They also may already have plans with their friends for the time period you are suggesting, thus creating a conflict of interest.

The fact of the matter is that with proper planning and input from the adolescents, teens will continue to enjoy holidays with their families for many years to come.

If teens are made to go places that they have not chosen, particularly with little notice, they will see the decision as an arbitrary one that does not take their opinions and ideas into account. The result is that no matter where you plan to go, whether it be Hawaii, Paris or the beaches of the Riviera, teens will protest. This makes the vacation miserable for everyone and no one gets the rest and relaxation that vacations are supposed to provide. This situation also perpetuates the myth that the teenagers do not want to spend time with their parents so that the elders may actually stop planning family outings. The fact of the matter is that with proper planning and input from the adolescents, teens will continue to enjoy holidays with their families for many years to come.

Parental Actions

The first step for parents is to begin planning a vacation well ahead of time. Whether it be as simple as a weekend of skiing or as complex as three weeks in Europe, the process should begin early. For a weekend outing, planning a month ahead is probably sufficient. Few teens can plan that far ahead unless a major event, such as a school dance or an important game, has been scheduled by other organizations. For a major summer vacation, the planning should start as early as February.

This allows sufficient time for the teens to get used to the idea and to actually look forward to it.

This planning process should be a consultative one. In other words, the whole family should be involved. For short holidays the meeting can be a quick one where the children are informed of the tentative destination, schedules are checked and any objections noted. Parents should try not to become defensive if teens object to the destination or the timing. Instead they need to listen to the reasons and discuss ways to overcome the obstacles. This can usually be done if enough notice of the event is given.

For major vacations, parents should create an occasion of these preparations by making the meeting a festive one. It can even become a family tradition, with snacks and drinks provided. The meeting should start with the parents asking for suggestions, even if they already have a destination in mind. Usually the teens will not have many ideas, but they might have, and it is important that parents listen to them and discuss them. Parents can then put their ideas on the table and again discuss their merits. Once again a key component of these meetings is receptiveness on the part of the parents. If they become angry or defensive because their teens don't like their ideas, then a family argument will result, instead of an enjoyable family event. If their teens raise objections to the parental suggestion, then ask for ways to modify it so that everyone can accept the proposal. The main idea is to come to a consensus so that everyone accepts the eventual decision. Then the process of looking forward to the holiday can begin.

For major vacations, the planning process should not stop once a destination has been decided on. The nature of teenagers requires some extra preparations if the holiday is to be a success. The key component of teen personalities to consider is their restless energy. Vacations need to be planned with this in mind. For example, there should be no prolonged travel in an automobile involved. The reason for this can be seen graphically in *National Lampoon's Vacation* starring Chevy Chase. This movie is a "must see" for parents of teenagers as the character of Clark Griswold makes every mistake possible in planning a summer vacation with his teenagers. The biggest one was his decision to drive across the US from Chicago to Los Angeles. The result is hilarious for audiences, but parents of teens will recognize many of the problems Griswold experienced as they occur whenever teenagers are confined together in a small space for lengthy periods of time.

The restless energy that characterizes the majority of teenagers often results in their becoming bored. This boredom quickly leads to whining and complaining, which can be a major problem in any holiday. To forestall this, good planning is necessary. Whatever the destination, teens need a wide variety of activities to keep them happy. Parents need to include these activities in their vacation preparations. To ensure that the trip is not too busy, with the result that parents do not get any rest, it might be a good idea to alternate busy days with relaxed ones. In the Griswold's case, one day they could go to Wally World (a thinly disguised Disneyland), and the next they could relax on the beach.

Finally, with teenagers it is not wise to plan extended vacations. Two weeks of togetherness is usually enough for them. A month-long holiday, no matter how exotic, will usually prove to be a strain on family harmony. With exceptionally good planning it can probably be enjoyed, but generally long holidays are not a good idea. It is much better to plan two short ones if this is feasible.

Successful Vacations with Teenagers

- *Start the planning process months before the actual vacation.*
- *Have a family meeting to decide on a destination. Make it a festive occasion.*
- *Include a wide variety of activities for teens.*
- *Alternate busy days with relaxed ones.*
- *Keep the vacation relatively short (usually two weeks).*

Arguments and Anger

One of the biggest surprises that parents get when their child enters the teen years is the anger that can be displayed when the teen's wishes are frustrated. This ability to go from zero to hellcat in milliseconds is partly the result of the teen's need for independence. Adolescents need to be able to make decisions for themselves, but their immaturity often causes them to want to do inappropriate things. When parents say "no," teens feel their maturity is being questioned and resent this. The result is usually an argument that very quickly results in the teen becoming angry.

Another factor in teenagers' quick tempers is their emotionality. The hormones that cause physical maturity also play havoc with the emotions, making teens change moods almost as fast as they change their taste in clothes. Frustration is enough to trigger these emotions and blow a simple disagreement all out of proportion. Saying no to an all-night rave suddenly becomes equivalent to violating their most basic rights and a tremendous explosion can then occur.

Unfortunately, the anger displayed by many teens today does not fall into the category of normal teenage behavior. Many teens get to the point of explosion far too easily and often. In these cases it is vital for parents to find the reason for the anger and deal with it quickly, because without treatment, serious anger problems can lead to violence and even death.

Even if these displays of anger are within the limits of normal teenage behavior, parents cannot just accept them. Angry outbursts cause too many problems in a family for them to be allowed to go unchecked. Parents need to be aware that teens will at times become angry, and develop strategies to deal with these explosions. Anger that is outside the normal limits will require the same strategies from parents, but will probably also need professional intervention to find the root of the problem and provide counseling to both the parents and the angry teenager.

The Problems

The biggest problem with anger is the loss of control that accompanies it. When in the throes of great frustration, teenagers and adults alike can be irrational. This results in things being said and actions being taken that can be very hurtful to family members. In the simplest cases, teens may tell parents that they "hate them" or that they're "the worst parents in the world." Rarely do they mean this, but these words often tend to provoke an angry or defensive response from parents. At this point both sides say things they don't mean simply to wound the other and the only result is hurt feelings or sullen resentment all around. In more serious cases physical action is taken; one party is so angry that pushing or hitting occurs. This causes even more damage to family relationships. Allowing anger to enter a discussion is just asking for trouble and virtually guarantees that nothing will get solved. Since teens are far too emotional to get control of themselves once they become angry, the responsibility falls to the parents to maintain control of the situation.

While frustration over not getting their way is the most common reason for angry teenage outbursts, it is not the only one. Anger is also used by teens as a form of communication. When teens are upset either by their parents' behavior or by something that is going wrong in their social life, they may use anger to approach an issue that they can't otherwise talk about. Parents are always amazed when they discover that their teens can't talk to them when upset. The fact is that most teens are very poor communicators for a number of reasons. The main cause is that they are afraid they might upset their parents if they bring up the issue that is bothering them. Issues that cause them to be angry are usually sensitive ones such as the mother's new boyfriend or the way dad seems to favor the younger brother.

Another reason that they are poor communicators is that parents are often poor listeners. Teens often feel that even if they did have the nerve to bring up a sensitive issue, they wouldn't be listened to anyway. As a result they often use angry outbursts to try to get their parents attention. A typical example might be as follows:

> Mom: *Robin, time to clean up your room.*
> Robin: *Why are you always bugging me about my room?*
> Mom: *I'm not "bugging" you, it's just that it's a bit messy and it's time to clean it up.*
> Robin: *You're always on my back. Why can't you leave me alone?* **I hate you!**

At this point "Mom" is probably very puzzled and frustrated. There was no real reason for Robin to be upset. If asked she would probably agree that her room was a mess. The problem is parents rarely see that their teen is trying to give them a message. Instead they often react with anger in response, resulting in a major blowup that solves nothing. Anger for no good reason requires investigation, not revenge.

> ### Messages Teens May Try to Give Through Anger
>
> * *I hate your boyfriend (girlfriend).*
> * *You are too strict.*
> * *I want you and dad back together again.*
> * *I'm having trouble at school.*
> * *My social life is a mess.*
> * *You favor my brother (sister).*
> * *I need more rules.*
> * *You should enforce the rules you set.*
> * *You never listen to me.*

Teens also use anger to get their own way. Many parents are intimidated when their teen explodes and eventually give in to the request, despite their misgivings. This pattern often starts well before the teen years with tantrums in the supermarket to get a chocolate bar. If parents are unable to deal effectively with this behavior, it becomes a staple part of the personality. The result can be disastrous in adolescence as this can lead to the teen becoming out of control (see Chapter 4: "Out of Control Teens"). Here is an actual conversation that took place in the author's office.

> Jennifer: *Are you going to the dance on Friday?*
> Jane: *I can't, I'm grounded.*
> Jennifer: *Just tell your mother that you're going anyway. That's what I do.*
> Jane: *My mom would get really mad at me.*
> Jennifer: *Then just yell at her. It works for me every time.*

The frightening part of that conversation was that Jennifer was not kidding. She got her way by intimidating her mother with anger. This tends to occur with children who are naturally more aggressive than others. They keep pushing until they get their way. This can be particularly upsetting for siblings who are not as aggressive. They see their brother or sister doing things that they know they shouldn't be doing, but the less aggressive one can't because he or she is unable to be so forceful. Naturally, this causes considerable friction within a family.

Whether a teen is angry about something in his or her environment or whether the anger has resulted from years of using it to get what is wanted, if not dealt with it may accumulate to the point of an eventual explosion. This explosion could take any form, such as running away from home, physically attacking the parents or a peer or, in the most extreme cases, actually killing someone. The anger tends to become incorporated within the personality so that, rather than just being directed towards the root cause, usually the parents, it becomes directed at anyone who frustrates the teen. This can result in rejection by peers, as they can no longer tolerate their angry and obnoxious friend. Not only will teens reject their angry peer, but they may also start to tease and harass this person. This results in a snowball effect as the teen's anger drives away his support group, which in turn makes him or her angrier.

As can be seen from the above discussion, anger in teens can occur for many reasons and it is not really their fault. Teens do not lay awake at night plotting how they will use anger to get their way or to send a message (Jennifer, above, was not really angry, she was just being verbally aggressive). The behavior comes naturally from trial and error, and it will not only persist, it will get worse if parents cannot recognize its purpose and deal with it effectively.

Parental Actions

No matter what is causing an angry display from your teenager there is one cardinal rule that parents need to follow — STAY CALM. If anger is responded to in kind, then nothing will get solved and hurt feelings are sure to result. It is the parents' responsibility to maintain direction of a discussion as teens are constitutionally unable to get control of themselves once they have lost it. Can you imagine a thirteen-year-old suddenly stopping her mother in the midst of a long harangue and saying, "Now mother, you really need to calm down and discuss this reasonably?" In the unlikely event that this did happen, it would probably infuriate mom even more.

> *It is the parents' responsibility to maintain direction of a discussion as teens are constitutionally unable to get control of themselves once they have lost it.*

It is easy to advise parents to stay calm,

but when your teenager is screaming that he hates you and you're a rotten parent, and you've had a long day at work and the bills are due and it's cold out, it's almost impossible to keep your cool. One key is to recognize the signs that you are getting frustrated and take a long, deep breath. Then, try to calm your teenager down. As soon as your teen starts to raise his or her voice, take that breath, then quietly advise the angry one to slow down and discuss the issue rationally. Let's look at a sample conversation.

> Lindsay: *Can I go to the Ghastly Ghouls rock concert on Saturday?*
> Dad: *No. Don't you remember that we're going skiing this weekend.*
> Lindsay: *"That's not fair. All my friends are going."*
> Dad: *Sorry, but you know that we've had these plans for over a month. You'll have to see them the next time they're in town.*
> Lindsay: *You're really mean. I hate skiing. It's stupid and so are you.*

This is the point to take the breath. You've just been called mean and stupid at the same time. It would be easy to get angry at this instant and retaliate with all the wrongs Lindsay has been guilty of for the last six years. Instead, Dad needs to take control.

> Dad: *Ouch, that hurts. How about slowing down for a minute and we'll talk this through.*
> Lindsay: *I don't care what you say, I want to go to the concert.*
> Dad: *I realize that you really want to go, but you probably forgot about the skiing in your excitement. We already have the reservations and we really want to make this a family weekend.*

If Lindsay does not calm down in the face of Dad's calm approach, then he will have no choice but to end the conversation. He can do this either by saying that he will discuss it further when she is calmer or, if Lindsay will not cease her belligerence, he can send her to her room. Dad should continue to try to calm her down until his patience starts to run out. This is when the scene should be ended.

One of the big advantages to having two parents in the house is that it allows the one not involved in the confrontation to intervene for the purpose of keeping things calm. This does not mean that the uninvolved parent should jump in on one side or the other. Jean's example illustrates this clearly:

> *"My mother and I argue about everything. Mostly it's about driving or watching TV or feeding our dogs. When we argue it turns everything around and then my dad gets in the middle and I get sent to my room for arguing with my mom and grounded for not listening."*

Instead, the calmer parent should try to defuse the situation by suggesting that everyone settle down and discuss things rationally. This has to be done diplomatically or both sides will turn on the would-be peacemaker. In other words don't shout, "For heaven's sake calm down, you two!" As an alternative, quietly suggest that everyone take it easy and discuss things reasonably. If necessary, take over for the overwrought parent, but it is usually best just to ensure that both parties are calmer and can resume the discussion more rationally.

Another key to remaining calm is for the parent to practice not taking any of the insults personally. A caring parent whose son says that he hates him is bound to be wounded and hurt. This can lead to retaliation, which causes the discussion to get out of control. Parents of teenagers need to gird themselves against these insults. Be prepared for them and do not react when the teen's anger bubbles over. The words are rarely meant literally; they are only said to shock and hurt when teens are not getting their way.

When parents begin to realize that their teen is getting angry frequently for no good reason, it is vital that they seek the cause.

Humor can be very effective in bringing an angry teen down to earth. When insulted, tell the teen to wait a minute, you're not ready. Then go and put on a hard hat and say, "OK, now you can throw those insults at me. I'm ready." You can also simply say something like, "That's not much of an insult. Can't you be more creative? How about calling me a 'pusillanimous polecat.'" The teen's initial reaction will usually be to get angrier, but if you keep it up the laughter will suddenly begin.

These suggestions are useful when there is a clear cause of the teen's anger. In cases where the fury is a form of communication, a slightly different strategy needs to be pursued. While keeping calm and using humor are still important tools, a further step needs to be taken. It now becomes important to not only control the situation, but also to discover what is bothering the teen. This requires good communication skills and a very open mind, since the underlying problem might well be rooted in the parents' behavior. When parents begin to realize that their teen is getting angry frequently for no good reason, it is vital that they seek the cause. If communication within the family is relatively good, then the parents must sit down with the teen to find the cause. More frequently, counseling intervention will be required to get to the bottom of the anger. Parents who truly care for their teens must be prepared to work with the problem and not expect the counselor to find the cause then fix the teen.

The most difficult type of anger for parents to deal with is that which has been rooted in selfish behavior from an early age. Children maintain behaviors that work for them, and aggressive children quickly learn which buttons to push to get what they want. If parents do not effectively deal with temper tantrums in early childhood, they will persist into the teens. This angry behavior then becomes a major problem because instead of using anger to get a chocolate bar at the supermarket, they use it to push their limits beyond what most parents would regard as safe. These limits include curfews and social activities such as drinking and drug use. Parents realize that their teens should not be engaging in these behaviors, but are intimidated by the anger and tend to give way to avoid an ugly scene. The irony of this approach is that the teens really don't want to get their own way. As discussed in Chapter Four, teens want their parents to set and enforce limits. Those adolescents whose parents are afraid to act tend to keep pushing to try to discover where the limits are, and often end up out of control. At this point only drastic measures will salvage the situation, and in the process the family goes through tremendous turmoil.

Parents should not give in to their teenagers in order to defuse their anger. Using the techniques of calmness and humor described above, they need to stick to their guns and enforce the rules they have set. A thorough review of Chapter Four would be in order for parents whose teens use anger to get their way as a reminder to set rules and ensure they are obeyed. If the situation has gone too far, then counseling will be required. Do not expect that an anger management course for your teen will solve the problem. As parents, you are an integral part of this problem; in fact you may be the main cause. In this case family counseling is required along with considerable practice of the principles learned from the counselor. If the problem has been ongoing since early childhood, it will not be fixed in a few weeks. It will probably take the better part of a year before relative calm returns to your household. While this may seem daunting, it is far better than losing your teen to the streets. The effort and expense will be well worth it if everyone buys in.

> *It is again ironic that by being afraid to discipline for fear of alienating their child, parents accomplish exactly that.*

An important point for parents to remember is that their angry teen does not want to be that way. He or she would much prefer the stability provided by parents who are in control of their household. It is again ironic that by being afraid to discipline for fear of alienating their child, parents accomplish exactly that. Teens want their parents to be in control — they just want that control to be fair.

Spying on Your Teen

The issue of searching your teen's room, reading a diary or listening in on telephone conversations to see if your teen is doing anything wrong is rarely discussed by parenting experts. This is unfortunate because it is an issue that can cause major rifts between parents and their teens. Many parents see spying or "checking up" on their teen as their right as the people responsible for their child and as the owners of the house. Unfortunately, while there is some logic to this position, it tends to cause more problems than it solves.

> *"The other day my dad said he didn't trust me.*
> *Then I catch him going through my things.*
> *I mean, he read all my notes. How can I trust him now?"*
> *— Bonnie*

The Problems

Sometimes spying occurs by accident, such as when you find a note in the pocket of your teenager's jeans as you are about to wash them. Or perhaps you pick up an extension phone just as your teenager is describing the happenings at the party on the weekend. These events occur frequently and parents are often at a loss as to what to do with the information accidentally gained. On the other hand, some parents, alarmed by a TV documentary or a story told by a neighbor, deliberately search their teenagers' rooms or listen in on the telephone extension to try to hear if their teens are involved in any dangerous or illicit activities. Usually parents want to know if their teens are drinking, using drugs, smoking cigarettes or having sex. In most cases parents are not looking for evidence of such activities in order to make trouble for their teens. Instead they want to protect them from the harm contained in these activities.

In some cases, where the relationship between the parent and the teenager is already dysfunctional, parents are deliberately looking for evidence with which to prove that the problems are the teen's fault and therefore not related to their parenting. Drug use, for example, is often thought to cause such major changes in a teen's behavior that it is the root cause of the teen being out of control. Some parents actually hope to find the evidence to charge their teen in order to have someone else (in this case the courts) deal with the problem. Fortunately, these situations are in the minority, although they are growing in number.

When teenagers feel they are not trusted, they tend to begin to do things that are forbidden, just because they feel they are already suspected of this behavior so there is nothing to lose.

The major problem with deliberately searching for evidence of wrongdoing is the atmosphere of distrust and suspicion that this breeds. The teen is almost sure to discover the spying eventually, and will feel betrayed and resentful. When teenagers feel they are not trusted, they tend to begin to do things that are forbidden, just because they feel they are already suspected of this behavior so there is nothing to lose. Teens from homes where sound moral behavior is taught may sometimes experiment, but they won't habitually do things that they know their parents will not approve of. The strong bond that normally exists between parent and teen ensures this behavior. Teens are often heard to say, "I wouldn't do that because my parents would be disappointed." However, frequent spying, on the grounds that this will prevent future misdeeds, will destroy this feeling and can actually result in the behavior parents are trying to prevent.

Parental Actions

The main action that parents can take in the case of spying is to not do it, even if they suspect problems. There are more effective methods of finding out the necessary information without taking the chance of destroying the trust, or what trust remains, between parent and teenager. In the simplest cases, if a note is found in a jeans pocket on washday, parents should simply file the information away for future reference, replace the note and wash it. Let's look at an example. Suppose the note describes the behavior of your daughter's friend at a recent party. The friend may have been drunk and the note might be asking if the friend had sex with her boyfriend while in this condition. Two factors come out in this note. The first is that there is drinking at the parties your daughter attends. The second is that some of your daughter's friends may be having sex. This is important information for parents to know, but it still says nothing about your daughter. The rule is, if there is no concrete information to the contrary, assume the best. There is no justification to start looking for evidence that your teen is engaged in these behaviors.

Let's discuss a more alarming example. The note may have been from the friend and might be describing your own daughter's drunkenness at a recent party and asking if she had sex at the time. Now you do have cause to worry. Should you start spying? Absolutely not! This is the time for open discussion on the subject. You should sit down with your daughter, describe how you found the note, and ask her about the drinking. This requires iron will to remain calm because your disappointment will be high, but it is important to do so. At least finding the note gives you some time to think about how you are going to handle the situation. A talk with your spouse is definitely in order, as he or she should also be involved, and a common approach decided upon. Open, honest discussion is required to determine if this is a frequent occurrence or just an experiment that went wrong. In either case a discussion of drinking and sex is required, along with assurances that it will not happen again.

The same approach applies to overheard conversations. If the information is not directly applicable to your teen, just file it away for future reference. If the conversation does directly apply, then open discussion is again called for. A similar approach is called for with the diaries teens often keep. Reading them is one of the worst forms of spying. Since diaries are

> **Communicate —
> don't snoop.**

difficult to read accidentally, there is virtually no excuse for this. These must remain private no matter what the temptation. Occasionally daughters (since teenage boys rarely keep diaries), deliberately leave them out in an attempt to get mother or dad to discuss an issue. Rather than reading it, take extra care to try to determine if there is anything that your teen wants to discuss with you. Take her shopping, out for lunch, or just sit down on the edge of the bed as you are tucking her in and ask if anything is bothering her. Communicate — don't snoop.

A new form of communication for adults and teenagers alike is e-mail. Parents who are computer literate may be tempted to read the mail from their teen's account. The same rules apply. Do not snoop, even if the computer is accidentally left on with the e-mail open. Trust between parents and teens is vital to a close relationship. Once trust is lost, it is very difficult to recover.

In cases where teenagers are out of control, spying is still not the answer. Parents often search their teen's room or listen in to conversations to try to find out what is causing their teenager's rebellion. Even if they do find drugs, weapons or hear incriminating conversations, parents are no closer to the root of the problem. As discussed in Chapter 4, out-of-control teens are usually angry. There may be one or many causes for this anger, but snooping will rarely find it. If the sleuthing is discovered, it will only exacerbate what is already a major problem. Find a good counselor or psychologist and invest some time and money in discovering the genesis of the teen's anger rather than resorting to emulating Sherlock Holmes. Elementary, my dear Watson!

Since the tragedy of Columbine High School in Littleton, Colorado, the question of parental responsibility to know what is happening in teens' lives has been raised. There is little doubt that parents do need to know what their teens are doing in their spare time. They do need to know if their children are depressed or angry, who they are associating with, and what their interests are. In families that are functioning well, this is not done through spying. It is accomplished by spending as much time as possible with your teens and communicating with them. As has been said many times in this book, teens want to talk with their parents. They need to discuss their dreams, hopes and fears with them. Parents who take the time to be with their teens as much as possible will know what is going on in their lives, and will not have to spy on them to find out.

Emotional Disturbance

Psychology is still relatively young as a discipline, and has changed radically over the course of its existence as psychologists have tried to discover the origin of "emotional disturbance." During the 1960's, for example, researchers were convinced that the serious psychological illnesses were mainly of environmental derivation. This meant that the experiences of life, and particularly those of the formative years, were instrumental in determining whether or not a person became mentally ill. Throughout this period, the role of heredity in this process was largely ignored. As the discipline progressed and genetic research became more sophisticated, it has now been well documented that, while the environment can certainly have a major effect on personality, many of the most serious psychological disturbances were indeed largely inherited. This list includes schizophrenia and many of the personality, mood and anxiety disorders. The National Institute of Mental Health in the United States estimates that one in ten children suffer from some form of serious emotional disturbance.

Research on psychological disorders has determined the most serious ones involve disturbances in brain chemistry, specifically a family of chemicals called neurotransmitters. These chemicals allow signals, such as thoughts and perceptions, to travel normally throughout the cortex of the brain. When not present in the correct amounts, the thoughts and perceptions become distorted, resulting in changes in how the world is viewed. Many researchers now think that the tendency to develop these disorders is inherited. The actual start of these problems can occur either as the result of the hormonal changes of puberty, a viral infection, or even of complications of pregnancy.

These emotional disturbances progress slowly and are not easily recognized in children and teenagers. Before they are eventually diagnosed and a course of treatment prescribed, they can have devastating effects on a family.

The Problems

Before examining the damage emotional disturbances can do to the adolescent and his or her family, parents need to know the nature of the problems that their teenager may face. Perhaps the most devastating of all of these mental health problems is schizophrenia. **Schizophrenia** is a chronic, severe and disabling brain disorder that affects about 1 percent of the population during their lifetime. There is now considerable research evidence to indicate that this disorder is hereditary and acts by affecting the balance of a neurotransmitter called dopamine in the brain. Dopamine allows nerve cells in the brain to send messages to each other. The imbalance of this chemical affects the way a person's brain reacts to stimuli — which explains why a person with schizophrenia may be overwhelmed by sensory information (loud music or bright lights) which other people can easily handle. This problem in processing different sounds, sights, smells and tastes can also lead to hallucinations or delusions, such as hearing voices. It can also cause disordered thinking, and social withdrawal. Schizophrenia appears to be extremely rare in young children; more typically, the illness emerges in late adolescence or early adulthood as a result of the hormonal and physical changes in the body brought on by puberty. However, research studies are now revealing that many of the aggressive or antisocial behaviors seen in young children may be early signs of this disease.

The first signs of schizophrenia in an adolescent may be failure to

> *Schizophrenia appears to be extremely rare in young children; more typically, the illness emerges in late adolescence or early adulthood as a result of the hormonal and physical changes in the body brought on by puberty.*

The first of these (mood disorders) used to be called manic-depression, but the new name is bipolar disorder

make expected progress at school, with delusions, hallucinations and psychotic behavior following later, according to Dr. Andrew Clark, Senior Lecturer in Psychiatry, University of Manchester. They may suffer from delusions relating to cartoon characters, or to idols of their age group. Or they may believe they are being persecuted at school. The adolescent schizophrenic often becomes a loner who finds it difficult to make and keep friends and mistrusts most people.

There are two major emotional disturbances experienced by teenagers that fall into the category of **mood disorders**. The first of these used to be called manic-depression, but the new name is **bipolar disorder**. Bipolar disorder causes extreme shifts in mood, energy, and functioning. Overly energized, disruptive, and reckless periods alternate with periods of sadness, withdrawal, hopelessness and other depressive symptoms. Unlike normal mood states of happiness and sadness, symptoms of manic-depressive illness can interfere with school performance, family relationships, peer interactions, and other everyday activities. Although manic-depressive illness typically emerges in late adolescence or early adulthood, there is increasing evidence that the disorder also can begin in childhood. According to one study, 1 percent of adolescents ages 14–18 were found to have met criteria for manic-depressive illness or cyclothymia, a milder form of the illness, in their lifetime.

The second mood disorder is **depression**. This differs from bipolar disorder in that there are no hyperactive periods. Large-scale research studies have reported that up to 3 percent of children and up to 8 percent of adolescents in the United States suffer from depression. This is a serious mental disorder that adversely affects mood, energy, interest, sleep, appetite, and overall functioning by causing the sufferer to feel so down that he or she cannot cope with life. It appears to be caused by fluctuations in the levels of a neurotransmitter called serotonin. In contrast to normal emotional experiences of sadness or passing mood states, such as when a close relative dies, the symptoms of depression are extreme and persistent and can interfere significantly with the ability to function at home or at school. There is evidence that depression emerging early in life often recurs and continues into adulthood, and that early onset depression may predict more severe forms of the disorder in adult life. One of the most serious dangers of depression is its potential to cause adolescents to commit suicide.

A **personality disorder** is identified by a persistent pattern of experience and behavior that is abnormal with respect to any two of the following: thinking, mood, personal relations, and the control of impulses. Personality disorders are not illnesses in a strict sense as, unlike schizophrenia and the mood disorders, they do not disrupt emotional, intellectual, or perceptual functioning. However, those with personality disorders suffer a life that is not positive, proactive or fulfilling. Not surprisingly, personality disorders are also associated with failures to reach a person's full potential in life. Once again heredity is thought to play a major role in their development.

In children and adolescents, two major personality disorders are identified. The first, **conduct disorder**, is the most serious. Adolescents suffering from this disorder tend to violate the basic rights of others. This means that they may be aggressive and show bullying behavior, or they may be physically cruel to animals or peers. They may also be very destructive or deceitful, and engage in criminal behaviors such as theft or robbery. As they grow older, teenagers with conduct disorder generally are not controllable by their parents.

The other personality disorder of youth is called **oppositional defiant disorder**. This problem is characterized by a pattern of negativistic, hostile or defiant behavior where the child often loses his temper, argues, defies adult requests and often blames others for his or her mistakes. While this describes the behavior of the majority of teenagers at one time or another, if this behavior persists to the point where it is affecting relationships both at home and at school, then the problem may be ODD.

At present there is no known cause for these personality disorders. It is understood that heredity plays a major role in their development, but to date they are not associated with disturbances in brain chemistry.

The major **anxiety disorder** affecting adolescents is **obsessive-compulsive disorder**. OCD is distinguished by intrusive, unwanted, repetitive thoughts and rituals performed out of a feeling of urgent need. Adolescents with OCD cannot control the thoughts that pop into their minds, many of them very frightening. They also may engage in repetitive behaviors such as hand washing, repeatedly checking that doors are locked, repeating words to themselves or counting things. Those suffering from this disorder know that their behaviors are obsessions or compulsions, but they still can't control them. Once again, research indicates that this disorder has a major genetic link and that drugs that alter the levels of the neurotransmitter serotonin are effective in its treatment.

Children and adolescents who suffer from any of these diseases present many problems for their parents. In their earliest stages they are extremely hard to diagnose because the symptoms are not clear-cut. The behaviors manifested by children with emotional disturbances usually fit into many categories, including that of poor parenting. The children may perform poorly in school or present minor behavior problems for many years before the symptoms become obvious enough to make a differential diagnosis. Chelsea's case clearly illustrates this point:

Chelsea first began seeing her school counselor when she was in Grade 7. She was one of the rare Grade 7 students in junior high who referred herself to the counselor, mainly for minor concerns about her relationship with her parents. She thought they were too restrictive, although when this was examined it appeared that they were being quite fair. In the meantime Chelsea was continually getting into minor scrapes with her teachers and the law. None of the problems were serious, some minor vandalism, a few fights and some defiance when confronted by her teachers. Although she was frequently in trouble, she was never actually in court or suspended from school. Her marks were low but she managed to pass all her courses.

Over the next two years Chelsea continued to see the counselor regularly, but her behavior gradually got worse. She started drinking on weekends and eventually started using drugs. She frequently got into fights with her peers, and her confrontations with her teachers became more serious. She was suspended several times. Her parents were concerned and worked with the counselor to try to straighten out Chelsea's life, but nothing seemed to work. During one counseling session she was describing a drug trip when she mentioned that she probably wouldn't need the drugs if it weren't for the voices she kept hearing. This statement greatly concerned the counselor and he immediately called home to have Chelsea given a psychiatric examination. The mother delayed this step for several weeks. In the meantime Chelsea became extremely agitated one day and was sent to the office for defiance. On her way to the office she met the counselor and began screaming at him that everyone hated her there and that she had had enough. She then produced a gun and threatened to kill every teacher in the school. She said that her voices were telling her to. After several very tense minutes she was talked into giving up the gun, and the police took her away.

The subsequent psychiatric examination indicated that she was schizophrenic and she was placed on risperidone, a relatively new anti-psychotic drug. Within a few weeks she was virtually a different person. She openly discussed her former problems and had no interest in pursuing her former life.

This case is typical of the various mental health problems that have been described above. One of the most puzzling features of Chelsea's case in its early stages was that she came from a relatively stable home. Her behavior problems were more typical of an unstable home situation where the teen was angry about her life. Instead she had probably the most serious emotional disturbance of all, and her behavior problems were early signs of this. Most of these mental health problems manifest themselves in similarly subtle fashion at first. It is usually only when the problem gets to a more serious stage that it can be diagnosed and treated effectively.

The emotional effects on the parents can be traumatic as they tend to blame themselves for the problems, not realizing the powerful role of heredity.

Serious emotional problems not only affect the teen; they affect the whole family. This is because the seriousness of the symptoms can force a family to concentrate on one child, to the detriment of the others. This is especially true in the period when the problem can't be diagnosed. Even if it is an only child, the emotional effects on the parents can be traumatic as they tend to blame themselves for the problems, not realizing the powerful role of heredity.

The effects on the child are equally traumatic, as children with psychological problems cannot control themselves and feel that they are "bad" or different from their peers. Many temporary and ineffective treatments may be tried over the years, such as special classes or the administration of Ritalin (on the assumption that the problem is ADHD), which emphasize the problem traits rather than eliminating them. This has a very negative effect on a child's self-esteem and this lack of self-confidence, in turn, compounds the behavioral difficulties.

From this discussion it is obvious that emotional disturbances present tremendous challenges for parents, both in diagnosis and treatment. Often the parents are left on their own to deal with the problems as even the experts have difficulty diagnosing them in their early stages. Even if they are properly diagnosed, there are few treatment programs for them. Fortunately the picture is not all bleak due to the many new drugs that have become available in recent years to treat these emotional problems.

Parental Actions

> If the troubled teen comes from a loving, two-parent home with a reasonable system of discipline, then the cause of the problems is probably not environmental.

One of the keys that counselors and psychologists use in the diagnostic process is the stability of the home. If the troubled teen comes from a loving, two-parent home with a reasonable system of discipline, then the cause of the problems is probably not environmental. Even if the home is a single-parent family or includes a stepparent, if there is no conflict detected then once again its time to look for organic causes of the difficulties. Parents should start the diagnostic process by doing an honest self-check of their parenting. This is very difficult for many parents, as they would rather believe that the problems are physical and not caused by their ineffective parenting techniques. The bald fact is that most of the serious difficulties presented by teens are caused by problems in the home. However, if an honest appraisal of the situation along with the opinion of an outside source, such as a counselor or psychologist, indicates that the problems are not due to unsuccessful parenting, then it is time to look for emotional disturbances. Keep in mind that the best estimates of the National Institute of Mental Health in the United States indicate that about 1 in 10 children suffer from mental illness severe enough to cause some impairment in behavior. That means that the other 90% do not have significant levels of emotional disturbance. These guidelines should help parents to know where to start looking for the cause of their teens' problems.

Once a mental illness has been diagnosed, parents and their advisers need to begin looking for treatment methods. Fortunately, tremendous progress has been made by the pharmaceutical industry in the last 10 years to help combat these illnesses. Many parents are upset by the recommendation that their teen take drugs, due to the poor reputation of drug therapy in the past. Parents do not want their children "doped up" so that they cannot function effectively in society. Fortunately, the majority of the new drugs have no such effect on those taking them and past prejudices now have little basis in fact. In reality, the new drugs have relatively few side effects and represent the best hope to combat these illnesses.

The major problem with schizophrenics and drug therapy is that it is hard to get them to take the medication regularly. Often after the medication has been effective for a while, the schizophrenic begins to believe that it is no longer necessary and discontinues its use.

The treatment of schizophrenia provides an excellent example of the treatment of emotional disorders by drug therapy. Three families of drugs are now used with excellent results in the treatment of this disorder. Risperidone, which is usually marketed under the brand name Risperdal, is one of the most common of these drugs, along with olanzapine (Zyprexa) and the closely related clozapine (Clozaril). Their use with teenagers is still under investigation, but several studies indicate that there is considerable promise in this direction. The major problem with schizophrenics and drug therapy is that it is hard to get them to take the medication regularly. Often after the medication has been effective for a while, the schizophrenic begins to believe that it is no longer necessary and discontinues its use. For this reason it is vital that psychotherapy accompanies drug therapy to help these sufferers to realize that they must take the medication forever. There is no cure for the "disease," but these drugs have been shown to be highly effective in its control.

Manic-depression or bipolar disorder has been shown in adults to respond to a well-known drug called lithium, especially when combined with psychotherapy. Its effectiveness with adolescents is also being tested. However, the major breakthrough in emotional disturbances in recent years has been in the area of depression. Depression is much more common in adolescents than is schizophrenia or bipolar disorder. The development of the selective serotonin reuptake inhibitors, or SSRIs, has been shown to be a safe and effective treatment for adolescent depression. These go under such brand names as Prozac, Zoloft and Paxil. Often no other form of treatment is necessary, although counseling to explain the nature of the disorder is highly recommended. Teens need to understand that they are not weird or crazy, but that they have a chemical imbalance in their brain. Unfortunately the bias against drug therapy is still strong. Many parents resist the use of these drugs on the basis of their beliefs alone. The fact that the rate of suicide among adolescents has doubled since 1964 is a compelling argument to try whatever is available to avoid the misery of depression and the related possibility of suicide.

The SSRI family of drugs has also shown itself to be effective in combating obsessive-compulsive disorder. Dosages in the neighborhood of 2 to 4 times those used for depression are usually necessary for this powerful disorder. Psychotherapy, especially a form of behavior therapy called systematic desensitization, is also highly recommended.

Unfortunately there are no drug therapies as yet for the personality disorders. Intensive psychotherapy, often in a controlled setting such as an adolescent institution, is the only treatment available at this time. Regrettably there are very few of these institutions publicly available, and the private ones tend to be extremely expensive. Along with psychotherapy, it is important that strong family support be maintained, despite the antisocial nature of adolescents with these disorders. They are not choosing to behave as they do, they are virtually compelled. Parental support is a vital component of any therapy.

The challenge for families with a child who has one of the above emotional disturbances is to avoid the situation where the afflicted child gets all the attention, to the detriment of any other children. This is difficult, as these disorders can be very demanding of parents' time and attention. Parents must do their best to equalize the time spent with their children. They must also be very forthright in explaining to the others the exact nature of the problem child's disorder. There should be no attempts to conceal or minimize the facts, as teens are able to understand far more than adults usually give them credit for. By understanding that their brother or sister has a psychological disorder and has trouble controlling his or her behavior, they can make allowances for the fact that their parents have to spend more time working with that child than with them.

The difficulties of dealing with a youngster with an emotional disturbance make it mandatory that parents seek psychological help, and not try to rely on drug therapy alone. The psychotherapy takes two major forms. Obviously the afflicted child needs therapy to learn the nature of the disorder as well as how to deal with the problems the disorder causes. Adolescents immediately conclude they are "crazy" when told that they have these types of problems, and this impression needs to be immediately dispelled. Counseling is also needed for the parents, to learn the nature of the disturbance. As well, parents need to learn effective ways of coping with the problems encountered and of maintaining the integrity of the entire family.

It is frightening for parents to discover that their teen has a psychological disorder, especially as so many prejudices against them survive from the past. As we learn more and more of the genesis of these disorders, they become less frightening but are still not easy for a parent to deal with. Utilizing medical and psychological support can go far in helping to return the household to a place of stability and happiness.

Chapter 7

Moral Issues

If ethical principles are not taught in the home, either directly or by example, then adolescents have no way to learn them.

The issues discussed in this chapter all require ethical decisions by both parents and teens. In previous generations, the teaching of morals came primarily from the church and, in North America, was generally based on the Ten Commandments of the Christian Bible. These moral principles were often reflected in school teachings as well. All parents had to do in those days was reinforce the teachings of church and school and set an example of the behaviors described from the pulpit.

The situation is very different today. Church attendance is by no means as universal as it once was, and schools have withdrawn from the teaching of Christian morals due to the wide variety of religions and beliefs that are represented by today's student population. This leaves moral teaching to parents alone. If ethical principles are not taught in the home, either directly or by example, then adolescents have no way to learn them. This can present many difficulties when teens are confronted by situations that require moral choices, such as whether or not to have sex or whether to engage in shoplifting. If teens do not have a firm set of principles to follow, they may find themselves in serious difficulties, ranging from problems with peers to trouble with the law.

Whether the family attends church or not, parents must act to ensure that their children learn a moral code which will help them to make appropriate decisions in a very complex and fast-moving society.

Teaching Your Moral Code

Parents in families that do not attend a church have an extra burden in today's society. Their task is to convey a set of moral principles that will help their teenagers cope with the pressures and temptations that exist in their world. Even churchgoing parents can face a dilemma if their church has either failed to keep up with the times, or is moving forward too fast for their comfort. An example of the first situation might be the stand taken by the Roman Catholic church on birth control, a position that is ignored by a large segment of their membership. Moving too quickly is exemplified by the question of homosexual marriages, which are being upheld by some churches despite the objections of a large number of their members. Whether the family attends church or not, parents must act to ensure that their children learn a moral code which will help them to make appropriate decisions in a very complex and fast-moving society.

The Problems

The very essence of being teenagers involves developing their own identities. Involved in this process is the desire to make decisions for themselves. This is not a problem when the decision is a simple one, like whether or not to wear a jacket to school. Unfortunately not all decisions teens are faced with are this easy. Issues such as whether or not to drink alcohol at a party or to have sex with a boyfriend or girlfriend are complex ones, especially when peer pressure is involved in the decision. Even such choices as which CD to buy can be more complicated than they seem due to the language and images used in some types of modern music. If teens have no foundation on which to make their decisions, then choices may be made that have dire consequences. This foundation needs to be a sound set of moral principles that has been clearly outlined by the parents.

Another aspect of being a teenager is their highly emotional nature. This trait often results in actions being taken or decisions being made impulsively. While teen emotionality can cause any teen to make mistakes in judgment, many fewer such mistakes will be made by adolescents who know that their parents will be upset and disappointed if they engage in behavior that is considered to be wrong by their elders. This is because a counterbalancing force to their impulsive and emotional nature is the need to have the approval of their parents. The great majority of teenagers need many signs that their parents care about them. Approval of their actions and decisions is one such sign. If they have clear knowledge of the behaviors that will gain their parents' approval, then teens will tend to display them. If they are unsure, the teenagers will have no standards against which to measure their behavior and will then tend not think before they act.

A further problem for parents and teens alike is the complexity of modern society. Teens today face far more complex issues than many of their parents did. Issues that were once black and white are now an amorphous shade of gray. An example of this is the use of marijuana. In previous generations the use of this drug was clearly illegal and the penalties for its possession were quite stiff. Now many jurisdictions have not only stopped charging users for mere possession, they have approved its use for medical reasons. Some countries have legalized marijuana use completely. This is bound to confuse teens who have not been clearly apprised of its dangers and the problems associated with frequent use. Premarital sex provides another example. While it has always been present in previous generations, it was not nearly as common or as public as it is today. Couples now openly cohabit before marriage with virtually no ostracism by society. From this teenagers easily develop the idea that there is nothing wrong with premarital sex, an idea that can lead to serious physical and emotional problems.

There seems little doubt that without a sound moral foundation teenage lives become much more complicated than they already are. Helping them to make sound decisions by providing clear moral guidelines has become a parental responsibility that should not be shirked.

Parental Actions

Imparting a moral code to children is really a three-step process. The first step involves the active teaching of what the parents believe are right and wrong. This is an ongoing process that should start at a very early age. At first it occurs mainly through the child's infractions. For example, hitting another child should bring a negative response from a parent. To be effective, this reaction should also include a short talk on why the action was wrong. Each time a child violates the parent's moral principles, a similar reaction should occur.

As the children become older, parents should seize positive opportunities to teach their beliefs. These are often called "teachable moments." They often occur while watching TV or a movie together. When something occurs that the parents believe is morally wrong, they should ask the teens what their opinion is. Swearing, violence and sex are examples of immoral behavior that is well represented in these media. Once again this should be followed by a short talk on what the parents believe. Newspaper articles and news stories are another source of discussion material. Stories on bullying are an excellent example of such material. Parents can bring up the article at the dinner table and ask for the teen's thoughts. This can also lead to a discussion of whether such things are happening in their lives. The parents can then summarize their thoughts on the subject, which could be something like, "Well, I hope that you kids realize how traumatic bullying can be for a young person and never engage in any yourselves. Also, be sure to let us know if anyone is ever bullying you."

Parents need to understand that they can not teach moral behavior to children and do the opposite themselves.

Besides active teaching of moral guidelines, parents also need to set an example for their children. This can be very difficult at times, but parents need to understand that they can not teach moral behavior to children and do the opposite themselves. Children love and idolize their parents in the early years and, even if as teens they want to establish their own identities, they still look to them for guidance throughout adolescence. If they see their parents bringing home office supplies from the workplace, then lectures about stealing will have no effect on them. If a colleague calls on the telephone and the parent instructs the teen to say that he is not there, then lying will have been condoned. Teens see things in a much more concrete way than do their parents so they cannot discriminate between lies and "white lies." That may be because there really isn't any difference.

One of the factors that help parents to set good examples for their teens is found in one of the behavioral attributes of most adolescents.

This is the strong sense of fairness and justice that develops as they begin to form their own moral standards. Adults will find that their teens will quickly point out the inconsistencies in parental moral behavior and will realize that it is "unfair" for parents to say one thing and do the other. In other words, if parents do not set an example their teens will immediately point this out, leaving them with virtually no ethical leg to stand on. Resorting to, "Do as I say, not as I do," will not work with teens.

The final step in imparting a moral code to children is to discipline them for infractions. This means that consequences must result for such offences as lying, stealing, swearing and physical aggression. These need not initially be considered as capital offences. In other words parents need not make a major issue of each offence as most of these mistakes are made out of ignorance or impulsiveness. They do, however, have to deal with them immediately and consistently. Consequences for swearing might range from simply saying, "That language is not acceptable in this house," for a first offence, to sending the child to his or her room for varying periods of time depending on the frequency of the inappropriate language.

Later in the teen years there may be instances where the offence is more serious. Coming home drunk or stoned from a party or shoplifting from a department store are major transgressions and need to be treated accordingly with appropriate consequences. If parents do consistently discipline moral infractions, such major errors in judgment will occur only infrequently as a result of peer pressure or experimentation. If there are repeated major offences, then counseling help should be sought, as the problems are more deep-rooted. Disciplinary action alone may be ineffective if the causes are not found and remedied.

The teaching of morals is an ongoing task that parents need to be doing, by active teaching, setting a good example and disciplining infractions. This takes place over many years. During their children's adolescence parents may feel that they have made no headway as their teenagers seem to question every value they espouse. Do not despair! This is normal teenage behavior. They will have absorbed much more than you think they have, but this will not become apparent in their behavior until the later teen and early adult years. Then you will see that your hard work over all those years has been well worth it.

> ### *Steps in Imparting Your Moral Code*
>
> - *Actively teach what you believe to be right and wrong.*
> - *Set a good example for your teenagers.*
> - *Consistently give consequences for moral infractions.*

Sex

There is a myth in society today that teenagers know more about sex than ever before. Parents believe that because there is so much sex in the media and because sex education is taught in the schools, their teenagers are well informed on the subject. This thought is a great relief to most parents as they find this subject extremely difficult to talk about. Even many sex education teachers gingerly skirt around such "racy" issues as oral sex, homosexuality and masturbation, due to their own embarrassment and lack of knowledge. For some reason adults find it difficult to talk about sex to teens. This may be because not many generations ago sex was virtually a forbidden topic. There does not seem to be any history of parents discussing this subject with their children. This is unfortunate because despite all the information that is out there, teens still have huge gaps in their knowledge of sex. The true anecdote below clearly illustrates this point.

Two Grade 9 (14-year-old) girls came into the counselor's office immediately after a sex education class. The counselor was busy updating some notes on his computer so the teens began discussing the lesson from the class.

> *Sally:* *Those STD's are gross. I didn't know about those yucky discharges.*
>
> *Laura:* *Yeah. I almost barfed. I'm really scared about them now.*
>
> *(By this time the counselor had finished his notes and joined in.)*
>
> *Counselor:* *You don't really have to be afraid of them. All you have to do is either avoid having sex or practice safe sex.*
>
> *Sally:* *You mean you can only get those diseases by having sex? What about water fountains and toilet seats?*
>
> *Counselor:* *That's why they're called "sexually transmitted diseases." You can only get the majority of them by the various forms of sex.*
>
> *Sally:* *What a relief. I was really worried for a while.*

The poor teacher would have been horrified to know that this major point had not been absorbed by these students. This kind of knowledge gap is common among youngsters and results from such factors as their short attention spans, distractions in the classroom and vague explanations by teachers.

While teenagers can joke about sex with each other, they cannot fill their knowledge gaps and reduce their fears and concerns by talking among themselves. They really need to be able to talk to their parents on this issue, and unfortunately most can't.

The Facts

Many parents assuage their guilt regarding not talking to their teenager about sex by convincing themselves that *their* youngster would never do such things. Some facts from numerous surveys might help to avoid this complacency. For example, in the US, 54% of all high school students have engaged in sexual intercourse, and 70% of seniors (Grade 12) have had sex. Canadian studies parallel these figures. By age sixteen over 40% of teenagers have had sex, and by age seventeen, 53% have had intercourse. By the time the teenage years are over about 80% will no longer be virgins. These figures continue to rise each year, as do the heartbreaks, pregnancies and STDs. While it is true that the surveys indicate that most of the younger teens who have sex either come from troubled homes, have been sexually abused, or have extremely low self-esteem, there is still a percentage who have none of this baggage. No parent can afford to assume that his or her child will not become sexually active, and will therefore not need to discuss the subject of sex.

Another important point for parents of teenagers to realize is that over the past few years a trend has developed among teenage mothers to keep their babies. Where once 95% of babies born to teenage mothers were given up for adoption, the reverse is now true. In fact recent figures indicate that only about 3% of teenage mothers give their babies up for adoption. Exactly how this trend has developed is vague even to sociologists, but the fact is that today's teenage mother wants to keep and raise her baby. This completely changes the lives of both the mother and her parents. These changes come from the fact that few teens have the resources to live on their own, so the mothers tend to stay in their parents' home to raise the baby. This causes major disruptions to family routines and an added financial drain on the teenagers' parents.

The babies' fathers are also affected more than in previous generations, as many want to be involved in raising the child, and often move into the home of one set of parents or the other. Further, the courts are much more adamant about fathers providing child support, if not immediately, then a few years down the road. It is no longer an easy matter for the teenage father to simply wash his hands of any responsibility, either because they don't want to or because the court orders it.

The Problems

"Sex education is a good way of knowing the physical problems involved with sex, but it doesn't target the idea that having sex at a young age would be an emotional problem. I mean, we don't know how it can hurt someone mentally or emotionally, we just know that having sex causes STDs and that we should always use condoms."

— Anna

Since parents rarely keep an open dialog with their teens about sex, teens miss a considerable amount of vital information. Facts like the rate of teenage pregnancy and the frequency of STDs in the population are taught and retaught to teens in the mistaken belief that the facts will frighten them away from sex. This approach is doomed to failure because of the basic nature of most teens — they think they are invulnerable. Facts alone will not do the job. What is missed in sex education classes is the teaching of sexual values and the role of feelings in the process. Schools shy away from teaching values, quite rightly, for fear of offending one faction or another. For example, teaching that abstinence is the best approach seems to make sense on the surface, but it can arouse a storm of protest in some circles. Lawsuits are all too common these days for teachers to go out on a limb in any way.

The feelings that lead to sexual intercourse and those experienced after the act are also missed by most educators because they are hard to research and quantify. Few teachers are close enough in age to the students to remember how they felt during their teens, and most texts do not explore these areas. As a result teens do not know what to expect when they get into situations where their desires can be aroused. If they don't know what to expect, then they have no way of knowing how to deal with the situation. Sex can happen as much out of confused feelings as it can from pure desire. The "feelings" part of sex is a subject that teens need to be able to talk about with their parents, because it is not likely to happen anywhere else.

Failing to discuss sex with teens has another negative side for parents. By not discussing this subject, teens feel that their parents aren't interested in their emotions and concerns. A curious spiraling phenomenon then begins where the less the parents discuss emotional issues with the teens, the less the teens think their parents are interested in their feelings. This causes teens to talk even less to adults, which in turn gives parents the idea that their teenagers do not want to talk with them. Parents then become hurt or resentful and do not try to initiate discussions. Eventually all important communication ceases.

This is definitely an undesirable situation, yet it happens in most households. It is vital that communication be kept open, as it is impossible for parents or sex education teachers to be able to anticipate every situation that teens can get themselves into. When something emotional does occur, teens need to be able to discuss it for several reasons. One is to prevent the same dilemma happening again. Another might be to be reassured that they handled the situation as well as possible. Finally, teens might need help to extricate themselves from a difficult situation.

A final problem with parents not discussing sex with their teenagers is the danger that the adolescents will get the idea that there is something wrong with having sex. The thinking is if their parents don't ever talk about it, then there must be something wrong with it. This is not what should be conveyed about sexuality. Instead, parents need to be able to convey the idea that sex is not only a natural part of life, but that is a very enjoyable part of living that is vital to a loving relationship. This can only be done if parents are relaxed and knowledgeable about the subject and can freely discuss all aspects of sex.

*"I don't think that teenagers should have sex.
I say this because a person doesn't reach full maturity until they
are in their 20s. I also believe this because I think that if a girl gets
pregnant, the parents will have no means of supporting the baby
and the teens' young lives are as good as garbage."*
— Ahmed

Parental Actions

Communication with teenagers is a difficult but vital part of raising them effectively. While good communication can be difficult on any subject, nothing seems as hard for parents to discuss with their youngsters as sexuality. A brief review of the communication skills outlined in Chapter 3 might be a useful place to start. Then we will examine some of the more specific areas of sexuality that parents need to discuss with their teens.

The main key to communicating with teens, or anyone for that matter, is to be a good listener. The key elements of listening effectively to teens are as follows:

- *Make it possible for teens to talk to you by making time available to them.*
- *Don't interrupt.*
- *Don't make snap judgments or conclusions — wait until you hear the entire story.*
- *Try not to show any emotion, including anger, disappointment or laughter.*
- *Don't relate the situation to your youth.*
- *If told something in confidence, keep it to yourself.*

The other side of communicating with teens is talking to them. This occurs either once the listening is finished or when something important needs to be brought up by the parents. This latter situation can happen either when something has been done incorrectly or when a "teachable moment" occurs and you want to get your message to your teen. The essentials of the talking process are:

- *Expand the conversation by asking more and more specific questions.*

- *Avoid lecturing. Make your point briefly and drop it.*
- *Don't nag. Remind with humor until the job is done.*
- *Try not to talk down to teens. Give reasons for your decisions.*
- *Never yell!*

That's a summary of the entire communication process in general. If this is insufficient for your needs, communication is discussed in detail in Chapter 2 of the author's first book, *Parenting Today's Teenager Effectively: Hear Me, Hug Me, Trust Me*. It is discussed in even more detail in Faber and Mazlish's book *How to Talk So Kids Will Listen & Listen So Kids Will Talk*. In addition to these general concepts, there are some communication skills specific to discussing sex that parents need to know. In order to be able to have discussions about sexual topics, parents need to be able to talk freely and frankly about any subject. They can not show aversion to anything that comes up. As hard as it might be, don't make any subject taboo or your teenager will recognize that you are uncomfortable in this area and stop talking about anything sexual. The hardest topics include oral sex, anal sex, homosexuality and masturbation. Many local health departments and parenting organizations publish pamphlets specifically for parents to help them discuss all aspect of sex with their teens.

Besides being able to communicate well with your teenagers, there are several topics specific to teenage sexuality that parents must ensure are discussed as early and as often as possible in their adolescent's development. They include:

1 How and why their bodies are developing. This is most vital with females as changes such as breast development and menstrual cycles are more obvious than the deepening of the voice and development of pubic hair in males. Nevertheless it is a topic that should be discussed with both sexes, both before any changes occur and while they are occurring. Never assume that they have learned it all in sex education classes. As mentioned above, their information is fragmented and incomplete at best. The changes of puberty often frighten and confuse teens. They tend to be very shy about their bodies, and reticent about discussing any changes that are taking place. Parents need to be vigilant so that they notice obvious changes in their child's body and must take the lead in discussing these with the youngster.

2 **What your opinion is on sexual issues.** Teens need to know where you stand on all issues related to sexuality. Typical attitudes might range from the idea that sexual intercourse should not occur outside of marriage to the notion that teens should not have sex until they are really sure they are ready. There may even be some parents who believe that sex between consenting teens is fine as long as the necessary precautions are taken. Whatever the beliefs, parents need to make them known to their teenagers so they have some standards to follow. The only caution in stating your opinions should be that this should not be done in a dictatorial and rigid manner. Rather, it should be accomplished during discussions and exchanges of information and ideas. Try to preface your statements with, "We think . . ." or, "We believe . . ." rather than, "The only way is . . ."

3 **Sexual feelings and desires.** This is one of the most difficult areas to discuss because even social scientists don't fully understand the reasons behind the feelings and emotions that surround sex. These include why we are attracted to others and what the difference between "crushes" and "love" is. Teens need to understand how powerful these attractions can be, and how they can lead to sexual encounters before their other emotions are ready. Teens also need to know that relationships in the younger years tend to be intense but brief, and that they don't last long because of the immaturity of their emotions. Many of these points can be made by encouraging the teens to talk about how they feel about their current girl- or boyfriend, then extending the conversation to the possible outcomes of the relationship. For example questions like, "Why do you think he's so attractive?" can lead to great discussions of how relationships develop.

4 **The circumstances under which sex tends to occur.** In contrast to the previous topic, this one is relatively straightforward. It involves discussions of mixed parties, peer pressure, drugs and alcohol and make-out sessions (particularly in cars and bedrooms).

These discussions can result either from teachable moments on TV or from other media sources. Teens need to be aware of the circumstances under which there is more likelihood for casual sex to happen, so that they can see situations developing, and take steps to avoid them. (Teens and alcohol and drugs is discussed later in this chapter, while peer pressure will be talked about in Chapter 8.) They should be able to recognize their reasons for considering sex in order to be able to decide to have sex, rather than having it happen while under the influence of drugs or alcohol.

Along with these discussions *gentle* reminders as they go out the door to a party or date can also be effective.

> *"Personally, I don't think young teens should be having sex.*
> *When they do it is usually carelessly and that's not healthy."*
> — Kelly-Ann

5 **How to resist sexual pressure.** Teenagers need to be prepared for as many as possible of the difficult sexual situations that can occur in their lives. Two types of these situations involve pressure to engage in sexual intercourse either from a member of the opposite sex or from their friends. In the first situation, the pressure comes from a partner (usually the boy, but not always) who uses such lines as, "If you really loved me you'd do it." Pressure from peers is usually more subtle, and results from seeing friends you admire engaging in sex acts. The teens feel that there must be something wrong with them to not want to do the same. They need to be given strategies to help them deal with these pressures and need to be reassured that not wanting to have sex is perfectly normal.

One such strategy involves teaching them how to cope with the various pressure "lines" that their partner may use on them. For example an antidote to the "if you really loved me" line is to say, "If you really loved *me* you would wait until I'm ready." Another important strategy is to make teens aware of how peer pressure works, and to let them know that they can be themselves and their friends will still like them. If teens know what situations they are liable to get into before they happen, then they will be more likely to handle them well (see Chapter 8 for a more complete discussion of peer pressure).

6 How to enjoy sexual feelings without intercourse. This is a difficult one for parents because it involves telling your teens that some sex is not only all right, but it is normal and natural. Teens should understand that they can give and receive some sexual pleasure from kissing and petting, but that they should stop as soon as they begin to feel uncomfortable or when their partner does not want to continue. If teens understand the physical and emotional dangers of intercourse, and have strategies to avoid it, then they should be able to enjoy the less dangerous but still pleasurable aspects of sexual encounters.

7 Contraception. If you maintain a close dialog with your teenagers about sex, then you will know when they are getting close to being ready to have sex with their partner. Even if you are not tuned into their social lives, the statistics on sexual activity (80% by the end of high school) should give you some warning that sexual activity is high. Even though contraception is generally well taught in school, various surveys show that it is used among teenagers between 38% and 66% of the time. From these figures one would conclude that, on average, about 50% of teens are having unprotected sex. Parents cannot assume that their teens know enough about this subject to look after their own contraception. Instead, they need to ensure that adolescents are knowledgeable and prepared. To do this, parents have to discuss the subject and, if need be, help the teen to obtain the necessary protection. Many parents hesitate to do this because they feel that such actions will hasten or encourage sexual activity. This will not be so if you continue to discuss such factors as your own moral code and how teens can tell that they are ready.

8 Masturbation. This is a subject that is rarely discussed by anyone. Despite the fact that it is virtually unanimous that masturbation is normal and natural, no one wants to talk about it. Teens continue to feel guilty about masturbating, and hide the fact that they do it — even from their peers. The obvious solution is for parents to discuss this subject, including where and when it should be done. Unfortunately this is very difficult. Recently the subject has become more public, such as in the hit film *American Pie.*

As it continues to be more openly talked about parents can use these "teachable moments" to bring the subject into conversation. Here is a sample, based on that movie:

Dad: *What did you think of* American Pie?

David: *It was OK. Kind of weird in places.*

Dad: *How did you feel about the masturbation scenes?*

David: *Aw, dad.*

Dad: *No really. Did you think they should show scenes like that?*

David: *I don't know.*

Dad: *Well, I'm not sure either, but masturbating is a normal part of life. It's a hard subject to deal with, but people do need to know that it is natural, and that they should not feel bad about it. It is certainly better to relieve yourself that way than to try to pressure a girl to have sex with you. What do you think?*

David: *I guess you're right. I feel embarrassed just talking about it.*

Dad: *I know, but you don't need to. If you feel the need just go ahead. As long as you do it in private, it's a normal, healthy part of life. Have you got any questions about this?*

That is all it takes. If your teen does have questions — great. Answer them. The chances are that even this frank conversation will not elicit a discussion. The subject is that hard to talk about. Nevertheless, that is all it should take. There is no need to say much more.

9 No means just that. It is vital that parents help their teens to understand that any time during a sexual encounter that one partner asks the other to stop, the session must end immediately. Stress that no matter how hard this may be, respecting your partners' wishes is not only important to a relationship, but not doing so can have serious legal implications. Both partners need to be ready for intercourse and if one isn't, then to continue is not only bad for the relationship, it can be considered sexual assault.

If the Worst Occurs . . .

"I think the right age for sex is 18 and up because
by then you are an adult and should have learned how to
make your own choices and fix your own mistakes."
— Dary

Despite the best information and a home where communication is open and honest, teenagers are still immature and they can make mistakes. If they happen to make a big one, like getting pregnant or contracting a sexually transmitted disease, don't abandon them. This is when they will need all the support they can get. Saying, "I told you so," will only make the situation worse. Instead, tackle the problem calmly and rationally and continually reassure your teen that he or she is loved no matter what. Close communication, loving support, and a combination of medical science and appropriate counseling can solve almost any problem. There may need to be adjustments in lifestyle, but society has come a long way from the days when pregnant teens were sent into exile to a distant relative to have their babies. There is far more acceptance and understanding than there once was, and if this process begins in the home, then the family can end up closer than ever.

If pregnancy is the problem, then the family should seek counseling to discuss the alternatives. There are a number of agencies in most jurisdictions that have counseling support for teenagers. In fact, simply looking in the yellow pages under "pregnancy counseling" will reveal several such agencies. Some have clear biases towards a particular solution, and parents need to be aware of these leanings from the start. If they do not correspond to your own religious or moral values, either find one that does or, better still, find one that can be objective about all possible solutions. This way parents can examine all the possibilities and weigh the merits of each. These solutions include the teen keeping the baby and trying to raise it herself, the parents taking the baby and raising it, giving the child up for adoption, and the teen having an abortion. Considerable thought needs to be given to these choices as each can have a huge effect on a teenager's life.

The other dire consequence of teenage mistakes in the sexual area is the contracting of a sexually transmitted disease. While teenagers certainly have been exposed to a wide variety of informational sources on this subject, the STD rates are still climbing. The biggest factor is for teens to recognize the symptoms early and seek treatment. This often does not happen because adolescents are afraid to face the fact that they have a problem and are worried about their parents' reaction. This will not occur if, during discussions about sex parents have reassured their teen that, while they would prefer them to avoid sex, they will always be there for them if an accident happens. Unfortunately such reassurance rarely happens because few parents discuss the subject at all. As a result most teens are ashamed and afraid and tend to leave the problem until they can ignore it no longer. This can have serious effects, including the permanent damaging of sex organs.

When parents do realize that their teenager has an STD, they need to seek medical help immediately. Once again the youngster needs calm reassurance and support from the parents, as the teen's emotional state is usually very fragile. With the exception of HIV and herpes, most of these diseases can be cured quickly if they are caught early. Even HIV and herpes can now be controlled with the right medications. Prevention, either by abstinence or the use of prophylactics, is still the best approach, and the intention here is not to minimize the risk or the consequences. The point is that accidents do happen, and when they do, this is when parental support and guidance is needed the most.

Shoplifting

Few parents would fail to be upset by a telephone call from the manager of the local convenience store or from the security department of a major department store stating that their child had been caught shoplifting. The normal reaction would be shock and disappointment that their child has engaged in theft. Related concerns about how often this has happened and whether or not it will lead to more serious crimes would also quickly enter parental minds. Generally, however, this is not a difficult issue for parents to deal with if they are prepared for the possibility and understand how shoplifting can occur with teenagers.

The Problems

Shoplifting among teenagers is an extremely widespread activity. It occurs not just among impoverished adolescents, but also among those from financially stable families. The reasons for this are varied, but they include the thrill and excitement of doing something illegal, peer pressure, showing off to friends and experimenting to see how it feels. It is part of being a teenager to push the limits and test the rules, and to many teens shoplifting falls into this category.

The main problem centers on the fact that teens generally don't think they are doing anything really wrong. They believe that stores have plenty of stock and they really won't miss the trivial items that teens tend to take. This attitude is somewhat akin to parents cheating on their income tax or taking stationery and supplies home from the office. The teenage outlook is often supported by the relatively mild penalties that are levied for shoplifting, such as being banned from the mall for a period of time or simply being made to pay for the item. However, shoplifting is definitely theft, and losses among retailers are becoming so high that many stores no longer treat this casually. Instead they are often laying charges against the offenders.

> *Being caught shoplifting is a frightening and humiliating experience for most teens.*

For parents the problem is to find the balance between overreacting and treating the offence too casually. It is very easy to overreact because of the disappointment and shock of discovering that your teen has done something illegal. Parents are often embarrassed and hurt by their teens' actions, adopting a "How can you do this to me?" attitude. As a result they become angry and tend to alternately lecture and threaten the teen. The difficulty with this extreme reaction is that it comes at the worst possible time for the teen. Being caught shoplifting is a frightening and humiliating experience for most teens. This situation is only made worse by an angry, threatening parent. Instead, at least in the early moments parents need to be supportive and comforting until the implications of the situation are fully known. There is plenty of time for consequences later.

On the other hand, it is equally problematic to react very mildly to a shoplifting incident. Parents risk tacitly encouraging further incidents by treating the first one casually. At the very least this approach teaches the teen that stealing is not a very bad thing, an attitude which could generalize into other areas in later life. A negative reaction is definitely called for, but how much to react and when are extremely important questions.

Parental Actions

The most effective parental response to a teenager being caught shoplifting is initial support followed by appropriate consequences. This early support should also extend to the authorities that apprehended the teen. Many parents attack these people in the mistaken belief that they are supporting their teen. This accomplishes little more than setting an example to your teen of contempt of authority. The sequence of events upon learning that your child has been caught shoplifting might be as follows:

- If called to the store to pick up your child, listen carefully to the circumstances and the actions that the store will take, then thank the security person politely and take your child home. Be calm and rational with everyone.
- If telephoned by the store to inform you of the circumstances, listen to the details and again thank the security officer.
- Once the youngster is at home, ask for his or her side of the story. Listen carefully to all the details before reacting. If the story differs significantly from the security officer's, ask questions for clarification. Stay calm.
- Once you feel you have the full story, it is time to consider consequences. For many teens the experience itself is consequence enough. You can usually tell if this is the case by their demeanor. If the store is going to press charges, this too may be sufficient. In either of these cases, insert a *short* lecture outlining your concerns, give your teen a hug, and let it go at that.
- If the teen does not seem to realize the severity of the problem, or if the store is not going to pursue the matter further, then home consequences need to be added. Ask the teen what he or she should get for this deed. Upon hearing the teen's opinion, decide whether that is sufficient. If not add consequences of your own. An example of a

typical consequence might be a one-week grounding from all activities followed by a one-month ban from going to mall or other shopping area. Add the lecture about why you are concerned, give the teen a hug, tell them you love them, and send them on their way. Make sure you follow through on the consequences.

Shoplifting among teens is a common event for the reasons outlined above. It calls for an immediate reaction from parents, but not an overreaction. If the steps above are followed, there is little likelihood that there will be a recurrence. If there is, this is symptomatic of deeper family problems, and counseling should be sought.

Smoking

Strictly speaking, smoking is not really a "moral" concern, and could easily be included in the next chapter on common teenage issues. However, it shares some important characteristics with topics that do have moral and ethical considerations. The similarity is that this problem cannot be effectively dealt with if parents do not share their views on smoking with their teens. As with moral issues, teens need to know where their parents stand on smoking, because they love and admire their parents (even if they rarely show it) and will usually tend to follow their beliefs if they know what they are.

Since teens do not have a well-developed ability to look ahead in their lives, they never really believe that they will become addicted or that they will contract any of the many diseases associated with smoking.

The Reasons

The physical dangers that result from teenage smoking are well known. They are taught in school, there are many active public awareness campaigns that place advertisements on TV and posters in public places and there are even warnings on cigarette packages. Teenagers know these facts as well as adults — yet still they smoke. In fact, smoking has recently seen a revival of popularity among teens, especially teenage girls. There appear to be several reasons for this phenomenon.

The first is rooted in the nature of teenagers. Many teens, especially those with lower self-confidence, need to show their bravado and fearlessness to their peers. Doing dangerous things accomplishes this, and one thing that is known to be dangerous is smoking. Since teens do not have a well-developed ability to look ahead in their lives, they never really believe that they will become addicted or that they will contract any of the many diseases associated with smoking. They honestly believe that they will be able to quit whenever they want to.

Another major reason for teen smoking is the feeling of congeniality they get from sharing the rituals of smoking with their friends. These rituals include lighting up, borrowing cigarettes from others, taking long drags, and butting out. These little ceremonies bind teens together and enhance their sense of belonging. This feeling is especially important for teens with low self-concepts.

Not to be ignored when searching for the reasons that teens smoke is the well-known experience of peer pressure. Teens who see their friends smoking feel that they should do it too. It is rarely the case that they are verbally harassed if they don't smoke. They just "feel" that they should. This happens often as teens tend to put considerable importance on popularity. Among young teens, the popular ones are usually the most aggressive and outgoing. If these adolescents smoke, then many of their admirers will want to do it too, as they think that this will make them liked by their more popular peers.

Another cause of teen smoking is a result of the active ingredient in cigarette smoke, nicotine. It is well known that this drug initially has a calming effect on the nerves, and teens today have more stresses on them than ever before. They often find that cigarettes relax them when under academic, social or familial stress. Unfortunately, the body builds up a tolerance to nicotine so that it takes more and more of it to maintain this calming effect. Eventually addiction sets in. There are also some calming effects derived from the rituals of smoking, as it is necessary to pause to light up a cigarette and to smoke it. These rituals provide a break from stresses and allow for the teen to relax for a few minutes.

The reasons for the rise in smoking among girls are still somewhat vague. It may be related in some to the newly emancipated status of women in general, but as yet this is not documented. Whatever the cause, this is an alarming trend, and education as to the dangers of smoking alone does not seem to help. More research needs to be done in this area.

The Problems

The physiological problems associated with smoking are well known and need not be listed here. However, there are several problems that result from how parents treat the issue of smoking. The first occurs when parents themselves smoke. In these cases, if their teenager starts smoking it is almost impossible to say anything that will make the youngster stop. When they see the people they love and admire most in the world smoking, an example has been set that words alone will not undo. Parents in this situation will often use the argument that they don't want their kids to get hooked they way they are. While this is logical, it is not enough to deter their teen from following their example. After all, unless mom or dad gets lung cancer, the teen does not see any really negative effects from parental puffing and, being unable to see much beyond the present day, cannot project any negative effects onto themselves.

Another problem is the manner in which many parents attempt to deal with teenage smoking. In an effort to control the smoking, they decree that if the teen must smoke, he or she should do it at home. This does little more than legitimize the habit because now a parent has said that smoking is all right under certain circumstances. The fact is that it is not right at all, but this is not the message the teen gets. Other parents do not allow smoking in the house, but instead send the teen outside. All this says to the teens is that that their parents do not want smoking in their house, but otherwise it is fine. Again this is not the message that needs to be conveyed.

If parents are serious about helping their teen control a smoking habit, then they have to ensure that the message they are giving, either by example or verbally, is that smoking is wrong and should not occur at all. While there are no methods that are guaranteed to end teen smoking, there are certain steps parents can take to ensure that their teen is receiving the right message from them.

Parental Actions

As a result of several of the above reasons, the teenage desire to smoke may be stronger than their parents' attempts to end the habit. Nevertheless, parents have a responsibility to do everything they can to discourage their teen from smoking. There are several positive actions they can take in this quest. They include:

- **Give up smoking yourself.** Without the example of their loved ones indulging teenagers will be less amenable to the many arguments against it.
- **Let your teens know very clearly that you disapprove of smoking.** Parents must let their teens know where they stand. Knowing their parents do not approve will prevent many teens from ever starting.
- **Do not allow smoking anywhere near your property.** Make this a clear rule well before your teen smokes and emphasize it frequently if you suspect your teenager is starting.
- **The instant you believe your teen is smoking, discuss the subject in depth.** Try not to lecture, but definitely discuss all aspects of the subject. This not only includes where you stand but why you feel this way and what the consequences will be if your teen continues. Try to make this a dialog where you listen to the other side of the story as well. You can be sympathetic while still being firm in your convictions.
- **In your discussions, concentrate on the immediate disadvantages of smoking.** Remembering that teens have only a limited ability to look ahead, do not dwell on diseases that may someday occur from prolonged use of cigarettes. Instead concentrate on the yellow teeth and stained fingers, the bad breath, the smelly clothes, the cigarette burns in clothing and upholstery and the cost of the habit. Elaborate on how non-smoking members of the opposite sex will feel. (Hint — kissing a smoker is like kissing a full ashtray.)
- **Discuss how to deal with peer pressure.** Teens need to know that other kids like them for themselves, not for what they do. Teach them how to say "no" without offending and reassure them that they can refuse to smoke and still be accepted by a smoking

group. For a more detailed discussion of this topic see the "Peer Pressure" section in the next chapter.

By following these suggestions, parents will be doing all they can to prevent their teen from getting addicted to the filthy weed. As already mentioned there are no guarantees, but these steps will definitely minimize the risks that your teen will become an addicted smoker.

Lying

Few things upset parents more than finding out that their teen has lied to them. They usually feel that they have been betrayed or that their love for their child has been exploited. This is especially true when the lie is initially believed, then later discovered as an untruth. Parents feel that this is an attack on them personally. Parents also worry that this lie may be only the tip of the iceberg and that many more lies may already have been believed. A definite loss of trust occurs that is hard for the teen to regain, even when the lie is an apparent first offence. Parents tend to remember lies and weigh each hard-to-believe story against the previous prevarication. The truth is that there are many different reasons that teens lie and, while some of them involve the parents, only in the most serious circumstances is the lie used as a personal attack.

The Reasons

The major reason that all children lie is to avoid punishment for something they have done wrong or think that their parents will disapprove of. Teens generally know when their actions are wrong and do not want to be grounded or lose privileges. Related to this is a desire by many teens to protect their parents from the disappointment they know their parents will feel if they discover that the teen has done something that will hurt or upset them. In other words, they're lying because they love their parents and don't want to hurt them.

Another main reason teens lie is to gain more control over their lives. Teens tend to believe that they can handle any situation and get upset when their parents try to restrain them. If the temptation is high enough, the teens will take matters into their own hands to prove to themselves that they are right and can actually deal with a situation. A typical example would be a 15-year-old teen whose parents refused to let her date a 20-year-old. The girl could take control of the situation by going out with the older boy and making up excuses as to where she was going to be. The most common lie would be going over to a friend's house or the library to work on a school project. Teens have difficulty realizing that their parents have much more experience in life than they do and know the kinds of things that can happen. They try to protect their teens from potential dangers by restricting their actions through rules and consequences. When teenagers disagree with their parents' ruling, the adolescents often take matters into their own hands, sometimes with disastrous results.

The Double Whammy

Erin really wanted to go to Ted's party. His parents were going to be away, and everyone was invited to stay the night. Shelly wanted to go too, but both 13-year-old girls knew that their parents would never give permission. They each decided to tell their parents that they were going to sleep over at the other's house. The girl's had been friends for years and knew that their parents would never say no to this, nor would they bother to check with the other girl's parents.

The plan worked perfectly. Both parents agreed and the girls had a great time at the party. Unfortunately, before they got home the next day, Erin's parents remembered that she had a piano lesson that day and worried that she would forget. They called Shelly's place to remind her, only to discover that Shelly's parents thought that both girls were at their place. Both girls arrived home to a very warm reception. Neither went to another sleepover for a very long time. Ted didn't give any more parties either, once his parents had been informed.

These girls were lucky that nothing serious went wrong at the party. The potential for trouble at unchaperoned teen parties is always high.

Teens also lie for reasons involving their own inner problems. These are usually teens with low self-esteem who use their lies to gain attention or to show their peers that they are in control of their lives, not their parents. These lies are usually about things they have done, places that they have been, or things their parents own. These lies are different because they are frequently lying to their peers rather than to their parents. Parents may not even find out about them unless a friend brings one up by accident. A typical lie of this type would be about a fictitious boyfriend or girlfriend who goes to another school. This increases the teen's social status because it shows that he or she is not a loser and can get the interest of a member of the opposite sex. In the most highly insecure, these lies can escalate to the point where a teen claims she is pregnant or a boy claims that he got his girlfriend pregnant. Both garner a considerable amount of attention from the peer group for a while. Lies of this magnitude get difficult to maintain because many other lies have to be told to keep the story going. It doesn't usually take too long for the peers to catch on and eventually the very peer group the teen is trying to impress rejects the teen.

Attention-seeking lies to parents include such things as lying about a teacher's behavior, by saying things like the teacher hit them or made racist remarks. Teens also might exaggerate situations their friends get into, such as claiming a friend was pregnant or that the friend got drunk at a party. These lies get their parents' attention because they make the teen's behavior look better than the friend's. Teens with this type of lying problem usually need more help than parents alone can provide, and counseling may be required.

Melissa's Whopper

Melissa was new to her junior high at the start of her Grade 8 year. She was quite outgoing so she quickly found a group of friends. One day the group got into a sharp disagreement, blaming Melissa for starting a rumor about one of the girls, so they decided to take the problem to the school counselor. As it became clear what the problem was, Melissa suddenly blurted out, "You'd be upset too if your mother was dying." This immediately garnered Melissa considerable sympathy from everyone, and the immediate problem disappeared.

Thereafter, whenever she got into social difficulties, Melissa reminded her friends about how upset she was about her mother, and the problem tended to fade away. Unfortunately, whenever she was asked about what kind of illness her mother had, Melissa was either very vague or gave a different diagnosis. Eventually her friends became suspicious and asked the counselor to find out the truth. A call to her mother quickly elicited the information that her mother was fine — there was no life threatening illness.

Even when confronted with her lie, Melissa was not able to admit the truth. She could only say, "Well, she was sick, and I thought it was serious." The result was that Melissa became an outcast from her peer group and throughout junior high was shunned by the majority of her peers.

Finally, teens often lie to get parents who ask too many questions off their backs. Good communication with teens is highly desirable, but some parents need to know every detail of their teen's life. This frustrates teens and often causes them to lie to get the parents to stop prying or to omit events entirely. Parents need to find balance between having a genuine interest in their teenager's lives and attempting to control them by making teens describe every detail of their day.

The Problems

Teenage lying is obviously a more complex phenomenon than most parents think. When they catch their teens in a lie it is just as important to try to ascertain the reason for the lie as it is to give consequences for the behavior itself. The problem is that parents tend to react emotionally to the lie and to take it as a personal affront to their parenting. The result is often an overreaction which involves the parents losing their tempers and harsh words being said. At best, parents may deal only with the lie without searching for the reasons behind it. This is not a major problem when the situation is fairly simple, such as wanting to do something that the parents forbid. On the other hand, lying to gain attention is serious and failing to look for the causes of the behavior may result in the problem not only continuing, but actually getting worse.

Parents need to remember that lying is rarely done to attack them, but instead is caused either by their parenting style or the teen's inner needs. Action is definitely needed but it should be more insightful than just a tongue-lashing and loss of privileges.

Parental Actions

An important fact that parents need to remember is that teens will rarely lie if they know deep down that their parents are always willing to help them with a problem, are truly interested in what they are doing and trust them to do the right thing. All teens will tell an occasional lie, but the behavior will not be frequent if the teens are convinced that their parents support them and will listen to them when they have a problem or make a mistake.

One way to minimize teen lying is for the parents to set a good example in this regard. If teens see their parents lying, they will tend to follow the example of the people they love. Simple examples of this behavior occur when parents tell their teens to say they are not home to an unwanted caller or call in to work sick in order to go golfing for the day. Many parents do not even consider this lying. Unfortunately, their teenagers usually do.

Since teens tend to lie to avoid getting into trouble, ensure that your household rules are fair and the consequences for breaking them are just. Parents who are too strict in their teen's eyes will be lied to far more often than those whose disciplinary systems are considered by the teen to be fair and reasonable. Parents must ensure that rules are set in consultation with their teens (see Chapter 4 for more details). This does not mean that the teens set the rules. It simply means that the process to make the rules should be a consultative one where the teens have a chance to voice their opinions of the disciplinary system. Teens who have such a voice in the process tend to adhere more readily to the rules and do not feel the necessity to lie about their behavior.

In a similar vein, parents who overreact to rule infractions by exploding in anger are also lied to frequently. Parents hate being lied to even more than they dislike their teenager breaking the rules, and often get very angry when they catch their teen in a lie. Teens who fear this parental wrath will try to avoid an angry response by rearranging their stories so as not to upset their parents. A typical example would be a teen who loses track of the time and comes home after curfew. This tardy teen might fabricate a story about having to help a sick friend get home to avoid an angry scene. Teens hate having their parents yell at them and will try to avoid this at all cost. The solution is for parents to listen calmly to the reasons for rule infractions, determine if a consequence is required and, if so, administer this consequence equally calmly. A hug or an affirmation that the teen is loved after this step helps to reassure the teen that no affection has been lost by his or her mistake. Teens know when they have made mistakes and generally expect consequences to occur. If they can expect them to be delivered without anger and histrionics, they will be far more likely to tell the truth.

Teens who tell lies to gain attention from parents or peers require a different approach. These are usually adolescents with low self-concepts who feel that the only way they can gain attention is by impressing people. Their lies either involve exaggerations or downright fabrications. Some examples of lying for attention might be:

"My uncle is really rich." — *The uncle is of average wealth.*
"My boyfriend is a real hunk." — *She doesn't have a boyfriend.*
"When Jody went out with Nick last night she slept with him." — *Jody gave Nick a goodnight kiss only.*
"We're going to Hawaii for our holidays." — *The family is going camping for a week.*
"When I turn 16 my uncle is giving me a car." — *The uncle has made no such promise.*
"My dad beats me." — *His dad is loud but does not get physical.*

> *One principle that is extremely important to the long-term relationship between parents and their teens is to always believe your child's story unless there is clear evidence that they are telling a lie.*

The solution to this type of lying starts with parents talking to the teen about the problems of "crying wolf." The fact that they will very quickly lose their credibility with both friends and relatives alike must be clearly pointed out to them. However, this alone is not enough. Since a low self-concept underlies the problem, steps must be taken to build up the teen's confidence level. This involves finding activities at which the teen can be successful. This may be sports, volunteer activities or interest clubs. In fact, one of the best possible activities for building self-esteem is martial arts. Counseling may also be necessary, as this is a very persistent personality trait and does not respond quickly to either reason or confidence-building activities. Generally a comprehensive approach is required to solve this type of lying problem.

One principle that is extremely important to the long-term relationship between parents and their teens is to always believe your child's story unless there is clear evidence that they are telling a lie. Teens need to be trusted by their parents and, knowing that the truth is sometimes stranger than fiction, adults must trust first. To constantly be suspicious is to undermine the trust relationship and, if the teens do not feel that they are trusted, they will tend to become untrustworthy.

It is vital to understand that all teens lie periodically. Even those with loving parents who set fair and equitable family rules will occasionally lie just to avoid disappointing their elders. While lying of any kind must be dealt with immediately (remember — keep the lecture short and stay calm), if the lying is infrequent, it is not a major problem. However, if a pattern develops, parents need to ascertain the reasons for the problem and remedy them rather than just disciplining the teen.

Teen Suicide

Suicide today is not the moral issue it once was. Many of the organized religions considered it a sin to commit or even to attempt to kill yourself. While this is still technically true, it now seems to be more of a social issue than strictly a moral one. Nevertheless, there are still many who consider a choice to commit suicide to be morally wrong as this decision adversely affects so many other people, especially parents and close friends.

Whether or not this is truly a moral issue, the fact remains that teen suicide is a serious problem for modern society as its incidence continues to rise. This is occurring despite a wide variety of resources, such as suicide hotlines, school preventative programs and organizations dedicated to disseminating information on this subject. Obviously there are circumstances in our modern society that act on teenagers so strongly that even these resources are inadequate. While parents can do little to change society, there is no need to despair. Through recognition of the danger signs and knowing what to do when they see these signs, there is much that parents can do to prevent their children from killing themselves.

The Facts

Few parents believe that their children could be so distraught as to commit suicide. Perhaps because they do not want to consider the possibility, they take an ostrich approach and avoid even talking about the subject. Few are aware of how many teenagers contemplate suicide at one time or another, or of how common the act itself actually is. These are the major facts, summarized from Statistics Canada and numerous Web-based suicide information sites:

- Suicide is the second leading cause of death for teens in Canada and the third leading cause among youth 15-24 in the US.
- Teen suicide rates have tripled since 1970.
- For every completed suicide there are an estimated 50 attempts.
- For every two homicides in the US, there are three suicides.
- Females account for 75% of the attempted suicides, but males complete suicide 4 times more often. This is because males tend to choose violent means such as guns and hanging while females usually choose slower means such as drug overdoses.
- 70% of suicides occur between the hours of 3 pm to midnight.
- 90% of adolescent suicide victims have at least one diagnosable psychiatric illness at the time of death. The most common is depression.
- Only 15% of suicide victims were in treatment at the time of death.
- About one third of teen suicides have made a previous attempt.
- Having a firearm in the home greatly increases the risk of adolescents completing the act of suicide. In the US, 64% of victims in the 10-24-year age range used a firearm.

These figures probably tend to underestimate the true seriousness of the problem as many parents are ashamed to report suicide attempts and many successful suicides may be reported as accidents for the same reason.

The Problems

The main problem for parents is that they rarely are able to see the warning signs that their teen is considering suicide. Articles often appear in the newspapers describing how a normal, well-liked teenager committed suicide without any warning signs whatsoever. This is rarely true. Studies have shown that at least 75% of all completed suicides showed clear signs that they were in deep despair in the weeks prior to their deaths. In many other cases there may have been signs, but busy or distracted parents missed them. The fact is that nearly every individual who attempts suicide will show some warning signs before actually committing the act. The majority of these signs are those of depression, but they are there to see if parents are paying attention. Here are some of the most common early warning signs:

- A change in sleeping or eating patterns.
- Withdrawal from friends and family members. Spending more and more time alone.
- A low tolerance for rewards, compliments or awards.
- Frequent complaints of not feeling well or of feeling "weird" inside.
- Appearing to be despondent or to be sulking.
- A sudden drop in grades and/or beginning to skip school.
- Finds no joy in anything, including former hobbies, sports, classes or friends.
- Neglect of personal welfare, such as no longer paying attention to personal grooming.

Signs that an attempt may occur very soon include:

- Has recently been in trouble or has experienced a disappointment or rejection.
- Sudden disappearance, for no apparent reason, of depression that has been characteristic of recent behavior.
- Statements to the effect of, "It doesn't matter, I won't be around much longer," "You won't have to worry about me anymore" or, "I want to go to sleep and never wake up."
- Giving away favorite possessions.

It should be emphasized that all of these symptoms of suicidal thoughts may not be present in each case. There may be only one or two. While depression is common among teens for many reasons (see the section in Chapter 8), if it lasts longer than a few days it must be treated, especially if any of the signs of imminent suicide appear.

The other major problem for parents is that they don't know what to do if any of these signs do appear. Often it is difficult to distinguish normal teen depression, such as that caused by being "dumped" or failing a major test, from the more serious form that can lead to suicide. There are also a number of myths about suicide that can interfere with parents' ability to effectively deal with the problem, even when warning signs are recognized. These are listed in the box below.

Suicide Myths

The following are beliefs that many hold about suicide, but which have been shown by experts in the area to not be true:

Myth: *People who talk about suicide don't do it.*
Fact: *Talking about suicide is one of the major signs that it is being contemplated.*

Myth: *If someone is going to commit suicide nothing can stop it.*
Fact: *The suicidal person is ambivalent — part of them wants to stop the pain by dying, while the other part still wants to live. While the person is still alive there is always hope.*

Myth: *Talking about suicide may give someone the idea.*
Fact: *Calmly asking the person if they are contemplating suicide shows you care and may help to open up a dialog on the subject.*

If any signs of serious depression or possible suicide are present, parents must act immediately. The longer the depression goes on, the more chance there is that the teen will go through with the act.

Parental Actions

The key action for parents to take if they believe their teen may be considering suicide is to sit down and talk to them about it. Parents must be patient and understanding, and need to carefully listen to the teen's problems. No matter how minor these problems appear in the great scheme of life, it is vital that they be taken seriously. To the teen they are extremely important and parents should avoid being judgmental about them.

The next step is to come right out and ask the teen if he or she is considering suicide. If the answer is "yes," then further probing is necessary. There are three criteria that indicate that immediate hospitalization is required. These are:

- **Does the teen have a plan?** If so ask what it is and determine whether or not it is realistic.
- **Does the teen have the means?** Is it possible to actually carry out the plan? For example, if the teen plans to shoot himself, does he have ready access to a gun?
- **Is the teen ready to do it?** When is the plan to be carried out?

If these criteria are all present the teen should immediately be taken to the psychiatric emergency department of the nearest hospital. Most hospitals have crisis teams available for any kind of psychiatric emergency, and potential suicide is one of them. Do not leave the teenager alone and be sure to remove any components of the means of suicide from the house if, for some reason, you can't immediately make it to the hospital.

If no plan is present, parents have some time. Start by calling the local suicide prevention hotline for advice as to where to start. Simply look under "suicide" in the telephone directory for the number. The majority of cities and towns have them. Try to get the name of a psychologist or counselor who specializes in the area of teen depression and suicide, and make an appointment for as soon as possible. There is no need for panic, but rapid action does need to be taken. Do not be surprised if the counselor wants to involve the whole family, and do not resist if medication is recommended (once again, check the section on depression in Chapter 8). While waiting for an appointment, check the wealth of resources on the Internet. There are literally hundreds of sites with pertinent information that will reassure you that you are doing everything you can.

Suicide can usually be prevented if parents are aware of the signs and symptoms of depression and if they know what to do when they see these signs. In order to do this, parents must be attuned to their teens' feelings and be aware of what is happening in the lives of their children. It is all too easy for parents to get caught up in their own lives and problems and miss seeing these often subtle signs of depression and imminent suicide.

Drugs and Alcohol

While many parents like to distinguish between drugs and alcohol, the fact is that alcohol is as much a drug as any of those that generally fall into that category. Parents tend to feel more comfortable with their teens using alcohol, rather than such drugs as marijuana, LSD or amphetamines. This is probably because they are more familiar with alcohol themselves. They realize that you can drink without becoming inebriated, whereas if you use a drug, you are virtually certain of becoming intoxicated. Unfortunately the use of any of these drugs has serious dangers associated with it. Not only that but a recent US government survey indicates that the level of alcohol use is strongly associated with both illicit drug use and with cigarette use. In fact 40% of current alcohol users in the 12- to 17-year age group had also used an illicit drug within the past month of the survey. For these reasons alcohol and drug use by teenagers are discussed together in this section.

The Problems

The teenage years are a time of experimentation as teens try to find out who they are and what they are capable of doing. Many of these experimental behaviors are harmless, such as their clothing and musical tastes. Unfortunately, some of these behaviors can be dangerous. This is particularly true when it comes to the use of drugs and alcohol. Teens use these intoxicants for many reasons, including curiosity, to reduce stress, to feel grown up, to fit in with their peers or simply because it lowers their inhibitions and allows them to be more sociable. The majority of teens try alcohol and soft drugs, typically around the age of 13 or 14, but do not carry on with the practice. Others are at serious risk for developing alcohol and drug dependencies. These teens are those who:

* Have a family history of substance abuse.
* Are frequently depressed.
* Have low self-esteem.
* Feel like they don't fit in with their peers.

Teens who becomes substance abusers find that drugs relieve their anxieties about their lives, so they continue to use them. Besides alcohol, the drugs of choice for teens today are marijuana or its stronger derivative, hashish, LSD (yes, it has made a recovery), crack cocaine (much cheaper than cocaine itself) and ecstasy. This latter drug is a relatively new one and it is often called a designer drug because besides the main ingredient (MDMA), which is an amphetamine, various other chemicals are added to these pills depending on the tastes of the maker. While the MDMA itself is dangerous, the additives can range from harmless to deadly.

Parents who suspect that their teen may be abusing drugs or alcohol should look for the following signs:

* Frequent smell of alcohol on the breath or sudden, frequent use of breath mints.
* Abrupt changes in mood or attitude, such as breaking rules, starting arguments or withdrawing from the family.
* Sudden decline in attendance or performance at school.
* Loss of interest in sports or other activities that used to be important.
* Sudden resistance to discipline at home or at school.
* Heightened secrecy about actions or possessions.
* Associating with a new group of friends who are less interested in standard home and school activities than were the previous friends. These are often ones of whom the parents do not approve.

Along with the hazard of becoming dependent on drugs or alcohol, their use has another major problem. This involves the tendency to indulge in dangerous activities when under the influence of an intoxicant. The ability of these substances to lower inhibitions not only makes teens more gregarious, but it makes them think they are capable of doing almost anything with no danger to themselves. Some of these dangerous activities are:

- Many teenagers' first sexual experience results from being under the influence of alcohol or drugs.
- Sexually active teenagers are more likely to not use condoms during intercourse if they are under the influence of drugs or alcohol. A recent survey indicated that 60% of college women diagnosed with a sexually transmitted disease were drunk at the time of infection.
- Despite massive media campaigns, teenagers are more prone to drive while intoxicated than are adults. According to Mothers Against Drunk Driving (MADD) teenage drivers make up 6.7% of the total driving population, but constitute 13% of the alcohol-involved drivers in fatal accidents.
- Fights at parties, often involving weapons, are far more likely to happen when one or more of the participants is intoxicated.

The above dangers of alcohol and drug use among teenagers are well known, yet the substance-abuse statistics continue to rise. This rise is very likely related to the increased stress that modern teenagers feel, their increased affluence, which gives them the means to purchase the substances, and the easy availability of most of these intoxicants. It may also be related to the examples set by their parents and idols. Teens are quick to follow the example of people they love and/or admire. If either their parents or the people they look up to, such as rock stars or sports heroes, are seen or known to use drugs or alcohol, then teens assume it must be acceptable for them as well. This occurs even when parents' advice to the teens is to the contrary. The "do as I say, not as I do" approach does not work with adolescents. They see the hypocrisy in these words and tend to follow the example instead. Parents who feel they must use alcohol need to do so sensibly and sparingly if they expect their teenagers not to follow their example.

Parental Actions

The most important action parents can take to prevent their teens from using and abusing intoxicating substances is to make your views on the subject clear to them. Talk to them often, using "teachable moments" from TV and press reports, to let them know the dangers of using drugs and alcohol. Ideally these talks should begin as early as the age of nine years. A recent survey by an organization called Partnership for a Drug-Free America showed that teenagers whose parents talk to them regularly about the dangers of drugs and alcohol are 42% less likely to use these substances than those whose parents don't talk to them about these matters. Unfortunately, the study also showed that only one in four teens actually had such conversations with their parents. This latter fact once again indicates that parents are either too busy to talk to their teens or don't know how to do so. This is regrettable because it is clear that simply discussing these matters and their dangers frequently can have a tremendous impact on preventing the adverse effects that come with the use of these substances.

Another vital parental action to prevent the use of these substances is to set a clear example, either of abstinence or of limited use. It is a common sight on television and in the movies to see adults using alcohol in times of stress, saying something like, "I've had a rotten day. I need a drink." This type of behavior clearly links stress with alcohol use, and it is not limited to the media. Indeed, this behavior is mirrored in families everywhere. Teens then get the idea that if they are under stress they should use alcohol or a drug to relieve it.

Teens absolutely hate seeing their parents get drunk. Despite this, viewing their role models in an inebriated condition clearly conveys the idea that drinking to excess is acceptable. After a night on the town parents will often dismiss their condition the night before as a relatively minor event and even rationalize it as just "letting off steam." What message can this possible convey to the teens except that occasional inebriation is allowable?

Besides talking about the dangers of drugs and alcohol to their teenagers and setting a good example for them, parents must also set firm rules about the use of these intoxicants. These rules should indicate that any use of these substances before the legal drinking age, in the case of alcohol, and ever for the case of drugs is forbidden and will be met with consequences. Do not allow any use on your premises. Parents often do this in the mistaken belief that by allowing it in the home, they can teach moderation in a controlled environment. While this approach seems to work in Europe where the cultures are very different, it rarely works in North America. The only message it seems to convey is that the use of these substances must be all right because the parents are allowing it.

In support of this point, a recent study by the National Center on Addiction and Substance Abuse, based at Columbia University, found that parents who impose strict rules on their teenagers have a better chance of raising drug-free children. The study showed that teenagers who lived in "hands-off" households were twice as likely to abuse drugs as the average teen. It also showed that only 27% of teenagers live in "hands-on" households where rules are set and consequences imposed for breaking them. A "hands-on" parent was defined as one who took such actions as:

- *Turning off the TV during dinner.*
- *Banning music with offensive lyrics from the house.*
- *Finding out where their children were after school.*
- *Imposing curfews.*
- *Assigning regular chores.*
- *Eating dinner with their children at least six nights a week.*

These are not exactly draconian measures; they are just common sense rules and actions that show teens that their parents care about them. Not only do these rules and actions help to raise more confident children, they also greatly reduce the risk of their ever abusing drugs or alcohol.

Consequences for any detected infraction of these rules must convey the seriousness with which you view this subject. Any form of drinking or drug use should have at least two weeks withdrawal of privileges. This can range from total grounding to removal of TV, Nintendo or the telephone for this period. Actual inebriation would call for even more severe penalties. *There can be no exceptions in this area*. It is too important an area to display your reasonableness or flexibility.

Since peer pressure is a fact of life among teens, parents need to ensure that they instruct their children about how this is related to the use of drugs and alcohol. Teens need to know that true friends will accept them whether they drink or smoke up or not. They need to know how peer pressure works and how to stand up to it. For a thorough discussion of this subject, read the section in the next chapter.

Finally, parents cannot naively assume that their children would never abuse these substances. Without being paranoid on the subject, they must be vigilant for the signs of abuse listed above. Remember that most teens will experiment and all teens will be exposed to drugs and alcohol sooner or later. By spending time with their teens, communicating with them, and setting firm rules parents will usually avoid any problems. But there are no guarantees. If any signs of problems are seen, seek help immediately. All municipalities have a wide variety of resources for this problem. If you cannot find them in the telephone book, call your child's school counselor and discuss the problem with him or her. Counselors have access to the majority of available resources, and can point you in the right direction.

Preventing Drug and Alcohol Abuse

- *Clearly communicate your feelings about teenage use of these substances and the dangers that are inherent in them.*
- *Set an example of temperance or moderate usage of alcohol and abstinence from any drugs.*
- *Set firm rules about the use of intoxicants and give immediate consequences for catching teens breaking these rules.*
- *Teach your teens about true friendship and the workings of peer pressure.*
- *Never assume that your teen will not become dependent, especially if there is any history of substance abuse in the family.*

Homosexuality

This is a topic so fraught with emotion and controversy that it is tempting to leave it out of this book altogether. Unfortunately there are many teenagers in our society who must go through years of fear and self-loathing because a large segment of the populace refuses to accept homosexuality as a fact of life. No child deserves to undergo the physical and emotional abuse that is heaped on these bewildered teenagers. Yet still it happens. These adolescents literally have no one to talk to. They certainly can't turn to their friends, since these are the people who are constantly making gay jokes and teasing each other by calling their peers "fag" and "dyke." The saddest part of all is that, because parents do not understand this condition, the teens can't turn to them for comfort and guidance either. Even many counselors are uncomfortable dealing with gay teens. For years these teens are doomed to a lonely and fearful life through no fault of their own. It is vital that parents understand as much as possible about homosexuality if it becomes apparent that their teenager is gay.

The Problems

The most serious problem for both gay teens and their parents is the prejudice against homosexuality that continues to exist in our culture. The heritage of religious intolerance, possibly stemming from mistranslated or misinterpreted Bible verses, combined with the hitherto unknown cause of this condition has resulted in a massive bias against homosexuals. This bias creates a powerful fear in teens who suspect that they might be gay. They fear being found out, being called names, being assaulted or even being killed. These fears are difficult enough for adults to cope with, but are even more difficult for teens to handle. They do not have the life experience and the skills to cope with these fears, so that they often become overwhelming.

Sexual preference is not always clearly defined in teenagers; it often takes many years for the teen to understand why they don't share the same sexual interests as their peers. As they begin to suspect their homosexuality, they have no one to turn to for advice, as they are well aware of the biases against gays and lesbians. They have heard the jokes and taunts, not just from their peers, but in the media and even from their parents. They usually don't know anyone that is homosexual, so they tend to keep their secret hidden or "in the closet." The result is often a loss of self-esteem and depression. Studies have shown that gays and lesbians comprise up to 30% of teen suicides annually, and they are up to 6 times more likely to attempt suicide than their straight peers are. Here, in part, is how Jenny defined being a homosexual teenager in an article on the Internet:

Being gay is:

- Listening to your friends talking about "queers" and making jokes about effeminate males and athletic-looking females as you stand there and know they would say the same thing about you.
- Awakening every morning, living every day, and going to sleep at night fearing discovery and rejection by your family and friends.
- Dating people of the opposite gender when you really don't want to, just to maintain a cover.
- Pretending to be ignorant about homosexuality and quietly listening to your straight friends display their ignorance while you dare not correct them.
- Being taught to hate yourself knowing that you can not change, knowing you can never share that wonderful feeling of being "in love" with your family and most of your friends.

(source: http://www.alumni.imsa.edu Copyright 1998, SKYWIND)

No matter what opinion a person holds about homosexuality, it is clear that teens are suffering because of the homophobic segment of society. The exact percentage of homosexual people in the general population is still in doubt. Kinsey's pioneering work on human sexuality placed the figure at 10%, but there were many design flaws in his studies. More modern figures estimate there are only 1% to 2% of the population that prefer their own sex. Even using the lower figure, that would mean that in a medium-size high school of 1500 students, there would be at least 15 very unhappy and confused teenagers. That is too many to ignore.

Part of the reason for the continued societal bias against gays and lesbians is the fact that the cause of homosexuality is unknown. Many people believe that sexuality is a choice, and that people do not have to be homosexual if they don't want to. While scientists are starting to lean towards a genetic cause of this condition, there is still no overwhelming proof. It is hard to imagine, though, that any young teen would choose to live in fear of the taunts, jibes and even beatings that homosexuals must endure throughout their lives. Teens are notorious for following the crowd, for being subject to peer pressure. Why then would any teen choose to be so different from the rest as to become an object of derision? Viewed in this light, the concept of their having a choice of sexual preference seems quite far-fetched.

Parental Actions

The key action for parents is to understand that homosexuality exists and cannot be changed. Parents need to model tolerance for gays and lesbians, just as they would for people of other races and ethnic groups, whether any of their teens turn out to be gay or not. This means that parents should avoid gay jokes or any other forms of belittling homosexuals, and should discourage any such behavior displayed by their children. Parents need to teach, whenever the subject comes up, that homosexuals are people with feelings too, and should not be used as objects of derision.

If parents begin to suspect that their own teen may be gay, then they need to ensure that communication is good with the youngster, because the teen has no one else to turn to. The teenager will not usually be able to broach the subject first, so the parent will have to do this. Unfortunately, since many teens are slow to exhibit sexuality of any kind, it will usually be in the later teen years when parents begin to have their suspicions. This means that the teen may have to suffer several years of fear and confusion. In the spirit of "better late than never," parents need to bring up the subject in as straightforward and objective a manner as possible, as soon as they are aware that their teen may be homosexual. Do not avoid the subject in the hopes that the problem will go away. Gently describe why you think your teen may be gay, and then listen calmly to the answer. If there is a flat out denial, then simply let the teen know that no matter what their sexual preference is, you will always be there to listen to their problems. If homosexuality is admitted, then the teen will need counseling and to be put in touch with a local gay/lesbian support group. As parents you are there for support, but you cannot be expected to fully understand the teen's feelings.

If your teen turns out to be homosexual, then take the time to learn as much as you can about it. There are many resources in the bookstore (such as *A Catholic Mother Looks at the Gay Child* by Jesse Davis) and on the Internet that can help parents to understand homosexuality. Work at accepting the situation, especially the idea of your teen bringing home same-sex boy- or girlfriends. It is still your teen, and they need your love and support even more than a heterosexual teen does, due to the prejudices that still exist in society. Also, teach the same lessons about sexual behavior as you would with any other teen, such as abstinence until ready and safe sexual practices, so that they learn to be responsible in this very dangerous area.

If You Suspect Your Child Is Gay

- *Model tolerance for gays and lesbians.*
- *Initiate a discussion of sexuality as the teen will probably not be able to.*
- *Learn as much as you can about homosexuality.*
- *Contact a gay/lesbian organization.*

Chapter 8

Common Teenage Issues

The issues discussed in this chapter are those experienced by many teenagers and their families. These are the areas that bother parents the most because they are completely new to them. Until teenage behavior starts, and that can be anywhere from 10 to 17, parents are lulled into a false sense of security by the compliant and obedient nature of their children. Suddenly all that changes! They begin to argue, wear strange clothing, listen to disgusting music and spend most of their waking hours with their friends. This rapid behavior change baffles most parents, leading to strained relationships, bitter arguments, and long periods of silence. This does not need to happen. If parents understand the needs that drive the behavior of their teens, and have effective coping strategies, the teen years can be both rewarding and enjoyable. In fact, these years can be even more pleasant than the preceding 12 or so, as the teens are now thinking, reasoning beings who parents can talk to on an entirely different level. Remember, though, that teenagers are still not adults, so this thinking and reasoning may often not be as logical as that of adults. Still, by understanding where they are coming from, parents can avoid getting angry and simply deal with the behavior. That is what this chapter is all about.

Teens and Their Friends

"My friends are important to me because you can talk to them about anything and everything. The laugh with you (sometimes at you) cry with you and rejoice with you. Friends are something everyone needs so emotion doesn't swell up inside you."
— Kelly Ann

During the teen years friends take on a new importance to teens. While most children have friends throughout their childhood years, parents notice a major change in their significance when teenage behavior begins. Suddenly it is almost impossible to pry them away from their friends, either in person or on the telephone. Usually, the presence of friends is a healthy sign in teens, just as their absence can indicate problems. Despite this healthiness, friends can create major difficulties in parent-teen relationships.

The Problems

Friends often become problems for parents in several different ways. Jealousy is one of them. Where once their kids wanted to spend all available time with their parents, now they rarely appear to want to be with their elders. While teens do in fact want to spend time with their parents, there is no question that this is much less time than it used to be. This can be very hard on parents who are close to their children.

Friends also create practical problems in scheduling of family outings and vacations. Often teens would rather be with their friends than, for example, visit Aunt Emily or even go skiing or to the lake. This frustrates and confuses parents who resent the arguments this reluctance creates. Where once they just planned the outing and went, now parents have to convince their screaming teen that it really is a good idea.

Finally, parents often feel their teenager is hanging around with the wrong type of friends. They either think that these friends are influencing their child in the wrong way, such as drinking or doing drugs, or that they are not doing well enough in school and their youngster may emulate their poor performance. Unfortunately, even hinting that their friends aren't good for them is enough to start a major battle. Actually prying them away from this group can be almost impossible. This is very frustrating for parents as their maturity and experience in life usually makes them good judges of the suitability of their teens' friends.

Why are Friends so Important to Teens?

Parenting experts have many theories as to why teens are so attached to their friends. David Elkind, a noted parenting authority, identifies three reasons for these attachments in his book, *Parenting Your Teenager*. The first and most important of these is to provide teens with transitional emotional attachments that help them to become independent from their parents. In other words they transfer some of their emotional dependence from their parents to their friends in order to begin the process of breaking away from them.

The second purpose of adolescent friendships, according to Elkind, is to help define their social status. The social group they fit in with is where they stand in their society. This helps teens to become independent by bolstering their self-confidence — they have an identity, even if it's that of a "skid" or "skater."

The final of Elkind's reasons for the importance of friends is to prepare the youngsters for heterosexual relationships. According to this theory, learning to handle close relationships with same sex peers, sharing confidences, likes and dislikes, helps in later years to deal with relationships with the opposite sex.

These theories make good sense to adults and parenting experts, but the teens themselves have more down-to-earth explanations. Christie's is particularly good. She says:

"My friends listen to me when I have a bad day when I need someone to talk to. My friends are people I can go to and hang out with and not get bored. They make me feel secure and safe sometimes."

Jacob has a similar thought when he writes:

"They respect my decisions. They share common interests with me, and they make me feel special"

Communication, especially listening, and bolstering of self-confidence is a theme that runs through most of the responses in these teen surveys. This makes sense, as the teenage years are those of the greatest feelings of insecurity. They need all the support they can get during this period. Mindy reinforces this idea when she writes:

"My friends don't judge me and they like me for who I am.
They help me when I'm sad and they listen."

Whether you listen to David Elkind, or the teens themselves, it is readily apparent that friends are a vital component of teenage lives.

Why Teens Need Their Friends

- *They provide teens with transitional emotional attachments that help them break away from their parents and establish their own identities.*
- *They help to define their status in society by showing which group they fit in with.*
- *Friends help the transition to heterosexual relationships.*
- *They provide a safe and uncritical environment.*
- *They can easily communicate with each other, while few adults appear to understand them.*

How do teens pick their friends?

One of the most misunderstood aspects of the teen need for friends is how the teen selects the friends and the friendship group that they associate with. Many parents believe that their teenagers are coerced into a group through peer pressure. This idea is particularly true when the teen's peer group is not acceptable to the parents. This is rarely the case. In fact, teens choose their friends on the basis of common interests or feelings. To be compatible they need to have mutual areas of discussion so that they can empathize with their friends and their friends can understand them. This is why the athletic group tends to hang out together, as do the academics, the musical types and the outcasts. They have things in common and can share their ups and downs with each other, knowing they will be understood. Teens will not accept anyone into their group who does not think and act the way they do.

The fact that teens choose their friendship group by fitting in with them is not a problem for parents if their teenager's peer group is made up of clean-cut, academically oriented youngsters with sound moral principles. It does become a problem for parents if the group is made up of scruffy, heavily pierced and tattooed individuals who stay out late and use drugs and alcohol frequently. In this case parents prefer to think that it is the group who are exerting an influence on their teen to join. This way of thinking is a protective mechanism for parents as they can blame the peer group for their teen's behavior and do not have to look for emotional problems within their own child. They also do not have to analyze their parenting practices for flaws.

Unfortunately this way of thinking does not solve problems for parents who do not approve of their teen's social group. Parents have to realize that if their adolescent is hanging around with individuals that they find unsavory, they need to look within their own teen to find out what that youngster has in common with these friends. This could involve a painful look into their own marital situation or parenting practices. It will definitely involve an examination of their teen's self-esteem and its origins.

Parent Actions

There are a number of positive actions parents can take if they feel their teen's friends are creating problems. It is not an easy task, however, due to the emotional nature of teens and the extremely strong attachment formed between these friends.

The very strong attachments between teens and their friends, like many other teenage traits, often catch parents off guard. Where once they ran to the door to great mom or dad on their arrival home, now they hardly seem to realize their parents are there — unless they want something. Parents who have been used to a relatively close relationship with their kids often resent the friends for seeming to pull the teens away. Barbara is typical of a teen in this situation.

"My mom says I'm always either at school, out with my friends, on the telephone or in my room. I argue with my mom every weekend over whether I should stay at home or go out with my friends."

It's vital that parents not take it personally that their children now want to be with their friends more. This is normal and natural. They are not rejecting you; they just need more time with their friends at this stage of life. It's also important that parents realize that teens still want to be with their parents sometimes, just not as often. Give them some space, within the boundaries of your family rules, and you will be well on your way to having a great relationship with them.

Prying Them Away

The subjects of outings and vacations with teens are discussed in detail elsewhere (see "Family Holidays" in Chapter 6), but since friends can often be the cause of adolescents not wanting to go places with their parents, the main points will also be covered here.

The two key ideas to keep in mind are to give the teens enough notice that you want to go somewhere, and get their input on where to go. If not enough notice is given, then there is a good chance that they will already have made plans with their friends. Given the prominent place of friends in teen's lives, parent activities almost always take a back seat. Let them know a few weeks ahead of time for major events, such as a ski trip or an excursion to the cottage. This amount of notice only applies to major events. If your teen is just moping around the house complaining of having nothing to do, don't hesitate to suggest you do something together.

Another very diplomatic concept is whenever possible let them bring a friend. As long as there is space and finances are not a problem, having a friend along will minimize any chance of boredom, and will circumvent the desire to be with friends rather than with you.

Visits to Relatives

In most cases teens heartily dislike visiting relatives because it is "boring." This means that there is either little to do or they have no one their age to associate with. To avoid battles about these very necessary visits, make some compromises. Either try to keep the visit short, or make sure there are some activities that your teens can partake in. Teens will buy into the visits if there is something in it for them.

For major events such as vacations, it is best to consult the family before deciding on a destination. Teens feel more grown-up and part of the family if you give them input, and you can avoid the miserable time that often results if you unilaterally decide on the venue. Consultation does not necessarily mean giving in to the teens, it just means listening to their ideas, and possibly compromising on the final decision.

Nothing is as guaranteed to start an argument than to suggest that a teen's friends are either not good enough or are exerting a negative influence.

The Wrong Friends

The subject of friends negatively influencing your teen is the most delicate of almost any issue you may have to address with them. As discussed earlier, they really need their friends at this stage in their lives, and criticizing the friends is seen by the teens as being the same as criticizing them. Nothing is as guaranteed to start an argument than to suggest that a teen's friends are either not good enough or are in some way bad for them. Nevertheless, parents are usually right in their judgments of their child's peers. How then should you handle this situation? Let's hear from the teens first. Lacey is quite adamant when she states:

"If my parents don't like my friends I think they should relax and let me live my life. I know some people I hang out with may not be the best, but I know my limits and my parents should respect that."

Joanne is equally unbending:

"I think they should back off unless it's involving violence or drugs. This is my friend and my friendships. We can choose for ourselves."

While both of these statements appear to indicate that parents should stay right out of the friendship situation, there are some useful hints here. One is the idea that teens will know their limits and will not do things that they don't want to do. There is much truth in this concept. If teens have been thoroughly taught right and wrong by their parents, these teachings will win out. It is usually best for parents to stay out of the friendship choices of their teens if at all possible. Michelle reinforces this point:

*"My parents should do nothing if they don't like my friends.
They should trust me enough to know my friends are OK, and that my
friends don't make me do things. I do something if I want to."*

I have already said that parents are usually right about friends. If they are truly worried about their teens' choice of peers, they should discuss the situation with them as calmly as possible. Kelly says this very clearly:

"Unless they have a good reason to dislike your friends they should keep their feelings to themselves. If they have a reason they should talk openly about it, never tell them that they can't be friends with these people."

In other words, discuss the situation and make your feelings clear by stating the reasons for your concerns. However, don't go as far as to ban the teen from seeing these people. Not only is this ban almost unenforceable, except in the home itself, it will just breed rebellion and sneaking around. Again, you will have to trust your teenager to eventually see your point. They usually will. Don't panic if there is no immediate effect to your words, as they may take a while to sink in.

Parents need to remember that their teen is choosing these friends, not the other way 'round. It may require a counselor's help to find out what your teen has in common with them that creates the attraction. If, with the counselor's help, you can raise the child's self-esteem, then there is little likelihood that the teen will continue to choose friends who themselves have self-esteem problems. The section on self-esteem later in this chapter will be useful in this regard.

If You Are Concerned About Their Friends

- *Don't take their desire to be with their friends personally. It is normal and natural. Give them some space.*
- *Give them as much notice as possible about an upcoming outing.*
- *Get their input on destinations.*
- *When possible, let them bring a friend.*
- *Plan activities for visits to relatives, or keep the visit short.*
- *Do not ban friends.*

- *When very worried about the choice of friends, discuss it with the teen calmly, clearly stating your reasons.*
- *Get counseling help if your teenager persists in the choice of undesirable friends.*

Giving them time and space to spend time with friends and having faith that they will choose the right friends, or at least see their faults in time, fall into the "Trust Me" category. The trust is that you have taught them your moral values and they will be able to apply this when they meet with difficult situations. Teens cannot grow up to become independent beings if they are never trusted to make their own judgments and decisions.

Part-Time Jobs

"Teens should work so they learn responsibility and so they have their own money. And they also get experience for when they get older."
— John

Most parents are pleased when their teenage son or daughter takes a part-time job. After all, jobs teach many skills that are desirable in later life, such as punctuality and responsibility. They also provide a measure of financial independence for teens, as well as a chance to learn saving and budgeting. Unfortunately, there is also a negative side to teens holding jobs that many parents do not realize. In fact, parents need to ask some key questions and take some vital responsibilities in this area if the job experience is not to become a painful one.

The Problems

The most important question to ask is why does the teen need a job in the first place. In some families the answer to this is obvious — they need to help take some financial responsibility off the parents. In this case a part-time job is certainly a positive thing to do. On the other hand, if there is no financial need, why does the youngster need the job? An adequate allowance should cover the necessities, which is all a teenager really requires. There are over forty years to work once a person enters the job market permanently, so what's the hurry? If the answer is a materialistic one, such as the teen wants to buy a car, stereo set or more clothes then there is no need for a job, and working should not be allowed. School, after all, is a teen's first responsibility. Jane certainly recognizes this when she says:

"If a teen wants to work, they should be allowed,
depending on what they need the money for.
I prefer to focus on school rather then money"

Time is the next problem to consider. Homework and household jobs remain whether a teen has a part-time job or not. If the teen is not a strong student, then he or she should probably not take a job at all. The same applies if the adolescent is involved in a number of extra-curricular activities. Money should be far less important than most of these excellent physical and mental outlets. One teen who clearly sees this point is Anna when she writes:

"Teens should get a job when they think they can handle all the
schoolwork and have everything under control and time to spare"

The next problem area is readiness to hold a job. This readiness is in two distinct areas. The first is readiness for the routine of working, also known as responsibility. Showing up on time every working day, indeed, just showing up every working day is difficult for many teens. They are generally emotional and distractible, two factors that make the routine of a job difficult. For example, teens often become absorbed in being with their friends and forget the time. Worse, if the teen is really having a good time, he or she can be tempted to call in sick. Those who employ teens are used to this behavior and do not tolerate it. Several of the surveyed teens recognize these factors.

"I don't think there is any specific age when a teen should look
for a part-time job, it's just how responsible they can be.
You kind of have to judge for yourselves because you know your kids."
— *Melissa*

*"Teens should be responsible and make sure they get all their homework
done so they can get good grades while having a part-time job."*
— David

The second readiness factor also relates to emotionality. Teens
often have difficulty accepting what they perceive as unfairness,
whether from a parent teacher or boss. Often when they feel that
they are being treated unfairly by their boss, they will explode — just
as they do at home. The same can occur when dealing with a rude
customer. This emotional behavior usually has disastrous results,
as employers will not accept it. There are many teens looking for
jobs and employers know this. Being fired is very hard on teens' self-
confidence, even when they feel they were treated unfairly.

*"I'm 14 and I'd probably get bored with the same
part-time job over and over now, but who knows in a year."*
— Mindy

Even when the teen is working successfully there can be problems.
Whenever they discover a reliable worker, employers have a tendency
to increase the hours to take advantage of this dependability. This is
because so few teenagers manage to hold a job for long due to the
readiness factors mentioned above. As the hours increase, homework
and sleeping time decrease proportionally, and school performance
tends to drop. While it is flattering for the teen to be appreciated and
while the extra money is nice, the long hours at work can really interfere with the things that should be important to a teen.

Parental Actions

Parents should play a key role in not only determining when a teen
is ready to take a job, but in monitoring the job performance to ensure
that it is a positive experience, both financially and emotionally, for
the teens. Their first action should be to determine if the teen really
needs to work. If there are no financial concerns it's probably best to
let the teen be a teen. With so many potential problems involved with
working too young, the risk should not be taken if there is no need.

If the "need" question has been answered in the positive, then the next parental action should be to determine if there is enough time available. If the youngster's grades are poor, a job is out of the question. Other demands on time can be extracurricular activities and household chores. There are many benefits to artistic and athletic endeavors, both physically and mentally, and teens should take part in them if at all possible.

When there is a need for money, and time is no problem, then the next factor a parent needs to consider is maturity. Is the teen responsible enough to hold a job? If not, then the parent has a duty to delay job seeking until a later date. There is a real need for clear and diplomatic communication here. Teens are very sensitive, and can easily interpret your reasons as criticism. Let the teenager know that it is simply a readiness factor and explain why the teen is not yet ready. Examples might be difficulties getting out of bed, frequent arguments with parents and teachers, or inability to complete chores. Promise to review the situation the next year if growth in maturity level is noted.

> *"Teens should work because they need a sense of responsibility.*
> *They should be able to purchase items on their own and not have*
> *to get money from Mom and Dad all the time."*
> — *Kristin*

Once this stage has been reached, parents can be a major asset to a teen by showing the youngsters how to go about looking for a job. It often does not occur to parents, who have been in the job market for years, that teens have no idea how to search for employment. Show them the want ad section of the newspaper and discuss what types of jobs to look for. Most teens will find it difficult to do "cold calls." This dropping into businesses that might hire students and asking for an application is hard for many teens. Parents can help to overcome this shyness by being supportive and encouraging, and even by driving the teen to the location to help keep the courage up.

Once a job is obtained, parents have a responsibility to monitor the situation and give advice and support where necessary. Parents may need to be communicating with their teen and actively teaching them how to deal with unfairness and rudeness. Explain that bosses and customers have bad days too, and a little kindness to the angry person may help defuse the situation. Teens should not be encouraged to simply quit if they don't like their boss or their customers as this is teaching the wrong thing. Life is rarely that simple. Similarly, the elders have a responsibility to ensure that the hours worked do not get out of control so that the teen can get sufficient sleep and has enough time to spend with friends in social activities.

There is no doubt that successful employment teaches young people many useful skills. Unfortunately, unsuccessful employment can have as many negative effects, especially on a teen's self-confidence. Parents must take an active role in determining readiness and monitoring performance, as teens usually do not have the maturity to regulate themselves. If parents do this, then the experience has a much better chance to be a positive one.

Ensuring Part-time Job Success

- *Make sure there is a financial need.*
- *Ensure the teen has enough time.*
- *Gauge the maturity level. Can the teen handle responsibility and the conflicts that may arise?*
- *Actively help in the job search by giving suggestions and driving the teen to prospective employers.*
- *Monitor their job performance. Give support where necessary and keep control of the hours.*

Summer Jobs

Working during summer vacation has one major difference from part-time jobs held during the school year. The difference is that the teen definitely has enough time to work for wages in the summer. Now parents can look more at the positive aspects of holding a job rather than at the negative ones. The only remaining concern is their maturity level. They still need to be responsible enough to endure the rigors of working. These include the discipline involved in getting up in the morning and getting off to work, and handling rude or demanding bosses and customers. If this maturity level is there then by all means let the teen have at it.

Teens usually signal their readiness to get a job by talking about it with their parents, but this is not always the case. Often it is the parents that suggest that it is time for the teen to look for a summer job, both to fill in their idle time and to reap the positive benefits that the successful holding of a job can bring. In either case, parents are often amazed that the summer is fast approaching yet their teen has not yet started to look for a job. In fact parents tend to get quite upset about this apparent lack of initiative. In most cases it is not laziness that prevents the job hunt, it is more likely to be a combination of disorganization and lack of self-confidence.

The lack of organization is partly the inability to know where to start and how to proceed that was discussed in Chapter 4. Organizational skills are generally learned and are not fully present in most teens. In the case of summer jobs, the disorganization is also the result of a lack of knowledge of the job market. Most teens do not know where the classified ads are in the newspaper, how to make up a resume, or who to approach in a business about a job. This is where the parents can be of great help. They should start in March to help the teen through the steps of a job search. Together you can make up a list of businesses likely to need summer help, type up and duplicate a resume (there's an excellent Resume template on Microsoft Word) and application letter, then make the rounds of these businesses to drop them off.

This brings us to the confidence factor. Many teens find it difficult to approach strangers and ask for a job. If your teen seems to be dragging his or her feet in the application process, this may be the cause. As soon as you see procrastination in this area, discuss the matter to see if timidity is the cause. If so, help out by driving the teen around to drop off the resumes or to pick up an application form. Teach the teen to ask for the manager only and to not be brushed off by an employee. Do not actually go into each business with the teens, as by doing this themselves they will gradually build up their confidence so that they will be able to do it entirely by themselves in the future.

Once the adolescent finds a job, then all the parental support concepts discussed above come into play. Remember that the teens are still very young and the working world is very foreign to them. Most teenagers will need considerable parental support both in finding a job and in keeping it once they are working.

"Teens should work so they know what the real world is like.
If they get fired, there is back-up (your parents). If you don't work,
when you grow up, there might not be back-up and you won't
know how to handle things."
— Sean

Self-Esteem

"The confidence that we have in ourselves
gives birth to much of that which we have in others."
— La Rochefoucauld (1665)

Self-esteem, or how well a teenager likes him or herself, is something an adolescent can never have enough of. The teenage years are the most self-conscious time of a person's life. Indeed, no teen can be tall enough, thin enough, smart enough, athletic enough or popular enough. This situation results from adolescents' attempt to break away from the shadow of their parents and establish an identity of their own. In this process, teenagers compare themselves to adult models, such as athletic heroes, rock stars, supermodels and even their parents, and find themselves wanting. The result is that they don't really know who they are, but they definitely aren't who they feel they should be.

Despite these pervasive feelings of inadequacy, most teens survive adolescence reasonably well because they have just enough self-esteem to see these years through. Unfortunately there is a minority of teenagers who suffer greatly during these years because their level of self-esteem is lower than average. These youngsters have such a difficult time that they often do not recover, and live relatively unhappy lives. It is vital that parents, who are the primary influence on their teen's self-esteem, monitor their child's progress and intervene if they see that the adolescent is suffering because of a low self-concept.

The Problems

Children with low self-esteem can be recognized through their possession of several common traits. One is their fearfulness to try new things. These children don't want to involve themselves in new activities for fear of not being good enough at them. This is very frustrating for parents who know that involvement in extra-curricular activities helps to develop a well-rounded personality. If this cause for lack of participation is not recognized, it can cause considerable friction between the parents, who are pushing the youngsters to expand their horizons, and their low self-esteem offspring who will resist this pressure due to fear of failure.

Another characteristic of children with low self-esteem is their inability to make friends. Once again, their fearfulness interferes with their ability to interact with others due to a concern that they may be rejected. Parents will again find this frustrating because they know the value of having friends and will push their children to form relationships. This only frustrates the youngsters because they do not themselves know why they can't make friends, and knowing that they are disappointing their parents only lowers their self-esteem further. This tendency becomes a serious problem during the teenage years when friends become much more important.

To compound the problems described above, low self-esteem in a youngster is usually detected and subsequently exploited by the peer group. Children instinctively recognize those that are weaker than they are and can use these youths to build up their own egos. They do this by teasing and picking on them, which again has the effect of confirming these kids' low opinions of themselves, making them feel even worse.

In order to feel better about themselves, youngsters with low self-esteem tend to develop compensation mechanisms. In psychology these are called defense mechanisms, and they serve to protect the ego, or self, from anxiety. In this case, the anxiety is the result of feeling inadequate in comparison to other children. It should be emphasized that these defense mechanisms develop sub-consciously and gradually. They are not the result of the child carefully analyzing the situation, then choosing a way to compensate. The particular mechanism chosen depends on other aspects of the child's personality and physical make-up, and develops as the child finds that acting in a certain way makes life easier. Most of these defense mechanisms work to relieve anxiety but tend to cause problems in other areas.

One of the more benign compensatory mechanisms children use to feel better about themselves is becoming the "class clown." Many children find that by getting their peers (and adults as well) to laugh, either at them or with them, they get the attention they need. While these children can be annoying in the classroom, they are not usually major discipline problems, and the reputation they develop among their peers helps them to feel that they are an integral part of the crowd, thus relieving their anxieties about themselves. Unfortunately, this humorous approach does not completely solve the problem and, inside, the youngster still has some self-doubts. These feelings are well known and have been immortalized in such popular songs as "Everybody Love a Clown" by Gary Lewis and the Playboys, and "Tears of a Clown" by Smokey Robinson. It is this mechanism that is often adopted by overweight children, and is the genesis of the "jolly fat man" syndrome.

A more serious form of compensation for low self-esteem occurs when the attention-seeking behavior is not humorous, but instead involves doing whatever is necessary to gain attention. In the classroom this can take the form of hair pulling, tripping other students, throwing spitballs or making fun of the teacher. At home it can be seen in the annoying of siblings or silly or "immature" behavior to get a parent's attention. In it's more severe forms, this behavior does not respond well to disciplinary procedures because they are also a form of attention. These children thrive on being reprimanded by the teacher or a parent because it momentarily makes them the center of attention. This is called "negative" attention, but to a child with low self-esteem, any attention can be important.

As discussed earlier in Chapter 5, some children compensate for their poor opinion of themselves by underachieving in school. While this too is negative attention, it serves the purpose by getting both parents and teachers to pay these youngsters some attention. Few things get parents more upset than when their children are not doing well in school. Underachievement is a very common manifestation of low self-esteem, but it is only partially effective in that, while it does garner attention from parents and teachers, it can eventually result in the youngsters actually believing that they really cannot achieve in school. No child likes to constantly receive low marks, but these children persist in their underachieving behavior to bolster their low opinion of themselves from the attention it garners. Obviously, if a solution is not found before the teen enters high school, then this compensation mechanism can have a lasting effect on the adolescent's future career and happiness, as the chance to attend college or university will be lost.

One of the most difficult compensation mechanisms for a parent or teacher to observe is displayed by those youngsters who adopt a reclusive approach to life. The basis of this mechanism is the idea that you can't be hurt if you just keep away from everyone. These kids are often seen alone in the school hallways before the start of classes or at noon hour, either reading a book or playing their portable video games. They also tend to cling to certain teachers for support, hanging around their classroom whenever they can. Parents may not notice a problem because at home, where they feel safe, the adolescents appear to be normal kids. The only outward sign might be of frequent depression or the lack of a constantly ringing phone in a house with a teenager. This is hard on parents because no amount of encouragement or cajoling can make much of an impact. Without a stronger self-concept, the youngsters just can not force themselves to interact with the people they fear.

While intoxicated, adolescents have the courage to socialize with their peers at a level that is not possible when sober.

Drugs and alcohol provide an excellent escape mechanism for many adolescents with low self-esteem. While intoxicated, adolescents have the courage to socialize with their peers at a level that is not possible when sober. While most teens will experiment with these substances, those who become heavy users are generally those with the lowest self-concepts. These are the teens that are drunk or stoned at every party, rather than just the odd time. Besides the obvious problems of addiction and physical harm that can result from substance abuse, an even bigger one for these teens is that the escape is only temporary. When not under the influence, these youngsters still do not like themselves. This can result in more and more frequent use, including during school hours, until academic performance may also begin to deteriorate.

The manifestation of low self-esteem does not always fall into clear-cut patterns such as those described above. More typical are combinations of these defenses, so that the disruptive, attention-seeking child can also be funny sometimes, and the reclusive types can also exhibit attention-seeking behaviors. However, if parents are aware of the major signs of low self-esteem, they can recognize the defensive patterns and act to enhance their youngsters' opinions of themselves.

Characteristics of Teens with Low Self-Esteem

- *Afraid to try new things*
- *Difficulty making friends*
- *Development of defense mechanisms such as class clown, attention seeking behaviors, underachievement or reclusiveness*
- *Abuse of drugs and alcohol*

Parental Actions

The basic principle that all parents need to understand is that when it comes to teenage self-esteem, they are the key. Genetics certainly plays a role, so that short boys, very tall girls and all overweight teens will struggle more than will those in the "normal" range. However, no matter what the genetic makeup, the parents have the greatest influence on the development of positive self-esteem, and they must work hard at this task if their adolescent is to successfully navigate the teen years. There are several affirmative actions that parents can take to ensure that self-esteem builds in their teenager.

. . . in this "hurry up" world of ours teens are becoming a neglected species as once they are old enough to look after themselves, their busy parents are becoming too involved in their own lives to spend time with them

The first such action is simply to spend as much time as possible with your teen. By planning activities as a family or just with the teenager alone, parents are showing that they care about their children. This in turn is interpreted by the teenagers to mean that they must be important to their parents, or they would not take the time and trouble to be with them. This makes the teens feel good about themselves because the people they love the most are showing that they feel good about them. This seems very simple, but in this "hurry up" world of ours teens are becoming a neglected species as once they are old enough to look after themselves, their busy parents are becoming too involved in their own lives to spend time with them. The message this gives is that their teens are not important. This is the opposite of what parents really want to communicate if they are committed to developing a positive self-esteem in their teen.

The next step is fundamental to both developing a strong self-esteem in teenagers and in building a positive relationship between parent and teen. Parents need to learn how to listen to their teens. This concept was covered in more detail in Chapter 3, but it is useful to review it briefly here. Parents who actively listen to their teen's ideas, dreams and problems convey a sense of worth to the teen. No matter how strange or immature their teen sounds, if parents take the time to really listen to them, the teen feels respected and important. The result is an enhanced level of self-esteem, with a minimal level of parental effort.

The previous two parental actions have not only been important to developing self-esteem, they are also fundamental steps in developing a strong relationship between parents and their teenagers. More specific to enhancing a teen's level of self-confidence is the ability to positively reinforce your child. Parents do this well with young children. They praise their first steps, their potty training and put even the crudest drawings on the refrigerator. Somehow, as the child reaches the teen years, parents seem to ease back on the praise, perhaps feeling that their adolescent will get a "swelled head." Nothing could be further from the truth. Teens badly need the praise and verbal support of their parents. The only difference is that they are now thinking beings and they can see through false praise and exaggeration. Here are a few guidelines in the positive reinforcement area:

- **Avoid teasing and sarcasm.** Teenagers are very sensitive and even when meant in a jocular fashion, such barbs are interpreted as criticism.
- **Praise all achievements.** Good marks (for them, not for you), a good recital or solid athletic performances all deserve unreserved praise.
- **If you must criticize try to be as positive as possible.** If they fail a test or perform badly at some task, try to pick out any positive aspects, then reassure them that they will do better

next time. They feel badly enough as it is, they don't need you to critique them as well.

- **If you need to reprimand them about their behavior, make it clear that you still love them.** Teens will make mistakes that need correcting. However it is the behavior that you do not approve of, not the teens themselves. Make this clear by giving the consequences, then telling them you love them.
- **Accept the fact that they may be very different from you.** Don't try to mold your teenager in your image. If they have different interests and talents than you did, support them the way they are rather than criticizing them for being different.

One of the essentials of developing positive self-esteem in anyone is by achieving successes. This is especially true for teenagers. Every time they succeed at something their opinion of themselves goes up a notch. The key for parents then is to find an activity that their teen can be successful at. This may be easy. If the youngster is athletic for example, both school and community provide many activities in which to participate. On the other hand it may take considerable attempts before the parents find the right fit for the teen. One of the best activities for enhancing self-esteem is any of the martial arts. Not only do they teach physical skills, but if well instructed, they also teach mental strength and self-control. Non-physical teens might benefit from chess clubs, computer clubs, youth drama programs or volunteer work at the local hospital or seniors home. It is up to the parents to keep trying until they find the right activity, as many teens do not have the confidence to try new things. Simply telling them to go over to the hospital and volunteer will usually not work. Instead take them there and introduce the teen to the volunteer coordinator. After that the activity will either interest them or it won't. Don't be discouraged if the first few don't take. Keep at it until you find the right match.

One parental action that is rarely connected to the development of a healthy self-esteem is an effective discipline system in the family. In fact, many parents believe that disciplining their teen will have a negative effect on them. Nothing could be further from the truth. Teens who are not disciplined tend to be more dependent and feel that they have less control over their world than teens that are.

Rules protect teens from having to make difficult decisions, thus giving them the feeling that their lives are in control. This feeling of control gives them the confidence to make decisions within the rules framework, and these "safe" decisions lead to a feeling of self-confidence. Rules and consequences for breaking them also show teens that their parents care about them and this too increases their confidence in themselves. A more thorough discussion of this subject is found in Chapter 4.

Finally, self-esteem in teenagers can be greatly enhanced by gradually giving them more and more independence. While they rarely need as much as they often want, teens do need to feel that their parents trust them to make their own decisions and their own mistakes. This means that the rules should be loosened a little each year so that the teen gains more and more independence and therefore more decision-making power. This process should be gradual but steady. If the teen fails badly in handling independence, it can be always be reined back in. It is amazing how well teens will handle themselves if they see that their parents trust them to do the right things.

Steps to Building Positive Self-Esteem

- *Spend time with them*
- *Listen to them*
- *Use as much positive reinforcement as possible*
- *Find activities they can succeed at*
- *Maintain an effective system of discipline*
- *Foster independence*

Depression

It will come as no surprise to parents of teenagers that adolescence is an emotional roller coaster. The hormones that trigger puberty bring with them many sudden changes in the emotional, physical and mental areas. Of these, the changes in the emotional area baffle parents the most. The once happy-go-lucky pre-teenager can go from a towering rage at being told "no" to a sullen, moping drudge in minutes. In between, are periods of relative normalcy when the teen is almost understandable. Being moody or "down" is a well-known aspect of this roller coaster that most teens experience at one time or another. Unfortunately, for some teens, these "down" times occur too frequently and too intensely to be considered a normal part of their development. These are adolescents that are subject to a more serious form of depression than can be explained by the hormones of puberty alone. It is estimated that about 10% of teenagers suffer from either clinical depression or a milder form called dysthymia that interferes with their functioning as normal teenagers and which can lead to suicide if not discovered and treated in time. The challenge for parents is to determine whether the moodiness of their teen is a normal part of adolescence or whether the teen is suffering from a more serious form of depression and needs to be treated for this problem.

The Problems

One problem related to depression is that the world is much more complex today than it was even a generation ago. Teens that may have survived their depressions through family support and the process of maturity are now faced with complex issues that can tend to increase the severity of their depressions. These issues include non-traditional families, increased exposure to a wider variety of drugs, gang violence and such sexual pressures as potential pregnancy and a wider and more deadly variety of sexually transmitted diseases. Parents are also busier and more involved with their own lives than ever before and often tend to miss the signs of serious depression. This tends to cause the depression to deepen, which can then result in experiences that range from a miserable teen existence to eventual suicide.

Another problem for parents is that the signs of depression are often subtle and may be masked by other behaviors such as anxiety, eating disorders, hyperactivity and substance abuse. The main symptoms of depression are as follows:

- A low tolerance for rewards or compliments
- A feeling of being "down in the dumps" or really sad for no obvious reason
- A lack of energy resulting in not feeling like doing anything
- A lack of desire to be with friends or family members

- An inability to enjoy the things that used to bring pleasure, such as hobbies or sports
- Feelings of irritability, anger, or anxiety, with no particular cause
- An inability to concentrate for any length of time
- A noticeable weight gain or loss or either too much or too little interest in eating
- A significant change in sleep habits, such as trouble falling asleep or getting up in the morning
- Feelings of guilt or worthlessness
- Complaints of sundry aches and pains, even though no physical cause can be found
- A sudden drop in grades or skipping of classes

Teens may have several of these symptoms without the parents needing to be concerned about the depression being clinical, as long as a good reason can be found for these feelings. These reasons can include:

- A recent break-up with a boy or girl friend
- A poor mark on a major test
- Failure to be selected to a sports team
- Rejection by a close friend (of the same sex)
- A rumor being spread around the school about them

However, if five or more of the above symptoms last for at least two weeks, especially with no obvious cause, then this is clinical depression and immediate help should be sought. Clinical depression tends to come and go, so that parents can be fooled by periods of relative normal moods in their teenager. Those suffering from clinical depression will go through many bouts of despair, usually of about the same intensity but of varying duration.

There is also a lesser form of depression, called dysthymia, which is not as serious but is still a problem for some teens. In this form fewer of the symptoms are present at any one time, but the depression lasts for at least a year. Depression of this duration has a serious effect on the social and academic life of the sufferer, but the risk of suicide is generally much less than it would be with a teen that suffers from clinical depression.

Parental Actions

The first thing parents need to do if they suspect that their teen may be depressed is to take the problem seriously. Depression has a long history of being seen as shameful or a weakness so that families have a tendency to deny its existence rather than face the fact that it might exist in their family. Parents need to do some reading on the subject in order to reduce these prejudices. There is a wealth of information on the Internet, and many books on the subject, such as "Understanding Teenage Depression" by Empfield and Bakalar.

If parents do this research they will find that many important discoveries concerning the origins of clinical depression have been made in recent years. Researchers have shown that the cause appears to be a lack of certain chemicals in the brain, called neurotransmitters, and specifically one called serotonin. This seems to be an inherited disorder caused by defective genes. The really exciting part of these discoveries is that a new family of drugs has been synthesized that have been shown to be highly effective in combating clinical depression. These drugs are called Selective Serotonin Re-uptake Inhibitors, and they act by increasing the amount of serotonin available in the brain by preventing it from being reabsorbed after it has been released. These drugs are marketed under such brand names as Prozac, Paxil, Zoloft and Luvox. They usually take from 2 to 3 weeks to become effective and they generally have very few side effects. Parents whose teens are diagnosed with clinical depression should not be afraid to have their children take these drugs as a result of a bias against taking drugs in general. They act to correct a biological deficiency and can change a teen's life in a very short time.

Parents need to realize that it may take some probing and active questioning to determine how serious the problem is as a depressed teen does not feel like talking and will try to brush off the parents with short, negative answers.

Drugs alone may not completely solve the problem, so psychotherapy may also be required. A particularly effective form is called cognitive therapy, and it works by teaching teens to look for connections between thoughts and actions and to challenge their negative thoughts by looking for evidence to back them up. If none is found, then the thought must be erroneous. In this way the teens learn to be more positive about themselves.

Above all the most important parental action is to keep the lines of communication open. If parents are able to openly discuss their teens' depression, they will be able to determine much sooner whether there is a cause in the local environment, such as being "dumped," or whether the problem is more serious and help needs to be sought. Parents need to realize that it may take some probing and active questioning to determine how serious the problem is as a depressed teen does not feel like talking and will try to brush off the parents with short, negative answers. However, if parents persist they can not only begin to understand the depth of the problem, but they can convey to their teenager that they have their parents support and understanding. This by itself can help to alleviate the symptoms of depression as it shows them that their parents care about their welfare and that they are not alone in their battle against depression.

Peer Pressure

When parents hear the words "peer pressure" they cringe. Most envision groups of teens hovering over their youngster taunting him to go along with their negative behavior. If their teen comes home drunk, many parents place the blame on the peer group for pressuring their adolescent into this situation. There is little question that peer pressure can be a negative influence on teens. However, it does not usually work in the way that parents think it does, and peer pressure can even be a positive influence on teenagers. It is important to understand how and why peer pressure works, so that parents can teach their youngsters how to successfully resist its negative effects.

What is it?

"Teens who act a certain way because they believe their friends expect that from them are feeling peer pressure, whether or not the expectation is linked to a threat of being left out."
— *Leslie S. Kaplan, "Coping with Peer Pressure"*

It has been said many times in this book that the teenage years are the most insecure of a person's life. To bolster their low levels of confidence in themselves, teens turn to their friends for support. This is also a time of questioning parental standards so teens try to be as different from their parents as possible. The result is a tremendous reliance on peers and teen idols to set their standards of behavior, fashion and music. The peer group that has the most influence on any teen is their immediate circle of friends. A study by the national Institutes of Health in the U.S. found that the single most important factor in determining teen standards is the behavior of their five closest friends. It is important to the teenagers to "fit in" with this group, so they mimic each other's behavior. The main form of peer pressure then is simply to want to be like their friends. This is much subtler than most parents think.

The influence of the peers can be in either direction, good or bad. If several of a teenager's friends are in their church youth group, that teen will probably want to join as well. The same goes for 4H clubs, athletic teams and marching bands. On the other hand, if a teenager chooses to be friends with a group of drinkers and smokers who do not participate in any positive activities, then that teen will mimic this behavior.

The more well known form of peer pressure also exists, but to a lesser degree. This is the taunting form where teens say things like "Don't be a wimp, have a drink" or "Don't be such a goody-goody." This does not usually happen from within a teenager's own circle of friends, but can occur when different groups get together, such as at large parties. A teenager's chances of succumbing to this form of peer pressure often depend on how much the taunting person or group is admired. If it is a member of a "popular" group, then the chances of going along with the behavior are considerably higher.

Giving in to peer pressure is also related to age. The most susceptible group is youngsters in the 11–13 age range. This does not mean that older teens will not give in, because peer pressure susceptibility is a function of self-esteem as well. Those with lower opinions of themselves are much more likely to succumb to peer pressure than are teens with a positive self-concept.

The Problems

> *Parents need to remember that teens actually do choose their friends. The peer group does not suck them in like a human vacuum cleaner.*

Peer pressure will rarely be a problem if a teenager chooses a group of friends who tend to engage in positive behaviors. It is every parent's dream to see their teen a member of a clean-cut group of adolescents who have good manners, attend church and have high marks in school. Unfortunately this is not always the case. Teens who choose less savory friends are definitely more apt to be subject to pressures to engage in risky behaviors. Parents need to remember that teens actually do choose their friends. The peer group does not suck them in like a human vacuum cleaner. If the teen does not have common interests and tastes as their friends, the group will reject that person very quickly. Choice of friends is the key element in which behaviors a teenager mimics as a result of peer pressure. If the teen has the "wrong" friends, then parents need to look at what that group has in common with their adolescent. Blaming the friends or trying to forcefully separate your teen from the group will not be effective, and may result in actually strengthening the bond between the members of the group.

Besides the friends they choose, researchers have linked several factors to susceptibility to negative peer pressures. One such factor is lack of discipline in the home. Teens who come from permissive homes have been shown to be much more prone to harmful activities such as drinking and smoking. This situation results from the fact that teens who come from homes with few rules feel insecure and unable to make their own decisions. They then turn to their peer group for guidance. Insecure teens, or those with low self-esteem, seem to find each other very quickly, and tend to follow the lead of the more assertive members of the group. If this lead is towards drinking, smoking or using drugs, then the less assertive members of the group will follow along.

Another factor that research has shown to make teens more vulnerable to peer pressure is a lack of affection in the home. If adolescents don't receive enough affection and approval from their parents, they tend to look for it from their friends. They then fear offending these friends in case their source of approval is withdrawn, so they follow along with whatever behaviors the friends indulge in. In extreme cases, such teenagers go to the extreme of joining gangs because these groups not only provide approval (in the form of loyalty) but safety as well. Teens who do not feel safe and secure at home find it instead in the tight bonds of gang membership.

> *Teens need to know what their parents believe in order to have guidelines to follow when out with their friends.*

Parental Actions

Parents can have a tremendous effect on their teenagers' resistance to peer pressure. One vital component of developing peer-resistant teenagers is to thoroughly teach the family values (see the section on this subject in Chapter 7). Studies have clearly indicated that teens who reported that their parents would be upset if they were caught drinking or smoking were much less likely to actually indulge in these behaviors. Teens need to know what their parents believe in order to have guidelines to follow when out with their friends. Knowing that their parents would disapprove helps to take away the need to make a decision on whether or not to indulge in risky behaviors. They can then say "no" more easily when a choice is presented.

A positive self-esteem is another weapon in the arsenal against peer pressure. Building this self-esteem is thoroughly described in the preceding section. The value of a positive self-concept to a teen lies in not needing to rely on the approval of others to know how to behave. Coercion, whether overt or subtle, can not sway teenagers who have confidence in their own ability to make decisions.

Another way that parents can help their teenagers resist peer pressure is to frequently and clearly show your affection for them. This helps to build a positive self-esteem, which in turn helps to oppose the pressures exerted by their peers. The same goes for a comprehensive system of discipline. This not only shows teens that they are loved, it also makes them feel secure. Knowing their boundaries allows them to make decisions within that framework that could not be made under a more permissive system where teens are unsure what is expected of them.

Finally, parents can help their teens to stand up to peer pressure by discussing with their teens how this pressure works at an early stage.

The best time to start is probably when the youngster starts attending mixed parties. These discussions should not only include the two kinds of peer pressure, the subtle imitation of close friends and the overt taunting of other peers, but also should include how to say "no." Parents need to teach their teens that the most effective method of turning down the advances of a close friend is to do it so that the pressuring teen is not being put down. If the pressuring teen feels that he or she is being belittled, then the tendency is to either get angry with the refusing teen or to try harder to get that teen to accept. A simple "No thanks," for example, is much more effective than "No way. Drinking is stupid." One of the most successful ways to do this is to use humor. When a cigarette, drugs or a drink is offered, lines like "Sorry, it's against my doctor's orders" or "I can't, I'm allergic" are very effective. The offering teen is not offended and the pressures will more than likely disappear.

Parents should be prepared for their teen to argue that peer pressure does not exist. That's because they really don't notice it on a conscious level because most of the pressure that they are subject to is of the subtle kind. They honestly believe that they like the clothing they do because that is their taste. The same goes for their music and any fads that are popular at the time. Patience is necessary in these discussions. It might help to get out your old yearbooks and show your teenagers the styles that were popular in your day. They will probably seem quite ridiculous to the teens but you can reassure them that you thought you were pretty cool. Don't be discouraged if you don't seem to be getting anywhere. The teens absorb far more of your words than you think.

While peer pressure is definitely a force to be reckoned with, parents can minimize its effects by taken an active role in combating it.

How Parents Can Combat Peer Pressure

- *Clearly state your values.*
- *Help build a positive self-esteem.*
- *Make your affection for your teen obvious.*
- *Actively teach your teen how to deal with peer pressure.*

Piercing and Tattoos

Every generation of teenagers has its share of fads and styles. These go along with teenagers' need to develop an identity separate from that of their parents. Teens show they are different by dressing differently, styling their hair differently, developing their own language and often by experimenting with risky behaviors. These are all signs of breaking away from the shadow of their parents by showing them that they are different.

One of the essentials of these fads and styles is that they must be different enough to bring comment from the older generation. Often this commentary is in the form of outrage and, while this extreme parental reaction is not mandatory, it is not discouraged either. There has to be enough difference to distinguish the teens as separate people, with different likes and dislikes from their parents. Looking back over the past 50 years, most of these fads now seem harmless and even laughable. Nevertheless they raised parental hackles at the time.

The predominant fads at the present time are piercing various parts of the body with stud or hoop earrings and tattoos of various sizes on a wide variety of body parts. These fads are particularly frightening for parents in that they involve the body. Most previous fads, like Hula-Hoops, Pet Rocks and Rubik's Cubes have all been external to the body. Even the mop-top hairstyles of the Beatles, although shocking at the time, were not as scary for parents as hair can always be cut.

It is always difficult to explain why any one thing becomes popular with teenagers and young adults, but the interest in piercing and tattoos may stem from the relatively banal clothing and hairstyles that are presently in vogue. The really outrageous styles belong to previous generations and little is new to parents in these areas. The result may be that the teens are turning to the body to get a reaction and show their independence.

The Problems

Aside from the negative associations that piercing and tattoos have with sailors and bikers, there are also some practical concerns. For example piercing, and the subsequent insertion of a foreign object into the body, can result in some very painful and even potentially dangerous infections. If they are to be done, they must be done by a qualified person and not be a friend with an ice cube and a needle. Piercing the tongue can also result in impaired speech, which can be an impediment, at a part-time job. Otherwise, while a pierced eyebrow, nipple or belly button may look strange to an adult, there is little harm in them.

Similar concerns about infection can also be applied to tattoos. These too need to be done by an expert. An added concern is the difficulty they present if the teens want to remove them at a later date. While this is possible, it is still difficult and expensive, so that size and location should be considerations to avoid embarrassment in the future.

While a small tattoo on the ankle or a pierced belly button should not be of major concern to a parent, alarm bells should go off if the teen insists on a number of large tattoos or piercing in multiple parts of the body. Teens with strong self-concepts do not need to decorate their bodies so ostentatiously. Only those with low self-esteem go to such great lengths. If a teen shows interest in multiple piercing (except for the ear in girls) or several tattoos, parents can assume the teen has a self-concept problem and should seek help to rebuild it.

Parental Actions

The key for parents is to remember the purpose of these body decorations. They are meant to bring attention to the teens as being distinct from their parents. They are not instruments of the devil. If kept within reason they are of no harm to anyone and parents should not be concerned about their teens wanting to pierce or tattoo. The secret lies in compromise.

When a teen wants to pierce a body part or get a tattoo, the parents should discuss number, size and placement. Explain that you understand why the teen wants to do this but that you have some concerns. The teens will usually be delighted that you have not turned them down flat and generally enter willingly into the discussion. If the subject is a piercing, ask where it is proposed to be and who will do it. If the location is acceptable, then discuss the hygiene concerns. If the planned location is not acceptable (the tongue or genital areas are usually the only locations that need to be forbidden) suggest an alternative. This is also the time to insist that it be done by a professional, with the teen raising the money for this. Remember to stay calm as emotions can very quickly enter these discussions.

If a tattoo is desired size as well as location should both be of concern. Once again if the proposed location is too visible, suggest an alternative such as the ankle or shoulder blade. Discuss the fact that they may want it removed at some later date so that it should be relatively small. Also discuss the design. If the teen is not sure, have him or her visit a tattooist and check out the possibilities. Have the teen check out the hygiene considerations (they can be found on the Internet) and make sure that the tattoo parlor of choice follows the health guidelines. You might want to check this out yourself, as an error in this area can result in a very serious illness. Insist (gently) that you approve the design before you OK it, and that the teen pays for the tattoo. Be sure to listen carefully to the teen's arguments and reasoning, but stay firm on your major principles. A calm compromise is always preferable to a bitter shouting match.

Hair, Clothing and Music

While these issues were discussed in Chapter 2, it might be useful to review them here, as the motivation for teenagers' strange habits in these areas is similar to that of the desire for piercing and tattoos. Hair styles, clothing tastes and musical preferences are all part of the teenager's desire to create an identity separate from that of their parents. Each teen is different in the need to create this identity, so that some need to be different in all three of these areas, while others may be content with normal hairstyles and clothing but their own type of music. Levels of self-esteem tend to dictate how different the teens need to be. Generally, the lower the self-esteem, the more manifestations of difference are required.

Usually parents do not need to worry about these strange teenage habits. Remember the greasy ducktail haircuts of the 50's, the Beatle cuts and hippie clothing of the 60's and the polyester and bell-bottoms of the 70's. Get out your old yearbooks and see how strange you looked in your teen years. However, if your teen has magenta hair, multiple piercings and all-black clothing, you should suspect a low self-esteem and try to find the cause. A counselor may be necessary in this case.

While normally parents do not have to worry about these fads, here are a few guidelines that you should want them to follow:

- *Clothing should be clean, in good repair and decent (by your standards or the schools)*
- *Music with bad language or violent themes should not be allowed in your house*
- *Hair should be clean and styled in some fashion (as opposed to unkempt)*
- *Music volumes should not be so high as to disturb the rest of the household (Diskmans are a great answer to this problem)*
- *If the clothing they want is too expensive or too bizarre by your standards, have the teen pay all or part of the cost*

Remember: If it's not life threatening, don't worry about it.

Eating Disorders

Unlike the majority of topics in this section, eating disorders do not affect a large percentage of the teenage population, and those they do affect are about 95% female. In fact, recent studies show that about 1% of females in the 12 to 18 age range are anorexic while other studies show that between 4.5% and 18% of females of college age have a history of bulimia. Overall it is estimated that about 10% of teenage and early adult females suffer from an eating disorder. While these are not huge figures, they do represent a significant portion of the teenage population and the results of these disorders can be extremely serious. Of even more concern is the fact that the incidence of these illnesses is on the rise, for reasons that are not yet understood. Parents need to understand the seriousness of these problems and know what symptoms to look for, as it is vital that eating disorders are diagnosed and treated as early as possible.

The Facts

As most people are now aware, there are two major types of eating disorders, anorexia nervosa and bulimia nervosa. While these disorders have quite different symptom patterns, anorectics occasionally display some of the bulimic symptoms. The definitions of these disorders, according to the American Psychiatric Association, are as follows:

Bulimia Nervosa

- *Recurrent episodes of binge eating (average of two binge eating episodes a week for at least three months)*
- *A feeling of lack of control over eating during the binges*
- *Regular use of one or more of the following to prevent weight gain: self-induced vomiting, laxatives or diuretics, strict fasting or dieting or vigorous exercise*
- *Persistent over-concern with body shape and weight*

A typical example of a bulimic was recently seen for consultation by the author. She was a young lady in her early 20's who stood 5'9" tall and weighed 85 pounds. She stated that she still felt that she was too fat. At one sitting she would eat as much as two large boxes of corn flakes before she would go to the bathroom and stick her finger down her throat to induce vomiting. She came for only one visit at the insistence of her husband but refused to return as she felt that she did not need any help.

Anorexia Nervosa

- *Refusal to maintain weight that is over the lowest weight considered normal for age and height*
- *Intense fear of gaining weight or becoming fat, even though underweight*
- *Distorted body image*
- *In women, three consecutive missed menstrual periods without pregnancy*

Causes

As yet there are known causes for these disorders. Studies have shown that teens with these symptoms also have more depression, anxiety disorders and substance abuse that do normal teenagers. Researchers are not yet clear whether the eating disorders are symptoms of such problems or whether these problems develop because of the loneliness of these sufferers, the pressures from well meaning friends and relatives, or the body changes that these disorders cause. Anorexia has also been shown to be associated with perfectionists and high achievers as well as those with a need to gain control over their lives.

The role played by our society's emphasis on being thin in developing eating disorders is also not yet understood. Being teased about weight, participating in sports that require thinness, such as gymnastics, and traumas such as rape or the death of a loved one can precipitate the beginning of an eating disorder. This certainly makes sense. What does not is why the anorexic cannot stop once an ideal weight is reached. It may be that some changes take place in the brain chemistry that makes it almost impossible to start eating normally after dieting or bingeing/purging has gone on for too long.

Early Signs

The early signs of an eating disorder are often subtle, but if parents recognize them and seek treatment near the beginning, the chances of success are reasonably good. With anorectics, parents might notice a sudden interest in exercise, which becomes taken to an excessive level. They may be preoccupied with calories to the point of counting them for such trivial items as the glue on a stamp. They also may move the food around the plate for long periods of time without eating it or cut it into very tiny pieces to prolong eating and make it seem like they are eating more than they actually are. Anorectics may try to avoid eating with the family so that it is not noticed how little they are eating, and they may eat vicariously by watching cooking shows or cooking for the family. Because of their reduced body fat they may feel cold all the time.

Bulimia is even harder to detect in its early levels. One key sign is that bulimics often leave the table immediately after every meal to go to the bathroom. They may run the water or flush the toilet to cover the noises of their vomiting. Large amounts of food may disappear from the family larder, with no one admitting to eating it. Bulimics may also complain of a constant sore throat or hoarseness of voice caused by acids of the stomach as they are regurgitated. As they often use laxatives or diuretics, they may leave the evidence of these drugs in the bathrooms.

The Problems

The biggest problem for parents is failing to perceive the early symptoms of eating disorders, when the condition is more easily treated, so that it moves to a level where damage is being done to the body. Once eating disorders are well entrenched, they are so difficult to treat that parents often must forcibly take their teens to an in-patient treatment center. The damage to the body of these disorders can be significant, and can even result in death.

The extreme purging or vomiting done by bulimics soon begins to upset the body's balance of sodium, potassium and other vital chemicals. This can cause fatigue, seizures, irregular heartbeat and thinner bones. Damage can be done to the stomach and esophagus by the repeated vomiting, the gums can recede and the tooth enamel can be eroded to the point where the teeth must be pulled. Skin rashes, broken blood vessels in the face and irregular menstrual cycles can also occur.

With anorectics, the body responds to the slow starvation by slowing or stopping certain bodily processes. Blood pressure falls, breathing rate slows, menstruation ceases and the activity of the thyroid gland, which regulates growth, diminishes. Many other physical changes also occur. The skin becomes dry, hair and nails become brittle, and constipation and joint swelling may occur. A soft hair forms on the skin for warmth because the reduced fat causes the body temperature to fall. The body chemicals may get so out of balance that death can occur.

Karen Carpenter, the famous singer of such 70's hits as "Close to You," was an anorectic who also purged. She used syrup of ipecac to induce vomiting but died at the age of 33 because the drug built up in her system to the point that it irreversibly damaged her heart.

Parental Actions

If any of the early signs of an eating disorder are observed, parents should seek immediate help from an expert in this area. Many cities have eating disorder clinics attached to children's hospitals which

302

family doctors can refer to. If not, make sure that the psychologist or psychiatrist you choose specializes in this area because the wrong approach may be worse than doing nothing at all. In Canada the National Eating Disorder Information Centre keeps a registry of specialists in this area. Similar services are provided in the U.S. by the American Anorexia/Bulimia Association in New York City or the National Association of Anorexia Nervosa and Associated Disorders in Highland Park, Illinois.

Parents should avoid trying to force or tempt their teens into eating. This could cause more resistance to form and end up prolonging the disorder. The best parental approach is to maintain good communication with the afflicted teen by spending time with her and showing a genuine interest in her feelings and thoughts. If resistance to help is met take a gentle, persistent approach to getting counseling help. If the teen won't go to a doctor, suggest someone she trusts like a school counselor, church minister or youth group advisor or even a coach or favorite teacher. This approach is difficult for parents who know the dangers and want to act as quickly as possible. However, these disorders are incredibly powerful influences on the teen and are very difficult to attack directly, especially if they have been present for some time. Patience and persistence are needed, and parents should never give up the fight. The stakes are just too high.

> *The National Institute of Mental Health in the U.S. estimates that one in ten anorexia cases ends in death from starvation, suicide or medical complications like heart attacks or kidney failure.*

Bullying and Teasing

Bullying and teasing have always been present as children grow up. Kids are well known for being cruel to each other by picking out weaknesses or prominent physical features and taunting each other about them. Beyond this there has always been an element of the childhood population that goes much further than these normal levels of hazing. These are the bullies, children who repeatedly and systematically harass and attack others. These attacks may include such behaviors as:

- *Physical violence and attacks*
- *Verbal taunts or name-calling, often based on physical features, racial or ethnic group or gender*
- *Threats and intimidation*
- *Extortion or stealing of money and other possessions*
- *Exclusion from the peer group*

While these elements have always been present in society, especially in the school environment, attention has been increasingly drawn to them in recent years due to several prominent incidences of school violence that appear to have a bullying connection. Many of the teens involved in these incidents had been driven to the breaking point by bullying peers. This increased attention has had the effect of causing schools to re-examine their treatment of those who bully and harass others. It has also caused parents to ask what they should be doing to help their teens to survive the bullies of their neighborhood, as the traditional approaches of telling their children to "just walk away" or to "ignore them" do not seem to be effective for some adolescents. School officials and parents alike are now realizing that bullying is a complex issue that requires the combined approach of giving consequences to the bullies and bolstering the self-esteem of the victims.

> *Evidence as to the long history of bullying is given in Thomas Hughes' famous book "Tom Brown's School Days" written in 1857. The behavior of the bully Flashman varies little from that of the bullies of today.*

The Facts

It should come as no surprise to parents that the essence of bullying is a power imbalance. Children who are stronger, more aggressive, bolder and more confident than average often bully those who are weaker, more timid and who tend not to retaliate or act in an assertive manner. This power imbalance can also be created by children who are older or by those from a dominant culture as opposed to new immigrants or cultural minorities. Research has found that it is not generally true that bullies are insecure cowards who hide behind their bravado. Instead many tend to have self-esteem that is at least at the average level. They also tend to come from homes where they are poorly supervised, where there is a lack of attention and warmth and that model aggressive strategies to conflict resolution. These aggressive strategies may include use of physical and verbal aggression towards the child by the parents, or use of physical or verbal aggression by parents toward each other. According to the research, these family factors seem to act most effectively in producing bullies on young children who are active and impulsive in temperament. Those who become bullies tend to be defiant and oppositional towards adults, anti-social and inclined to break school rules.

The victims of bullies, on the other hand, tend to be quiet and shy in temperament and are usually physically weaker (especially with boys) and less skilled athletically than the bullies. These victims usually lack the ability to respond assertively to (or stand up to) bullying behavior, and tend to be unable to make friends easily. Since they do not retaliate to verbal or physical aggression, they are seen as easy targets for the local bully.

Most victims do not do anything to incite their adversaries. They are picked on because of their timid demeanor and possibly because of some physical characteristic such as being overweight or being of a different ethnic group. However, there are some victims who draw bullying attention to themselves through their irritating and inappropriate social behavior. They provoke anger in their peers by such behaviors as tripping them in the aisles, hiding their school materials or poking them in the back with their pencils. These irritating victims also do not make friends easily and may themselves pick on younger or smaller children. Their behavior is very hard to change because it is the only way they know how to draw attention from their peers — and it certainly succeeds in gaining attention, even if it is the negative kind. It is only when the attention becomes overwhelming, in the form of angry responses or perhaps physical aggression, that this type of victim seeks adult help. These children are the perfect targets of bullies because other children support behavior that will free them from this "pest."

Between the two classes of bully and victim is the bulk of the teenage population. Many of these children do not bully themselves, but they will follow a bully's lead in the early teenage years because the aggressive and outgoing teens are seen as the "popular" ones. This bystander group does not initiate the bullying but joins in when the harassment starts, giving the victims the impression that the whole school is against them. In actual fact, most of these bystanders do not enjoy the bullying process, they are just afraid to go against the "popular" teen.

A Bullying Summary

- *About 16% of the students in schools are involved in bullying with 9% being victims and 7% being bullies*
- *A power differential exists between the bully and the victim*
- *Bullies tend to be confident, aggressive, and lack empathy for the victim*
- *Bullies come from homes where there is poor supervision, lack of warmth, and modeling of and tolerance for aggressive behavior*
- *Victims tend to be quiet, passive children with few friends*
- *Victims do not respond effectively to aggressive actions*
- *Bullying is often done so that adults are not aware of it*
- *Victims tend to be ashamed and often don't tell adults*

Source: Suderman, M., Jaffe, P., Schiek, E. et al. (1996) A School-Based Anti-violence Program. London, ON: London Family Court Clinic.

The Problems

The major problem for parents is the effect that bullying has on their teens. Those who are bullied frequently tend to be very unhappy much of the time and generally suffer from fear, anxiety and low self-esteem. These teens often try to avoid school or, if in school, to avoid any social contact in order to escape the bullying. It should be noted that many of these "victims" were often loners in the first place and already had relatively low self-esteem, but bullying makes it worse. It has even been known to drive teens to suicide. While most teens survive the harassment with few emotional scars, some victims do experience long-term psychological harm that interferes with their social and academic development. Even into their twenties, these victims tend to suffer from more depression and continue to have lower self-esteem than their non-bullied counterparts. This combination can definitely interfere with career aspirations as a lack of confidence makes it less likely that the bullied person would be able to attempt new challenges and to cope with change.

A Note of Caution

It has been stated that bullying often causes teens to avoid school. Parents should use caution when presented with this reason for not wanting to attend school. Since bullying has gained prominence as a school issue, many teens are seizing on this as an excuse not to attend, when the real reason may be something else entirely. Other causes can be upset over a divorce or its aftermath, or finding the schoolwork extremely difficult. Parents should check their facts with the teachers and other students before accepting this reason for avoiding school.

Bullying also presents problems for the bullies themselves. There is a strong correlation between bullying other students during the school years and experiencing legal or criminal troubles as adults. One major study showed that 60% of those described as bullies in Grades 6 to 9 had at least one criminal conviction by age 24. Those exhibiting serious bullying tendencies seem to maintain these behaviors into the adult years, and this behavior affects their ability to develop and maintain positive relationships with other adults.

Signs That Your Child is Being Bullied

- *Fear of going to school*
- *Happy on the weekend but not during the week*
- *Lack of friends*
- *Missing belongings, torn clothing or frequent bruising*
- *Stomach aches, sleep difficulties or frequent headaches*
- *A change in behavior such as becoming withdrawn, excessively clingy, depressed or fearful*

Parental Actions

Few things are as frustrating and heartbreaking to a parent than to see their child being bullied. One of the reasons for this is that it is extremely difficult for an individual parent to stop. Many parents tell their children to "just ignore it" or "just walk away." This generally does not work as it enhances the image the bully has of the child as weaker and more fearful. Fathers often tell their children to hit back or retaliate. This too does not work as usually the victim is too timid to do this. It also conveys the message that violence should be answered with violence, which is a not a principle that parents want to teach. There are several steps that worried parents can take if they find that their child is being continually bullied. They are as follows:

- The school is the key, as this is where most of the bullying is taking place. Contact the administration immediately, let them know who the bully is, and monitor the steps they take to control this behavior.
- If there is no immediate action from the school, contact other parents of victims and meet with the administration together. In the rare instance that nothing happens again, contact the school superintendent.
- Try to get an anti-bullying program started in the school. This should include school-bullying policies, anti-bullying segments in the curriculum, a monitored schoolyard and halls and assertiveness training.
- Work on rebuilding your child's self-esteem. Find activities that the teen can be successful at and which are interesting and enjoyable for the youngster. (See the section on "Self-Esteem" earlier in this chapter)
- Be supportive and understanding. Encourage your teen to discuss how they are feeling and really listen carefully to these feelings.
- If in your research you discover that your teen is of the "irritating" victim type, get counseling help to point out these behaviors and help to correct them.

If it happens that you discover that it is your teen who is doing the bullying, there are also a number of steps that can be taken. These include:

- Make it clear that this behavior is not acceptable. Discuss how the victims feel, as the bullies are often unaware of how frightening they are to them.
- Give consequences for any bullying actions that you become aware of, but do not use physical ones.
- Do not model aggressive behavior either toward members of the family or to others.
- Increase your supervision of your child by setting rules and enforcing them, and by spending more time together.
- Work closely with the school to change the aggressive behavior. You need to know what is happening there so contact the teachers frequently to see if the behavior is improving.
- Discourage the viewing of violent TV shows, movies or the playing of video games. While these do not affect all teens, they may encourage a bully's aggressive behavior.

Whether your teen is a victim or a bully, do not expect instant behavioral changes as soon as you implement these corrective actions. Both personality types are very resistant to change because so many needs are being met by the behavior, so it's going to take a while. Be patient and supportive and do not hesitate to involve a counselor. If you do, expect to be part of the counseling process as family support is vital to the process of change.

Overweight Teens

Anything that acts to negatively affect the self-esteem of teenagers makes life even harder for them. Factors that can do this include being too short, too tall, having acne or having to wear the wrong clothes. However, these factors are minor compared to the effect that being overweight has on an adolescent's self-concept. Despite the fact that the effects of being overweight on teens are well known, the problem is growing rapidly. Experts blame the rise in obesity (defined by most authorities as being at least 20% over the recommended weight for the teen's height) on unhealthy food choices and increasingly sedentary lifestyles. Parents of an overweight teenager need to take positive action to help their child maintain a reasonable weight or the teen years will be devastating for the youngster.

The Problems

Most parents are well aware of the problems that obesity causes for teens so they will be listed here rather than discussed in detail. They include:

- Being teased by peers. This may not be as serious as bullying since most of the remarks are meant in fun. Nevertheless they hurt the teenager badly and emphasize his or her difference from peers.
- They are rarely popular with the opposite sex. When their friends begin dating they are often left out because being overweight is not considered to be attractive.
- Well meaning adults, including parents, often make pointed remarks about the teen's weight, without doing anything constructive for the teen, e.g., "You'd be so attractive if you only lost a few pounds."
- Popular clothing styles rarely fit or, if they do, only serve to emphasize the teen's weight. This leads them to wear baggy, shapeless clothing to try to disguise their shape, which again tends to set them apart from their friends.
- With the possible exception of football, team sports are usually out of the question.
- There are several future health problems that may result including heart disease, sleep apnea and asthma.

In recent years there has actually been a rise in teenage obesity. There are two major contributors to this rise. The first is modern eating habits. Over the past two decades there has been a decrease in the number of parents who cook meals for their teenagers. Instead many families eat on the run, with the members preparing dinner for themselves. Given the choice, teens tend to gravitate to high fat and high sugar foods and soda pop rather than having a balanced meal with lots of fruit and vegetables. A recent study by the American Journal of Health Promotion found that students decreased their consumption of breakfast, fruits, vegetables and milk as they moved from elementary to junior high school. Between the third and eighth grades fruit consumption fell by 41% and vegetable consumption decreased by 25%. In this time soft drink consumption tripled. With more pocket money than ever to spend, teens often discard their home-made lunches in favor of pop and chips at the local convenience store. As a result, in the past decade one study indicates that the prevalence of obesity in teenage girls has risen from 14% to 24%, and in boys from 18% to 26%. Many studies place these figures even higher.

Families also tend to eat at fast food outlets much more frequently than ever before. The fat content of most of these foods goes off the scale, yet the lure of cheap, tasty, almost instant meals is more than most families can resist. The result is that a recent study by American Demographics indicates that American families eat at fast food restaurants an average of 6 times a month.

Besides eating habits, the other key contributor to teenage obesity is the sedentary lifestyles that today's teens prefer. With a huge variety of television channels available and a wide assortment of highly entertaining and realistic video games on the market, teens tend to spend many of their leisure hours pursuing these sedentary activities. These activities are at the expense of such physically active pursuits as pick-up basketball and football games, swimming, street hockey or scrub baseball. Few students even walk to school anymore as the traffic jams outside the school in the morning and afternoon clearly illustrate. The box below highlights a few frightening facts about the fitness of modern youth:

Fitness Facts

- *Students today watch an average of 26 hours of television per week*
- *Only 6% of children aged 10–19 are active on a regular basis*
- *By the time they reach the 15–19 age group only 24% of girls and 50% of boys can achieve a recommended level of aerobic fitness*
- *On the average, children are up to 40% less active than they were 30 years ago*

The combination of poor eating habits and sedentary lifestyles are major problems in modern society, but they do not account for all teenage weight problems. Genetics also plays a part. If both parents are obese, there is a very strong chance that one or more of the children will also tend to be overweight. Metabolic rate, an inherited characteristic, plays an important role in weight gain. Some children can eat anything they want and still remain slim, while others have only to walk by a restaurant to gain weight. Generally, heredity alone can be expected to account for mild obesity, while greater weights are obtained by a combination of heredity, overeating and underexercising. Overweight parents have to be extra vigilant that their youngsters do not follow in their footsteps.

Parental Actions

As with other aspects of physical health, prevention is always easier than a cure. Preventing a child from becoming overweight will save him or her from the pressures and anxieties of being an overweight or obese teenager. Studies in the Netherlands show that parents have a major influence on their children's eating habits, when they choose to exert this control. There are many ways that they can do this. They include:

- *Set a good example with your own eating habits and weight control*
- *Eliminate unhealthy foods from your household rather than buying them and then trying to prohibit your teen from eating them.*
- *Keep healthy snacks in a place where your teen can easily get them, e.g., cut up carrots in smaller pieces and leave them in the refrigerator in a plastic bag.*
- *Take time to enjoy an active outdoor life with your children. Walk with them; ski with them; cycle with them; or swim with them. Encourage them to participate in sports or physically active endeavors. This is undoubtedly the key element in raising healthy and fit teenagers.*
- *Limit TV and computer time — for everyone.*
- *Eat dinner together, as a family, at a table — not in front of the TV.*
- *Prepare nutritious meals with plenty of fruits and vegetables, but little fat.*

If the teen is already overweight, the same strategies should apply, but extra steps also need to be taken. The first, and one of the most important, is to never use ridicule, sarcasm or scolding (lectures) to try to motivate the teen to lose weight. Comments like "Pretty soon you'll have to buy your clothes at Omar the Tentmaker's" do not help to motivate. Instead they make the teen feel even worse about the weight problem. The same goes for lecturing. Telling teens that they do not look attractive and will not be popular with the opposite sex may be true, but they only increase the teen's discouragement. These are not positive approaches and they will not work.

> *. . . never use ridicule, sarcasm or scolding (lectures) to try to motivate the teen to lose weight*

A more effective approach is to use encouragement and positive reinforcement to help the teen to shed the pounds. For example, encouraging the teen to join a weight-loss club such as TOPS or Weight Watchers is an extremely effective approach. If a parent is also overweight, join along with the teen and help to motivate each other. It's incredible how powerful a force for weight loss the weekly weigh-in can be. These clubs not only help to increase motivation but they teach the principles of sensible weight loss, so that a weight conscious lifestyle develops instead of the teen merely trying fad or temporary diets.

The Parent is Vital

Teens who are overweight generally do not have strong self-concepts. This leads them to be somewhat timid and shy about being out in public. Also teens in general tend to be personally disorganized. This combination makes it highly unlikely that overweight teenagers will take the initiative to enroll in an activity or club that will help them to lose weight. Recognizing these factors, parents need to play a leading role in this process. It is not babying them to help them to find the right activity or weight-losing club to join, then take them there to enroll. Also, do not expect them to instantly take to the weight losing process. Considerable encouragement and positive reinforcement will usually be necessary before the teen becomes fully engaged in losing weight and becoming fitter.

If parents do not join such a program with their teen, then they will need to do some homework on cooking nutritious, low calorie meals. Much has been written on this subject in recent years so that eating nutritiously does not have to mean bland and tasteless meals. One trip to a local book emporium should result in an abundance of excellent cookbooks that will allow the entire family to eat well but maintain a sensible weight.

An absolutely vital component of any weight loss program has to be a reasonable exercise program. Very obese teens cannot maintain a vigorous jogging program, for example, and quickly get discouraged. Instead a walking program that gradually increases the distance traveled, yoga or a beginner's aerobics class two or three times a week will be much more likely to be maintained. Once again it is best if a parent can also do the program as extra motivation for the teen. Eventually the teen might move up to a more vigorous program of jogging or swimming as the body begins to slim and the aerobic capacity increases.

Finally, parents need to ensure that their teen maintains an active social program. The more time the teen has, the more chances there will be for snacking. Encourage the teen to join activities such as music, drama, scouts or a church youth group. This may be difficult at first due to the tendency of most overweight teens to be self-conscious. Their low self-esteem may make them afraid to try. Once again gentle parental encouragement is the approach to take. Parents will usually need to take their teen to the first meeting or activity as the teen will often be afraid to turn up at these events alone. Part-time jobs are also an effective method of filling in spare time if the teen's school performance is adequate (see the section on Part-time Jobs in this chapter).

Three Steps to Positive Family Living

- ***Live Actively*** — *enjoy an active, outdoor life together by hiking, skiing, swimming or cycling as a family.*
- ***Eat Nutritiously*** — *prepare healthy, low-calorie meals and eat them together.*
- ***Be Supportive*** — *spend time together, communicate with each other and encourage your teens to live healthy lifestyles in positive, supportive ways.*

Teen Dating

As the emotions of youngsters develop to the point that they begin to find members of the opposite sex attractive, many parents begin to worry. They well know the dangers involved in sexual development and fear that they will not be able to control this process. Unfortunately for these worrying parents, the awareness of sexuality is a natural part of the process of puberty and cannot be stopped. Dating, in all its many forms, is the beginning of the long, emotional roller coaster that eventually leads teenagers to marriage and children of their own. Interest in the opposite sex can start as early as the fifth grade, but more commonly begins in the seventh or eighth grades.

Interest in "dating" is a key indicator of how the process of puberty is progressing. The earlier teens start showing an interest in activities with the opposite sex, the more advanced is their stage of adolescent development. For this to happen, the necessary hormones need to be present. Sexual interest can occur as early as 9 years or as late as 17 years of age. In fact, the differing stages of puberty will often cause changes in friendship groups. This results from one or more members of a group of long-time friends becoming interested in "dating," while the others maintain their childhood interests. Those with these more emotionally advanced interests tend to seek out other peers with similar interests, leaving their childhood friendship group. These breakups are very puzzling for the ones left behind. They cannot understand why the friend they have had since Grade 1 is no longer interested in hanging around with them. Unfortunately, neither can the ones with the more advanced hormones. They don't really understand why they don't want to be with their old friends any more, they just don't feel comfortable with them. This results in many hurt feelings, but is really nobody's fault. Parents need to be aware of these differences in development so that they can explain it to their upset youngsters if it happens to them.

Along with these stages of physiological development, parents also need to understand how the process of dating progresses throughout the teenage years. It starts with "going out." This first stage is confusing to parents because it is so inappropriately named. There is in fact no going out at all. It only requires that one person ask another to "go out." Often the youngsters are too shy to do this so a friend does it for them. They are then "going out" which may mean anything from doing absolutely nothing together to pairing off for brief conversations at noon hour or possibly meeting at a school dance. Even at the dance the "couple" may share only a few dances together. As soon as one or the other develops another romantic interest, which is often a matter of days, then that person "dumps" the other, or once again gets a friend to do it. Generally this stage predominates in the Grade 7 to 9 range.

> This is an indicator of how romantic the "going out" stage is. A girl asked her friend to dump her boyfriend for her. The designated "dumper" went up to the boy and said
>
> **"Roses are red, Violets are blue,**
> **You're dumped, boo hoo hoo."**
>
> The relationship was then considered to be over.

That first dating stage usually has little or no sexual content. A kiss would be a very big thing at the "going out" stage. The next step in the dating game could be termed "going with," and it involves a more advanced relationship. As teens mature their relationships tend to last longer, and involve more time spent together. While parents may not have even been aware that their teens were "going out," they usually know when their adolescents are in the "going with" stage. At this point there often is some real dating. The teens go to dances and parties together, to the mall or take in the occasional movie. Kissing and "making out" is now frequent and sexual intercourse may occur, but it is not yet common. At this stage you still have to be asked to "go with" someone before you can go to any activities with that person. Teens will usually "go with" several different partners for lengths of time varying from a few months to several years. While their attachments to these partners are often very strong, they are rarely "in love." The "going with" stage usually lasts throughout high school.

By the end of high school, serious relationships begin to develop. At this point 80% of the teens will have had intercourse, and a small percentage of relationships will lead to marriage. By this time, around 18 years of age, their emotional systems are capable of real love. This is the "in love" stage. At this point the teens can date without making a commitment. If there is no spark, then the dating of that person ceases. Unlike the previous two stages, during the "in love" stage you can date several different people at the same time, without females being considered "sluts" or the males being tagged as "players." Eventually one of these dating relationships will lead to engagement and marriage.

The Problems

As with most aspects of raising teenagers, dating presents many problems for parents. The first occurs when the teenager is ready for the dating process before the parents are. These adults have difficulty with the idea that their youngster is maturing and try to slow down the process by restricting it. They make rules such as "No dating until you are sixteen," presumably to try to protect their adolescent from the dangers of dating. While parents do need to be vigilant for the dangers of dating, such as abusive relationships, pregnancy and sexually transmitted diseases, they cannot delay the process for long. Usually, these are the parents of girls, but occasionally parents make these rules for sons as well. This is about as effective as pouring gasoline on a fire to put it out. Attraction to the opposite sex is a natural process and, while wise parents can and should control dating, it cannot be postponed entirely.

Most of the problems associated with teenage dating are experienced by the teenagers themselves. Parents become involved due to the mood changes of the teens, which often depend on the success or failure of relationships. The problem for parents is to understand what is happening to the teen, while being supportive and caring. For example, teenagers can feel the pressure to date, but not be ready. This can result in their being frustrated and depressed. Similarly, the teen may be friends with someone who is outgoing and attractive, and therefore popular with the opposite sex. They, on the other hand, may not be as attractive or outgoing and therefore not get the same amount of dating attention. To counter the depression that results from these situations, parents need to understand what is happening and to provide the appropriate counsel and support.

Another problem experienced by the teen occurs when they are "dumped" by their partner, or find out that the partner has been cheating on them. In the "going out" stage, most teens bounce back quickly and may not need any help. In the later stages, however, major depressions can result and parents will need to be on top of the situation in order to provide support and guidance. Parents often underestimate how powerful these feelings can be, especially with younger teens, and try to cope with the depressed teen by telling them to "snap out of it." This lack of understanding only serves to make the situation worse for a teen who really needs parental support at that point.

Many teens experience problems with their friends when they begin to "go out" with someone. The friends, who have been used to spending most of their spare time with each other, now find that this time must be shared with the teen's partner. Jealousies and misunderstandings lead to battles and disagreements. The teens themselves rarely understand what is happening or how to balance these relationships. The power of the attraction often blinds them to the needs of their same sex friends. Understanding parents can minimize these conflicts by teaching their teen how to balance their time more effectively. Interestingly, this situation is not much different from the golfing husband who fails to spend enough time with his wife. Balance can be a problem even for adults, but it is especially hard for highly emotional teenagers.

Yet another problem is created for dating teens in the early stages by the fact that the two sexes at not at the same stage of development emotionally. While there are many different possible explanations for these differences, parents need only realize that boys and girls are at different maturity levels. This is especially true in the "going out" stage. Girls at this level are more ready for relationships than are boys of the same age. This results in the girls being frustrated by the males' relative lack of interest in their liaisons. The boys are interested in "going out" with girls, but are equally interested in male pursuits and being with their same sex friends. There are two frequent results of these differences. One is that relationships at this level, usually the 12 to 15 year age range, tend to be very short. The other is that girls of this age often are more comfortable with boys two or three years older than they are. This really upsets many parents who see sexual motives in the older boys. This is rarely the case.

Rather, these relationships are the result of the older boys being more able to sustain an emotional relationship than their younger counterparts. Once again parental understanding of the nature of teenagers can save considerable friction in the family.

Parental Actions

The previous section clearly indicates that, while parents do have many worries about their teenagers' dating, the teens experience the bulk of the problems. Parents can be of most help by understanding the problems that their teens are going through and being as supportive as possible. This support consists mostly of empathetic listening. The last thing most teens want is direct advice as to how to handle dating situations. Teens really believe that parents are too far removed from the scene to really understand what they are going through. In more contemporary terms, they think their parents are "out of it." Teenagers also do not want to be regaled with stories of their parents' dating life back in the "dark ages." Instead they just need them to be a pillar on which they can support themselves when dating gets puzzling or depressing. Parental understanding allows them to avoid minimizing the situation by saying trite things like "You'll get over it," "It's not as if you're going to marry her" or "I told you so!" As true as these statements may be, they will only make the situation worse because they show that you do not understand how they are feeling. With parental support, teens will bounce back quickly and learn to handle dating situations with gradually increasing maturity. Without it the maturation process will be slower and much more painful for the teens.

Besides being supportive, there are two key actions that parents need to take to protect their teens from the dangers that exist in the dating world. The first is to ensure that they have thoroughly communicated their moral principles to their teenagers. Parental ideas on pre-marital sex, drinking and drugs need to be well established if teens are to have a set of guidelines to follow when interacting with the opposite sex. (See the section on this topic in Chapter 7.) While they will occasionally make mistakes, teens that have been well taught do not want to disappoint their parents and will try to follow the parental standards most of the time.

The second key parental action is to have a clear set of rules for the teenagers to follow. Curfews are particularly important as they limit the time teens have to succumb to peer pressure or a desire to experiment. Similarly, rules against unchaperoned parties will help to minimize the chances of these functions getting out of control and placing the teenager in a difficult situation. A clear, yet fair set of rules (see Chapter 4) helps a teen to feel safer and protect them from many of the dangers that are inherent in the dating scene.

Finally, as further protection for your teenager, make sure that he or she takes a cell phone on dates and to parties. It need not be their own phone, but this relatively new form of communication can be an important link to parental help if it is required. It can be handy in minor situations, such as wanting to stay out later if the party is good, to minor crises like missing the last bus, all the way to major predicaments like out-of-control parties or attempted date-rape. A cell phone provides parents with an increased sense of security that was not present in previous generations, while also removing that age-old excuse, "I couldn't find a phone" when the teen arrives home late or gets into a problem situation.

Helping Your Teen Handle the Dating Process

- *Understand their feelings.*
- *Teach your moral principles as regards premarital intercourse.*
- *Define clear rules about curfews and unchaperoned parties.*
- *Give them a cell phone when going to parties or on dates.*

Chapter 9

The Non-Traditional Family

Divorce was once a relatively rare event in society. In fact, it was so rare that there was a stigma attached to divorced people. It was as if they were considered to be failures in life. Perhaps the most famous example of this stigma was Wallis Warfield Simpson, an American divorcée who eventually married Edward VIII of England. British society was so intolerant of divorced people at that time (1936) that Edward was forced to give up the throne to marry her. This societal bias against divorce has gradually softened, with the result that the divorce rates throughout the developed world have risen dramatically since the brief reign of Edward VIII.

This dramatic rise in the frequency of divorce is clearly displayed by the statistics. In 1936, during the Edward VIII controversy, there were 16 divorces for every 100 marriages in the United States. By 1998, this figure had risen to 51 divorces per 100 marriages. While the incidence of divorce among developed countries is highest in the US, the figures for other countries are equally alarming. In staid, conservative Switzerland for example, it is projected that 42 out of every 100 marriages from 1998 will end in divorce. In Canada the rate is slightly less, at 36 out of 100 of the 1998 marriages. Nevertheless this represents a huge increase in divorces when compared to earlier generations.

The overall result of the increase in the divorce rate has been an acceptance of this trend as a normal part of modern society. There is no longer any stigma attached to divorce, a fact that may be helping to keep the statistics up. The thinking appears to be that if so many people are getting divorced, then it must be an acceptable thing to do. While this acceptance may be a fact, it does not mean that divorce does not have any negative effects. Slowly a body of information has been accumulating that clearly shows that divorce has serious negative consequences on the children involved. It is this data that parents should be considering before they contemplate divorce rather than the extremely high rate of acceptance that divorce presently enjoys.

Divorce Has Consequences

The growing acceptance of divorce as an integral part of our society has led to the development of a major myth about its effects on children. Divorcing parents want to believe that their children will suffer no ill effects from the breakup of the family. For many years the myth has grown that children are young and can "bounce back" from the disappointments of their parents divorcing. A word for this has even been coined — "resilience." Parents want to believe that their kids are resilient and will quickly recover from any emotional trauma. This is simply not the case. A recent monumental study by Patrick F. Fagan and Robert Rector, called *The Effects of Divorce on America*, and published by the Heritage Foundation of Washington, D.C. clearly shows the effects that divorce has on children. By surveying over two hundred research studies on this topic, they concluded that these effects are far more serious than even the most pessimistic researchers might have believed just a few years ago. The main findings are as follows:

- Children whose parents have divorced are increasingly the victims of abuse and neglect. They exhibit more health problems, as well as behavioral and emotional problems. They are more frequently involved in crime and drug abuse, and have higher rates of suicide. They even have shorter life spans.

- Children of divorced parents frequently do poorly in school. They perform more poorly in Reading, Spelling and Mathematics than their peers from intact two-parent families do. They are also more likely to repeat a grade and to have higher dropout rates and lower rates of graduation.

- Divorce generally reduces the income of the child's primary household and seriously diminishes the potential of every member of the household to accumulate wealth. For families that were not poor before the divorce, the drop in income can be as much as 50 percent. This decline in income is also intergenerational, since children whose parents divorce are likely to earn less as adults than children raised in intact families.

- Religious worship, which has been linked in many studies to health and happiness, longer lives, longer marriages and a better family life, is less prevalent in divorced families.

- Divorce permanently weakens the relationship between a child and his or her parents, and it also leads to a poorer self-image and destructive ways of handling conflict.

- Children of divorce tend to lose their virginity earlier, cohabit more frequently, have higher divorce rates later in life, and have less desire to have children.

- Divorce diminishes the capacity of children to handle conflict. For example, compared with students from intact families, college students from divorced families use violence more frequently to resolve conflict. Children from divorced families, both male and female, are more likely to be aggressive and physically violent with their friends.

- Divorce leaves most children feeling emotionally insecure and more likely to believe that the social environment is unpredictable and uncontrollable. This results in poor social skills and often rejection by the peer group. Children of divorce tend to have fewer friends and to complain more about the lack of support they receive from the friends they have.

- The divorce of parents makes romance and courtship more difficult for children as they reach adulthood. The older teenagers and young adults date more often, have more failed romantic relationships, and tend to have shorter relationships with their dating partners. *These effects on relationships seem to be the strongest when the divorce takes place during the teenage years.*

> *The marital instability of one generation appears to be passed on to the next.*

The inevitable result of the above points is that the risk of divorce for children of divorced parents can be as high as twice that for children of intact families. The marital instability of one generation appears to be passed on to the next. These effects seem to be greatest on females. Even marriages of children from divorced families that stay together suffer from weaker relationships. They tend to have higher levels of jealousy, moodiness, infidelity, conflicts over money and excessive drinking and drug use.

At this point you may have to catch your breath. This is an incredible list of potential effects of divorce on children. While not all of these effects apply to every child, there is as yet no way to predict how each individual child will be affected by a divorce. It can be stated, however, that every child will be affected in some way and that these effects can also affect the next generation as well. The inescapable conclusion, according to Fagan and Rector, is that "marriage is the best environment in which to raise healthy, happy children who can achieve their potential, and that the family is the most important institution for social well-being." Society needs to change its attitude about divorce, not necessarily all the way back to where it was in Edward VIII's time, but to something like, "If kids are involved, divorce is not acceptable."

These are strong words that many will not want to accept. Unfortunately the facts are becoming increasingly hard to argue with. Once married couples become parents, divorce should be avoided except in cases of physical or emotional abuse, or addictions such as alcoholism, drugs or gambling. The following sections of this chapter outline how some of the negative effects that divorce has on children are created, with the intention that parents contemplating divorce will think many times before they actually go through with it.

Further Reading on the Effects of Divorce on Children

- Amato, Paul, & Booth, Alan. *A Generation at Risk.*
- Gallagher, Maggie & Waite, Linda. *The Case for Marriage.*
- Heatherington, M., & Kelly, J. *For Better or Worse: Divorce Reconsidered.*

- Popenoe, David. *Life Without Father.*
- Staal, Stephanie. *The Love They Lost.*
- Wallenstein, Judith. *The Unexpected Legacy of Divorce.*
- Whitehead, Barbara D. *The Divorce Culture.*

After the Divorce

Few parents research the problems that divorce can create both for themselves and for their children. This may be because of the emotions that accompany a marriage in trouble. The tensions become so high that one or both members of the embattled couple just wants out. They assume that ending the marriage will solve all their problems and, because they will be happier, their children will be happier too.

The truth is that the children are almost never happier after a divorce. Even in the cases of abusive or addicted spouses, where the youngsters can clearly see that the marriage has to end, the kids still miss the non-custodial parent. They also still suffer many of the same consequences as do the children from divorces that may not have had such clear reasons for happening. Parents need to be aware of how divorce causes such emotional damage to children and, if they must divorce, take steps to avoid the most serious of the problems. Unfortunately, no amount of pre-divorce planning can nullify all the negative effects that divorce has on children.

Single Parenting

The inevitable result of marital breakups where children are involved is that the kids have to live with one parent or the other. Usually this parent is the mother. In fact, according to Statistics Canada, in 60% of the Canadian custody orders, custody was awarded to the mother. In another 30% of the cases, joint custody was ordered, although in most of these cases the children do not divide their time equally with each parent. Instead they live in one household, usually the mother's, and decisions about their welfare are theoretically shared equally between the two parents. In the US 84% of the children in single-parent homes live with their mother; this is probably a more accurate estimate of Canadian divorced households as well.

When families break up, the parents rarely take the time to determine what the consequences will be, not only for the children, but for themselves as well. These parents are usually in such an emotional state that they do not research the possible consequences of their actions. One major result of this lack of preparation is that they have no idea what to expect when they become the sole parent of the children for the majority of the time. Single parenting is an extremely difficult thing to do well, and it is very demanding on the parent. These demands come from several different directions, and can seriously affect the mental health of the parent, which in turn can have a negative impact on the children.

The Problems

The first problem to confront single parents, especially mothers, is the drastic drop in economic status. This problem is usually anticipated to a certain degree. In fact it often delays mothers from divorcing until they can figure out how they will be able to live on their own. The full effects of this drop in income, however, are generally not appreciated. A 1994 study at the University of Michigan reported that during the years children lived with two parents their family incomes averaged $43,600 (US) a year. When these same children lived with one parent, the incomes dropped to just $25,300. Other studies have confirmed that the drop in income for a single parent ranges from 28 to 50 percent.

The economic figures mean that money is a problem in most single-parent households, and this creates a number of spin-off difficulties. For one, it limits the activities that the family can take part in, resulting in less family togetherness and poorer family communication. It can also limit the extracurricular activities teens can involve themselves in, which lowers their enjoyment of life. Often teens have to work to get the money they need for school events, clothes and entertainment. The time commitment involved limits their extracurricular involvement and adds a fatigue factor that can impair their academic performance.

Limited financial resources also increase parental stress levels. This then tends to spill over onto teens via a lower parental anger threshold. Teen-parent conflict is common enough for all parents, but when their stress levels rise, their tolerance decreases and even the smallest events can trigger a family row. Single parents are subject to this stress for several reasons. One is that they are limited in the jobs they can take. Jobs involving travel, for example, are out of the question. Promotion is often limited as well as increased responsibility, which also takes time away from the family. This means that single parents are often restricted to lower paying jobs, which perpetuates their financial difficulties, and may decrease their job satisfaction. They also cannot just quit if the job becomes boring or onerous. The prospect of being without a job for any length of time is intolerable, as they need the money. All of these factors increase parental stress levels, and this tension is then passed on to other family members.

> *Single parents are caught in almost endless work cycles. The fatigue that results from this heavy workload also increases stress levels, which again is passed on to the children in the form of irritation and anger.*

Stress does not just come to a single parent through financial strain. It can also come from fatigue. Single parents bear a tremendous burden alone. They usually must work to support the family, then go home to run the household and parent the children. There is no second parent to spell them off from these duties, so single parents are caught in almost endless work cycles. The fatigue that results from this heavy workload also increases stress levels, which again is passed on to the children in the form of irritation and anger. This anger results from such things as failure to do chores, leaving a mess, fighting with siblings and even accidents like spilling a drink or breaking a dish. Teens generally have little understanding of what a single parent is going through and do not understand the relatively low tolerance levels that they often encounter. In fact, they start to think that their parent does not like them, which in turn causes their self-esteem to plummet.

While the stress caused by money worries and fatigue definitely has an effect on the relationship between a single parent and the children, there are other factors that affect these relationships as well. Studies of divorced parents show that divorced mothers, despite their best intentions, are less able than married mothers to give the same level of emotional support to their children. They are likely to be less affectionate and less communicative with their children and to discipline them more harshly and more inconsistently, when they choose to discipline at all. Other studies indicate that most single parents, male or female, tend to change from a rigid or structured discipline system to a permissive one. This may occur because single parents realize that the divorce has been hard on teens and they don't want to psychologically damage them further by being authoritarian. Often, too, they want the teens to support them rather than the non-custodial parent, so they try to avoid angering their children.

Single parents also tend to become more emotionally dependent on their children. This means that they rely on their children to listen to their problems and to support them when life becomes overwhelming. Unfortunately teenagers are not emotionally equipped to sustain this role for long, and they in turn become tense and anxious. Teens want their parents to support *them* emotionally and cannot assume a parental role just because the custodial parent has no partner to share life's burdens.

The reasons for these parental changes in attitude towards and treatment of their children are complex. They usually tend to involve the stresses that develop from continued conflict with the divorced spouse, the financial burdens of single parenting and the loneliness and fatigue of being the only parent in the family. While these changes are understandable, they have serious emotional effects on children. The following chart, reproduced from a 1996 Statistics Canada study entitled *Growing Up in Canada: National Longitudinal Survey of Children and Youth* summarizes these effects:

Problem	Single-Mother Family Percentage	Two-Parent Family Percentage
Hyperactivity	15.6	9.6
Conduct disorder	17.2	8.1
Emotional disorder	15.0	7.5
One or more behavior problems	31.7	18.7
Repeated a grade *	11.2	4.7
Current school problems *	5.8	2.7
Social impairment	6.1	2.5
One or more total problems	**40.6**	**23.6**

* Data for asterisked items apply for 6-11-year-olds. All other data in the table apply to 4-11-year-olds.

The final row in the table indicates that children from single-mother families are almost twice as likely to have one or more total problems than are those from two parent families. The probability of this data being due to chance is less than one in one thousand (p < .001), which means that these results will usually apply to the general population, and not just to that research sample.

Other studies in the US indicate that there was a positive relationship between the mental health of the parents and their child's mental health. In other words, the children of better-adjusted parents tend to have fewer emotional problems than those of poorly adjusted parents. Similarly, a relationship has been shown between the amount of conflict between the parents prior to, during and after the divorce and the emotional well-being of their children. As might be expected, the more conflict between the parents, the worse the mental health of the children.

Taken all together, the research indicates that children in single-parent families where the conflict between the parents has been bitter fare much worse emotionally than either children from traditional two parent families or children from single-parent families in which the parental conflict has not been as obvious. This would indicate that if divorce must happen, there are steps parents can take to minimize the emotional damage to their children. Since the children live with the mother the vast majority of the time, it falls to her to take the lead in minimizing the potential emotional damage. Non-custodial fathers can also play a major role; this will be discussed in the next section.

Parental Actions

The facts and figures discussed in the above section are not designed to frighten single parents but rather to alert them to the dangers that divorce and single parenting can create. It is entirely possible to raise emotionally healthy children in these situations, it is just harder. If single parents are aware of the dangers, and take steps to counter them, then the parenting experience will be rewarding and emotionally healthy adults will be the result. The following are some strategies that will help to counteract the problems associated with divorce and single parenthood.

- **Maintain a positive attitude.** There are many benefits to single parenting when compared to parenting in a poor marriage. These include less tension and conflict in the home, and more autonomy and independence in decision-making. Single parents need to be determined to focus on these positive aspects rather than taking a self-pitying attitude towards their circumstances. Many families become closer under these circumstances, so resolve to be one of them.

- **Be the boss.** Single parents, through fatigue, stress or misguided philosophies, tend to become permissive when it comes to disciplinary situations. This approach simply does not work. Teens want their parents to be in charge. They need discipline and limits to feel secure and loved. Single parents must establish firm, clear boundaries for their teens, leaving no doubt as to who is in charge. If rules are broken, then consequences must follow. Teens much prefer this approach to a permissive one. You will not damage them emotionally by being firm and fair, but you might by being permissive. (See Chapter 4 for more details on establishing rules and consequences.)

- **Be organized.** Single parents often feel overwhelmed by their responsibilities and duties. This can be avoided by being organized and efficient. Make sure that all children have assigned chores and household responsibilities and ensure that they do these tasks. Teens in single-parent households realize that they should be helping out, but they are still teenagers. They are not well organized themselves and are rarely self-starters, even when they know they should be. Arrange for car-pools to school and sports events and make up and post schedules of the weekly events. These schedules help to avoid conflicts and to remind everyone of the week's activities. They also help to plan time more effectively. Do not be afraid to ask for help from other parents when your schedule becomes overloaded, on the understanding that you will reciprocate when your schedule allows it.

- **Take care of your own mental health.** Realizing that single parenting is demanding, plan for some time for yourself. Try to get together with friends at least once a week for both a break and for emotional support. Enroll in courses that teach relaxation, meditation or stress reduction techniques. Watch your diet and build in some exercise time. These suggestions rely on good organization as it is easy to get so caught up in the chores and tasks that you forget your own needs. It is not only not selfish to allow time for yourself, it will benefit your teens, since by looking after your mental health you will be more relaxed and patient with them.

- **Treat your children as children, not as equals.** Teens can be understanding, but they are not emotionally ready to shoulder the problems of their parents. Do not discuss major problems with them or rely on them to make decisions for you. Certainly good communication is important, but most of that communication should be in the form of listening to their problems. If they notice you are worried about something, by all means tell them what it is, but do not expect them to help solve the problem. It is all too common for single parents to become emotionally dependent on their children. Teens need to be involved in their own world, which is complex enough. They need you to help sort out this world, they do not need to be trying to solve adult problems.

- **Maintain civility with your ex.** This may be extremely difficult if the breakup was bitter, but for the sake of the emotional health of the children it is vital that a veneer of civility be maintained. Cooperation between the ex-partners is necessary in many areas, such as disciplinary matters, finances, custody arrangements and attending the children's events. If a state of war exists then the cooperation disappears and there is constant tension for everyone. For the mental health of both the single parents and the kids, maturity needs to prevail. Try to remember that there was once love between you, so the ex-partner must have some good characteristics. Dwell on them rather than the things that broke up the marriage.

Single parents who can accept these suggestions have an excellent chance of raising mentally healthy children and so avoiding having the kids become part of a statistical table like the one reproduced above. Like any other skill, single parenting requires study and practice. If this is done it will not only be easier, but more rewarding as well.

"Social science research is almost never conclusive. There are always methodological difficulties and stones left unturned. Yet in three decades of work as a social scientist, I know of few other bodies of data in which the weight of evidence is so decisively on one side of the issue: on the whole, for children, two-parent families are preferable to single-parent and stepfamilies."
— *Dr. David Popenoe, author of* Life Without Father

The Non-Custodial Parent

For reasons that are hard to explain, the role of the non-custodial parent in helping to raise mentally healthy and happy children is rarely considered. Yet the non-custodial parent is one of the biological parents and the children almost invariably love this person, even if the other parent no longer does. As has been previously discussed, over 80% of the children of divorce live with their mothers. This then means that a similar percentage of the non-custodial parents are fathers. Once they are divorced and no longer live with their children, the lifestyles of the non-custodial parents tend to change relatively quickly. No longer do they have the daily parenting chores, such as driving the kids to their events, which they once had. Living alone, they quickly get out of the habit of marriage and parenting and develop new lifestyles, often with new partners. This can create many problems for their children who want the parent to stay the same as he or she has always been.

The Problems

Since the great majority of non-custodial parents are fathers, this section will mainly concentrate on them, even though many of the comments will also apply to n/c mothers as well. The importance of fathers in children's lives has been hotly debated over the years. The research leaves little doubt that two parents are generally more effective in raising emotionally healthy children than are single parents, but the actual significance of the father's role is not yet fully known. Recent studies by Paul Amato and David Popenoe (see "Further Reading" above) both indicate that being emotionally close to a father produces young adults who are happier and more satisfied in life. In other words, the actual role of the father may not yet be well understood, but it seems to be a vital one for children becoming stable adults.

The higher the level of conflict between the parents during the divorce, the more likely the distance between father and the children afterwards.

This leads to the major problem with non-custodial fathers. Surveys have shown that fully one-fifth of divorced fathers had not seen their young children in the past year, and less than half the fathers saw their children more than a few times a year. By adolescence (12 to 16) less than half the children living with their separated, divorced or remarried mothers had seen their fathers at all in more than a year, and only one in six saw their fathers as often as once a week. Such traditional custody arrangements as the non-custodial father having the children one night a week and every other weekend obviously break down rapidly in over half the divorced families. This has a serious effect on the children. They tend to feel rejected by the father, which is extremely hard on their self-esteem. They simply cannot understand how someone they love so much can abandon them so easily. To be fair, not all these fathers are actually abandoning their children. In many cases, especially in those of bitter divorces, the custodial mothers find all kinds of ways of circumventing the custody arrangements. They try to "punish" the divorced spouse by withholding the children. This can result in very expensive court battles, and not all fathers can afford them. Rarely do the children understand what is going on, especially the younger ones, and they tend to blame their fathers for not being available to them. Studies confirm this by clearly showing that the higher the level of conflict between the parents during the divorce, the more likely the distance between father and the children afterwards.

> *"Since he got a girlfriend I don't want to visit him any more.*
> *But I miss him — I miss a dad."*
> — *Megan*

Another problem presents itself when the father starts to have a social life. Since they generally live alone and have no parental responsibilities, fathers often start dating sooner than custodial mothers do. While this is understandable, it is usually devastating to the kids. Most children of divorce harbor secret dreams that their parents will reunite. These dreams are shattered when dad begins to date. After all, if he remarries, there will be no chance of the parents ever getting back together. The resentment and bitterness on the part of the children towards both the father and the new partner are frightening to behold, and play havoc with the relationship between father and the children. Naturally, the same reaction occurs if, by chance, the custodial mother starts dating first. This resentment will be more thoroughly discussed in the "Step-Parenting" section of this chapter.

Parental Actions

A non-custodial father can take several steps to remain a major part of the children's lives. The first is to choose a residence that is close to the mother's home. While it would be uncomfortable for both parents if the father chooses to live across the street, a few blocks away would help. This proximity helps the teens to feel more comfortable and more connected with dad, and makes the travel between homes relatively easy.

The second step is somewhat obvious, but still needs to be stated. Non-custodial fathers should spend as much time as possible with their children. If at all possible, visitation periods should be adhered to. The routine is very necessary for children, and it shows teens that their father really cares about them. Canceling frequently, even if for good reasons, has the opposite effect, casting doubt on whether their dad really cares about them. Events such as concerts, parent-teacher interviews, and sporting activities should be attended faithfully. Teens often give the impression that they don't care whether their parents attend these events or not. Don't be fooled! They want their parents there and greatly appreciate it when they do attend.

Having the non-custodial parent at these events can be uncomfortable if the custodial parent is there too. This is where maturity becomes important. Recognizing that the children love both parents is vital to the divorced couple. They must declare a truce for important events that both should be attending. This includes parent-teacher interviews, graduations and big games. At other times, it may be sufficient for just one parent to be present, and these events need to be agreed upon beforehand. This kind of civility between divorced parents is unfortunately a rarity. Many parents prefer to maintain the battle long after the breakup of the marriage for reasons of pride or revenge. Custodial parents often deliberately do not tell the absentee parent of these activities just so that they can appear to be the "good guy." Others try to give the impression that the kids do not want the non-custodial parent there. These are the actions of immature people. Even if the marriage did not work, cooperation for the sake of the kids after the divorce is vital to their emotional development, and it should continue throughout the children's adolescence. Fathers need to work hard to avoid the development of emotional distance, even if it means being civil and cooperative with the Ex.

Another vital action for non-custodial parents is to ensure that child-support payments are made. These payments are not important just for their economic benefits to the children. Making them regularly also shows a strong emotional commitment to the kids, and this dedication becomes extremely important as they enter the teen years. This is the age when they begin to understand the value of money and its importance in financing both the household and their activities in school and out. A father who does not help pay the bills is seen to not care for the well-being of his children who therefore feel that he does not love them. While this may not be true, that is the message that is conveyed. It also tends to make the mother more bitter and angry towards the non-custodial father, which often results in making the children less available for visitations. It also provides a weapon for the mother to draw the children closer to her if feelings remain bitter. Overall, while it is undoubtedly a burden on some fathers, making child-support payments regularly has a beneficial effect on the children both economically and emotionally.

A final step for non-custodial parents to take is to ensure that good communication exists between the children and themselves. As they only see their kids for relatively brief periods, it is vital that that time be used effectively. The communication skills outlined in Chapter 1, such as questioning techniques and good listening, need to be carefully applied so that the bond between parent and children stays strong. Communication can be aided by carefully planning the time the non-custodial parent spends with his children. This planning should include a balance between activities the teens enjoy, such as going to movies or professional sports events, and quiet times when discussions about what is happening at school and in their social lives can take place. Quizzing the teenagers about their custodial parent's habits or lifestyle should not be part of these conversations, nor should criticizing her in any way. However, keeping the children fully informed about the father's life, within reason, is important. They are interested and should be told, where dad is presently working, his social activities (this topic will be discussed in more detail in the next section) and any future plans he may have. The children's opinions on these topics should be carefully listened to and respected. This does not mean that dad has to do what the kids want, but it does mean that a thorough discussion should take place before the father makes any major changes in his lifestyle.

The role of the non-custodial parent is often a difficult one, especially in cases of bitter divorces. However, if the father works hard to ensure that his children enjoy visiting him and supports them financially and emotionally, then the natural bond that exists between parents and their children will remain strong. This will be beneficial to everyone in the family.

> ### How Non-Custodial Parents Can Remain Part of Their Children's Lives
>
> - *Live as close as possible to the children.*
> - *Spend as much time as possible with the kids.*
> - *Declare a truce with the ex for important events that both parents should attend.*
> - *Keep up child-support payments.*
> - *Maintain effective communication with the children.*

Parental Dating

Being single, for an adult, can be an extremely lonely existence. Whether the parent has custody of the children or not, needs eventually develop for an adult confidant and an intimate companion. While these needs may be natural, few aspects of divorce are as difficult for teenagers to adjust to than their parent dating someone other than their real mother or father. This is an emotional minefield that parents need to traverse with great care. If dating is not done in the right ways, then there is a real chance of a parent completely destroying the relationship with his or her children.

The Problems

The most serious hurdle for a single parent, whether custodial or non-custodial, to overcome is the fact that their children usually love both their parents. To the parents the causes of their breakup are clear. The children, on the other hand, do not see things the same way. Only in rare circumstances do they accept the grounds for the divorce. The result is that most children secretly hope their parents will get back together. The arrival of a new partner for one of their parents signals the beginning of the end of these hopes, and the children tend to take their frustration out on the stranger. The person could be as kind as Mother Teresa and as good looking as a movie star but it won't matter; the kids will resent the interloper. Teenagers are particularly good at finding ways to display this resentment, much to the puzzlement and embarrassment of their parent. The signs of this resentment can vary from rudeness to the stranger, to staying away from home whenever the new person is around, all the way to refusal to attend school. The really incredible fact is that parents believe that because they are interested in this new person, their kids will be too. This is almost never the case.

> *"I'll always love my mom, but she lets her boyfriend run our lives.*
> *She has only known him for two months and already he's moving in.*
> *It's like if they had met a long time ago and he was moving in,*
> *I wouldn't really mind, **but it's too soon!**"*
> — Cristal

The other problems with parents starting to date are related closely to the first one. As in Cristal's case above, a major concern is that the dating process often starts too soon for the kids and it progresses too fast for them. "Too soon" can mean anything from a few months to several years. The real problem is less the time interval than the thought that there is no longer any chance that the parents will reunite. This means that the parent has done little or no preparation with the children for the dating process to begin. The teens are allowed to harbor their dreams — and then suddenly the dreams are shattered by the new "friend." Parents need to be very aware of their children's feelings and talk about the dating process at considerable length with them before ever considering introducing the new flame to the kids.

The speed and intensity of the relationship between their parent and the new "friend" can also be an illusion to teens. They see the relationship as moving much faster than it may actually be. While they think nothing of changing partners every few weeks, and possibly even sleeping with them, their standards for their parents are much higher. Once they have accepted the fact that their parents are seeing other people, teenagers are almost Victorian in the standards they set for them. They do not want to see signs of affection, such as hugging or holding hands, for months, and they definitely do not want any hint that there may be a sexual relationship.

Many parents resent this teenage prudishness, feeling that the tail is wagging the dog. They do not want to have to listen to their teens, thinking that the children are being selfish or that they do not understand the situation. Parents who think this way simply do not understand the nature of teens. Teenagers hate the thought that any adults are sexually active — including their own parents when they live together. Teens would prefer to think that the only times their parents had intercourse was to conceive them. Otherwise the thought of parents copulating is repulsive to them. If this is the case for their natural parents, it is not hard to imagine how resentful they would be if they had any inkling that one of their parents was having sex with someone new. While it is true that they resent their parents dating at all, the reason they get upset about overt signs of sexual activity is actually a combination of the resentment of the new person with their natural abhorrence of the thought of adults having sex at all.

Despite these problems, parents who separate and eventually divorce will usually need another adult to share their lives at some point.

The ideal solution would be to postpone this until the children are out of their teens and better able to understand adult needs and feelings. Failing this, there are a number of steps parents should follow to help prevent a permanent schism between themselves and their children.

Parental Actions

Newly separated or divorced parents should understand at the outset that their teenagers will almost automatically reject any new person being brought into the family. They do not want to give up their dream that their parents will eventually reunite. However, if single parents must form new relationships, there are ways to minimize the impact on their teens. These include:

- **Leave as long a time gap as possible before beginning dating.** Ideally this should be years. Teenagers consider it extremely disrespectful to both themselves and the former partner to begin seeing new people shortly after the relationship ends. It is directly comparable to how society views someone who starts dating shortly after their spouse dies.

- **When you do want to start dating, be sure to communicate your intentions to your teens before beginning.** While teenagers usually resent their parents beginning to date, they are also capable of understanding why a parent would want to do so. Talk to the kids at length about your needs and desires before they see any signs that you are interested, such as telephone calls from members of the opposite sex or mysterious nights out. Keep them fully informed and this will tend to dampen their resentment.

- **Do not arrange for a new romantic interest to spend time with your children until you know him or her quite well.** The point here is: do not ask for trouble if you don't have to. Until you know your relationship is going to last for a while, there is no point in trying to deal with your children's resentment. You also need to know such things as how this new person will react to your kids and whether he or she can deal with the wariness and possible anger that this person will be exposed to. Until you reach this point, your teens can know that you are dating, but they do not need to spend any time with this person.

- **Expect an initial dislike when the teens meet the new romantic interest.** Do not be angry or upset if your teens do not immediately accept a new romantic interest. Be patient and understanding of their rudeness, cutting remarks or lack of enthusiasm. Talk to them about their resentment and by all means try to get them to give the new person a chance, but don't scold or lecture them about their behavior as that will only make things worse. Try something like this:

  "You kids were pretty hard on Griselda (Beauregard) last night. I understand why you are upset by my dating her (him) but I'd really appreciate it if you would give her (him) a chance to get to know you. I really like her (him) and I think if you give her (him) a chance, you will too."

- **Allow the teens to get to know this person gradually.** Once they have been introduced initially limit their exposure to this new person to short periods of time. Try not to leap into daylong outings or weekend excursions. Teens need a considerable amount of time to accustom themselves to this new addition to their lives. To rush it will only invite disaster. Parents can gauge the amount of adjustment time needed by the intensity of the dislike displayed by the youngsters. As it begins to wane you can gradually increase the exposure time. If it does not wane at all, then possibly you have selected the wrong person. In this case you need to talk to the kids about what the problems may be and why they continue to dislike this person. They may be seeing something that you have missed.

- **Keep the teens generally informed about the relationship, but don't force them to make decisions about it.** Communication plays a major role in the parental dating process. The teens will want to know how things are going and if the relationship is getting serious. However, they can not be forced into any decisions about whether they like this person or whether the person is right for their parent. Parents would be wise not to directly ask how their kids like this person but simply to listen for their comments and watch their behavior. The process takes time — a lot of time — and parents will not help themselves by trying to get their teens to give their romantic interest the stamp of approval.

- **NO SLEEPOVERS!** This is a remarkable reversal of roles that parents often resent. Nevertheless wise single parents, or non-custodial parents whose teens are visiting them, do not have their romantic partners sleep over, nor do they sleep over at their friend's place. Teenagers are extremely Victorian in their views of parental sex, and obvious signs like sleepovers will only upset them. Sex is a natural part of adult relationships, and it will normally occur, but not in the home and not for the entire night. Be discreet and the teens will have a chance to get to know the romantic interest. Be obvious and the teen resentment and disgust will overshadow any good qualities the new friend might have.

- **When dating begins be extra careful about criticizing the ex-spouse.** It is always a good practice to avoid denigrating the ex in front of the teens. They still love their natural parents and resent them being put down. This becomes especially true when a single parent begins dating. Negative comments about the ex-spouse will simply be seen as the parent making excuses to start dating. It is viewed as rubbing salt into the wound and will only make the dating process more difficult for the parent.

The entire process of dating and forming new relationships for both single and non-custodial parents is not much different than trying to negotiate a minefield. It is very dangerous to the relationship between the parent and the teens. If there are any doubts at all, parents should avoid the process, as the relationship with the children should always come first. On the other hand, if the above suggestions are taken into careful consideration, then dating can be accomplished without losing the affection and respect of the children.

The Visitation Shuffle

*"It feels so heartbreaking to live with two different types of families.
Each household is very different from the other and it is hard to
go from one house to the next each week and change my attitude
to blend in with my surroundings."*
— Jessica

When two distinct households have been established by separated parents, the lives of the children suddenly become extremely complex. Trying to live comfortably in two different places can become so difficult that some children eventually refuse to visit the non-custodial parent — or go to live with him on a permanent basis. An understanding of the difficulties that two households can bring will help separated parents to avoid many of the pitfalls.

The Problems

Shuffling between two households is much harder on teens than most parents realize. In fact, these hazards are rarely considered when parents contemplate a separation or divorce. Yet this is one of the most difficult aspects of divorce for both parents and children to become accustomed to. While the situation affects both parents, the main problems are usually associated with going to the residence of the non-custodial parent, as this is not "home."

When custody has been settled, the custodial parent and the children go about the business of making a home for themselves. If they have stayed in the home that they lived in before the separation, then there is no problem in doing this. If they have moved to a new location, then there are many adjustments to make such as to a new school, new friends and new transportation arrangements. Once these adjustments are made, then a home has been established. For the non-custodial parent it is much harder to make a "home" for the children.

The problems are many. The bulk of the children's clothing, toys and games, and personal decorations such as posters, trophies or other memorabilia, are all at the custodial parent's place. There is usually nothing to make them feel at home. Often the n/c parent's residence is smaller so that the children do not have their own space to personalize. These factors make it very difficult to allow the children to feel that they belong there.

Another difficulty with visiting the non-custodial parent is that the children's friends are usually back in their custodial parent's neighborhood. This gives them no one to play with during times that no activities are planned. While this is not a major problem for young children, it is a vital one for adolescents, to whom constant contact with friends is so important. In fact, teenagers have more problems than younger children when it comes to visitations.

Teenagers rely on their friends for emotional support while they are establishing their own identities (see the section on friends in Chapter 8). They want to spend as much time as possible with these friends and resent it when they have to miss activities, such as parties or dances, or even just "hanging out" together, to visit their other parent. Their basic insecurity makes them feel that if they are not with their friends they will be talked about, or worse, that their peers can get along without them and won't care to be friends anymore. While these fears are generally groundless, it does give teens mixed feelings about having to visit their non-custodial parent. This can be a serious challenge for the parent who does not understand these teenage anxieties and takes the resentment personally.

> *"I have to go to my dad's every second weekend. It's kind of a hassle.*
> *I would like my parents to remarry."*
> — *Ashley*

Another major problem that can exist for children caught in the "visitation shuffle" is the two sets of rules that may be in place in two different households. Non-custodial parents often have fewer rules, possibly with the misguided intention of winning the children's affection. Other n/c parents have stricter rules than their custodial counterparts because they are not as used to having children around so they attempt to have them interfere with their single lifestyle as little as possible. Whatever the reasons, having two sets of rules is frustrating and confusing to children, especially teenagers. They are struggling with rules enough as it is, but having them be different at school and in both homes is often too much for them, resulting in rebellion and frequent arguments.

The resentment of not feeling at home, missing friends or having different rules is natural for teens to feel, but they are not the only ones who resent these visitations. Many non-custodial parents resent the restriction in their lifestyle that having their children visit imposes on them. While most love their children and want them to visit, they can be frustrated by having to plan activities and having to curb their own social life every other weekend. This frustration can often be detected by the children, causing them to feel unwanted.

Probably the most serious problem involved in the "visitation shuffle" involves either parent using these visitations as a weapon against the other parent. This is done in many ways — by making the children unavailable for the biweekly stay, by constantly being late to pick them up or by making them feel guilty about spending time with the other parent. These practices will be discussed in more detail in the next section. They almost always backfire so that, rather than succeeding in punishing the other parent, the teenagers become angry and resentful at being used as weapons of war. Adolescents are old enough to understand this game and will withdraw from parents who insist on playing it.

Besides all the above problems, the visitation process eventually just wears down teenagers. The constant back and forth, the packing, the things they need being in other places and having two birthday parties, two Christmases and two Easter egg hunts all becomes too tiring and confusing for them. To maintain the positive aspects of having two parents, the adults need to work very hard for the visitation process to be successful and above all, they have to work together. Both parents need to accept that their children now have two homes, and they need to ensure that their children are relaxed and comfortable in both places. Parents also have to understand that they have to give up some of their control of the parenting process to the other parent, at least for part of the time. This is all very difficult for people who no longer love or respect each other, and even harder if a state of war exists between the parents. For the children's sake, however, it has to be done.

Parental Actions

The most important factor in ensuring that the visitation process works well is positive communication between the parents. The important areas include:

- *Always try to be on time, but when this is not possible, inform the ex-spouse.*
- *Give the other parent advance notice of any changes in your usual schedule.*
- *Let your former spouse know if any new people will be part of the visitation, such as a babysitter or a romantic interest.*
- *Share your vacation schedules and plans well in advance. Decide if the children are to be part of these plans or whether it will just mean a break in the normal visitation routine.*
- *Inform your ex-spouse of any changes in your address, telephone numbers or your job. This may seem like a non-issue, but it is amazing how many warring parents try to keep this information secret. It then becomes impossible for the other parent to communicate, except at the secretive parent's whim.*
- *Be flexible in your approach to visitation. While a routine is important for the children, some variations need to be allowed. As long as these variations are communicated, and don't upset any plans of the other parent, they should be accommodated.*
- *Keep the rules and consequences similar in each household.*

The next step is for the non-custodial parent to ensure that the children enjoy coming to visit. This process starts with making the home as comfortable as possible for them. Ideally it should be located as close as possible to the custodial spouse's, without impinging on each other's privacy. This helps keep transportation to a minimum, and can even make it possible for the teen to socialize with friends. The place should be large enough so that each child has his or her own space. They can personalize this space with posters, stuffed animals and other memorabilia so that it truly becomes another home.

The process continues with ensuring that the visits are opportunities for parent and children to get to know each other and to enjoy each other's company. To do this a balance needs to be maintained between planned activities and down time, where nothing elaborate is planned, but parent and children are together. This down time could include playing board games, watching a movie with pop and chips or just doing chores together. As the children get older, parents should seek their children's input into the planning of activities so that they are both enjoyable and age-appropriate. A note of caution needs to be injected at this point. Non-custodial parents should avoid trying to buy their children's affection by giving them expensive gifts or taking them on exotic trips. The kids already love them and all that is accomplished is upsetting of the custodial parent. In fact this is often the purpose. Teenagers very quickly see through this and, while they like presents, they just want to enjoy their time with their father (or mother). They do not want to participate in the battle between them.

Further Steps to Make the Visitation Process Work Well

- *Don't make teenagers babysitters for younger children while you continue your social life.*
- *Keep their grandparents in the picture by visiting them as often as possible.*
- *If possible, allow the kids to bring a friend occasionally.*
- *Spend some individual time with each of your children.*
- *Keep your promises.*

While the above points may seem like common sense to many parents, it is amazing how often these details are not considered to be important. This is especially true when it comes to promises. Teens will remember a broken promise for years, especially if it involves something important to them. Keeping promises shows teens that you really do care about them and, as has been said many times before in this book, teens need constant reassurance that their parents love them.

"My dad promised to take us to Disneyland. We were all packed and waiting on the front steps but he never showed up. He didn't even call. I cried myself to sleep every night for weeks. I guess we just weren't that important to him."
— *Corinna*

It is vital that parents understand how hard the visitation shuffle can be on their children. To ease the burden they must work together to make it successful. Divorce is difficult enough for teenagers without adding to the pain by making visitations a chore rather than a chance to enjoy the company of the non-custodial parent. Parents need to stop being preoccupied with their dislike of their ex and pay attention to the needs of their children. This can help to ease the emotional scars that tend to accompany the trauma of divorce.

When Visitation Breaks Down

In a minority of cases, teens get to a point where they either no longer want to visit the non-custodial parent or, conversely, they want to move in with the n/c parent. This situation is particularly common when the children enter their teen years. At this time, as has been said many times throughout this book, their feelings of independence begin growing and they start to want to make their own decisions. If they are uncomfortable about their living arrangements or about visitations they will say so — in many different ways. To the parents they want to be with, they will complain about the situation and try to enlist that parent's aid in arranging to live only with him or her. Rarely will they be as direct with the parent they do not want to visit or live with. Instead, they will begin to make excuses as to why they cannot visit, or why they should remain with the non-custodial parent longer. There will be more frequent arguments with both parents and such signs of emotional upheaval as frequent "illnesses," a drop in school marks or even outright refusal to attend school. Once these behaviors begin it is time for parents to undertake an honest review of the situation to try to find a solution.

The reasons that teenagers want to change their living or visitation arrangements are many. The most common is the introduction of a new person into one living place or the other. A new partner that the teenagers do not like or who does not relate well to the youngsters is deadly to parent-teen relationships. They do not take to new people in their family well at the best of times and if the new arrangements are not approached in a careful and considerate manner, then the teen will gradually not want to be in that household. (See the section on "Parental Dating" as well as the one on "Step-Parenting.")

Another reason for not wanting to visit or for leaving the custodial parent is that the parent simply does not treat the teens properly. This occurs in alcoholic situations, in physically abusive circumstances, or when the parent shows no affection or consideration for the teens. This latter can occur if the parents continue to treat the teenager as a young child, frequently use the teen as a babysitter for younger children while pursuing their own social life or simply do not make the visits enjoyable. Boredom is a major enemy of all teenagers.

No matter what the reason is, parents who find that their teenagers either want to stop visiting the non-custodial parent or want to go and live with them need to find the reasons for this behavior and try to correct it. Once teens are unhappy in a certain situation, forcing things is not the answer. For example, parents whose children refuse to visit them have been known to seek court orders to force visitations. That will never work. Even if the court orders these visits, the orders cannot be effectively enforced. You can't legislate love and affection. A better approach is to engage a counselor to help find solutions to the problem, then follow these solutions. This may require a very open-minded approach on the part of the parent who is being rejected. Many would prefer to blame their ex-spouse for alienating the teens rather than facing the real problems. The fact is that children who love their parents cannot be alienated from them by others. The rejected parent may even need to seek counseling to help to overcome the barriers that have arisen between that person and his or her children.

Weekends

Weekends now mean so much more than they used to. I find myself spending a large part of twelve days looking forward to the two days I spend with my children. Weekends are no longer filled with household duties and lawn maintenance. I do my best to get those things out of the way before the weekend arrives. When the weekends do arrive, or more specifically six o'clock on Friday nights, there is a kind of magic in the air.

It is difficult at times to distinguish myself as more than a friend, because all I want to do is have fun with my kids. I learned, after a few months, that it is still of the highest necessity to enforce rules. The rooms still need to be cleaned, table manners insisted upon, and time schedules adhered to. That is not to say I don't bend the rules often. There have been many a Sunday night that I have spent cleaning the kids' rooms because I didn't have the heart to ask their friends to leave so that they could pick it up themselves.

I always look at the time we spend together as a time for making memories. We take a lot of pictures. I have spent many a Saturday afternoon on my hands and knees, searching for that deceptive toad that hops around the outskirts of a pond, and more than once we have caught him. We have created several memories as we huddled over a piece of paper with crayons in hand, and the creative juices flowing. I have several private memories also. The ones that are discovered at two in the morning when I pull the covers up to their neck, or when I find the word DADDY written inside a heart that was drawn by small hands. The weekends are magical.

There have been some weekends though that just didn't turn out the way they were planned. Maybe the weather intruded, or one of the kids just wasn't feeling well or maybe the budget just didn't allow for certain extravagances. It used to be that those weekends would really bother me. I would almost feel cheated. Then I realized that the kids really didn't care about the extravagances, and sometimes it can be fun to play in the rain.

So, take it easy on yourself when things don't turn out just so, and try to live through the eyes of your child. If only for a moment.

I get forty-eight hours every two weeks, four days a month, forty-eight days a year, to spend with my children. It's not enough, but if nothing else, it will be full of memories.

— Chuck Houghton
From his Web site:
www.geocities.com/Heartland/Meadows/1259/weekend.htm

Inter-Parental Conflict

"The aftermath [of divorce] is horrible. Your parents fight over you as if you were a teddy bear and they were two little children pulling at each arm, stretching you out."
— Jessica

This is also called Parental Alienation. It means that the parents continue to be in a state of war long after the separation and divorce. Often the children are used as weapons in this war, with little or no thought given to how much this hurts them. The point that is so often forgotten by these warring parents is that the children usually love them both equally. To see them fighting is always hard for them. To realize that they are being used to try to hurt the other parent is even worse. Parents should never delude themselves that their teenagers don't know that they are being used. They always do — and they hate it.

The Problems

There are a wide variety of ways that parents carry on their marriage wars after the relationship has broken up. One of the most obvious is fighting in front of the children whenever the parents come face to face. This often occurs during pick-up and drop-off times, or when activities need to involve both parents, such as parent-teacher interviews, graduations or sports finals. The reasons for parents needing to continue their battles are generally emotional, such as having been hurt by the divorce and wanting to try to return the favor. This is immature behavior, and the teens know it. Generally these fights embarrass them, especially when they occur in public. Neither parent will win any points with their children in this way, yet they keep trying.

Another common method of displaying interparental conflict occurs when parents refuse to talk to each other and use the children to convey messages instead. They may want to remind the non-custodial parents that a support payment is late, change visitation times or perhaps just inform the other parent of an upcoming event. This is extremely wearing on the teens because at best, it puts the burden of remembering to tell the parent something that might be important on them, and at worst it puts them squarely in the middle of some very difficult problems. This can occur even through telephone conversations. The dialog below was recorded by a teenager out of sheer frustration at the impossible situation she was constantly being placed in:

The telephone rings.
    Amber: *Hello*
Father (with no preamble): *Tell that bitch to quit calling me. I'll give*
              her the money when I'm damned good and ready.
Amber turns and relays this to her mother.
    Mother: *Tell him I can do whatever I effing like.*
Amber cleans up the language and relays this to her dad.
    Father: *If she expects to ever get another dime out of me, she's*
          got another think coming.
Again Amber transmits this message.
    Mother: *Tell him that if he doesn't start paying on time*
        I'll take him to court.
By this time the mother is shouting so loudly that Amber does not have
to pass on the message.
    Farther: *Tell her to go ahead. She can't afford a lawyer anyway.*
    Amber: *Both of you shut up! I can't stand being in the middle!*
She drops the phone and runs to her room.

All that this kind of situation does is hurt the teen. In this case Amber's response was to refuse to attend school. She feigned one form of sickness after another in a vain attempt to get her parents to stop fighting. She continued this behavior for over a year, even after receiving counseling. This was not surprising, as there was no change in her parent's behavior during this time either.

"I wish my mom and dad would at least get along and like each other."
— *Raeann*

Besides being a conduit for information from one non-communicative parent to the other, teens are also often used to spy on their parents' behavior. As they move between parental residences, they are constantly quizzed about the lives of the former spouses. Sometimes this information is gathered to add ammunition for the actual divorce, but more often it is just used as fuel for the inter-parental battle. Indiscretions, disciplinary methods, or apparent lack of them, and financial difficulties are avidly gathered by one parent to throw in the face of the other. This extremely childish behavior is usually recognized for what it is by the teens and they learn to hate being pumped by their parents. In fact, the spying can end up being a huge barrier to communication between parents and teens. They would rather say nothing than give their parents more ammunition to use in the inter-parental war.

One of the key tactics used by alienated parents is withholding visitations. Obviously, since the mothers usually retain custody, they more commonly employ this tactic. It can take the form of saying that a child is ill, telling the non-custodial parent that the child can't go because of some social or athletic event, or just taking the teens out when the father is due to pick them up. Fathers or non-custodial parents can respond by returning the youngsters late from their visitation period, or not picking them up when they know that the mother has plans for the weekend. These are incredibly juvenile tactics, yet they are employed with impunity by a huge number of divorced parents. These people seem oblivious to the damage that this does to their children. The teenagers still love both parents, and realizing that they are the ammunition in the inter-parental war wounds them deeply. The teens also usually hate to miss their visitations and become frustrated by their lack of ability to do anything about it.

The Research

Research studies on divorce show that children in divorce situations usually develop a closer alignment with one parent or the other, but they still want to spend time with both parents. When there is little or no parental conflict, this pattern continues. However, when there is a high degree of parental conflict a child's preference for one parent over the other can become highly polarized and unyielding. The child then does not want to see or visit the other parent at all.

Another weapon in the inter-parental war is emotional blackmail. This is utilized in the form of making the kids feel guilty about either visiting the other parent or returning to the custodial parent. Statements such as, "I'm going to be very lonely while you're gone," or, "I sure wish you wouldn't go away and leave me all alone," are designed to make the children feel guilty about visiting their other parent. The ultimate goal is to get the teen to not want to visit one parent for fear of hurting the other. This is definitely an unfair tactic that disregards totally the feelings of the youngsters.

Finally, a common stratagem of insecure and angry parents is to try to win the affection of their teenagers by bribing them. Usually this is attempted through the giving of expensive gifts or by taking exotic trips that the other parent can't afford. This behavior is often accompanied by remarks indicating that the other parent could never afford to do these things. This ploy is normally utilized by the wealthier parent — usually the non-custodial father. Once again the children are rarely fooled by this tactic, but it does continue the inter-parental battle very effectively by emphasizing the difference in economic status between the parents. It may not fool the teens, but it almost always angers the parent with the lower economic status.

No matter what methods are employed, parents who continue their squabbles after the separation succeed only in hurting their children more than the separation already has. In the process they are losing the trust and affection of their children as the youngsters can clearly see that their parents are being more immature than they are. Separated and divorced parents don't have to like each other, but to continue their battles after they have broken up not only does not solve any problems, it makes the entire difficult situation even worse for everyone.

> *"I want my mom and dad to get back together — or at least be friends."*
> — *Stacy*

Parental Actions

Remembering that most teens love both their parents, the most appropriate approach for separated or divorced parents is to maintain an outward civility towards each other. The marriage is over and cannot be repaired. Even if it could, the right way to go about it certainly would not be by trying to get even with the ex for past wrongs. For the sake of the children, then, it behooves the parents to act like adults. Here are some guidelines to follow if civility is to be maintained:

- *Communicate messages directly to the other parent, not through the teens.*

- *Avoid contact with each other if tempers are still raw.*
- *Don't use the teens as spies. The other parent is out of your life and his or her affairs are no longer yours.*
- *Disagree in private. If there are matters to attend to, such as late support payments, discuss them out of earshot of the children.*
- *Do not say negative things about the other parent. Let the teens make up their own minds about them.*
- *Help the teens to remember your ex-partner's birthdays and other special occasions. Teens are highly disorganized and this small amount of thoughtfulness will go a long way towards maintaining peace between you.*
- *Keep to the visitation routine. If changes really need to be made, discuss these in advance with your former spouse.*
- *Do not try to buy your teens' affections. Try to keep gifts and trips at the same level of expense as they were before the breakup.*
- *Avoid stooping to emotional blackmail. This is very hard on teenagers as they rarely see through it. This causes them to feel very guilty about loving their other parent and unnecessarily increases their already elevated stress levels.*

When written like this, the above suggestions seem relatively simple and straightforward. Unfortunately when emotions get involved, few things are simple. It is essential that parents put their children's needs ahead of their anger and hurt. If they can't, they risk not only alienating their children, but, causing emotional damage that can seriously impair their children's ability to form stable relationships in the future.

Step-Parenting

Modern marriage ceremonies are often notable for the distinctive vows written by the bride and groom to more closely represent their unique situations. These often replace the traditional, "Do you John Smith take this woman Mary Jones etc." For those about to marry someone who already has children, thus creating a stepfamily, the vows should read as follows:

"Do you, John Smith, take this woman, Mary Jones, her kids, her ex-husband, her family, her financial obligations and her complicated life

to have and to hold from now on, while accepting that her kids will likely hate you from the start and that often you will not come first in her life and your marriage will more than likely be under constant strain for the first few years?"

It would be nice if this was a joke or an exaggeration, but it is neither. It is an accurate portrayal of the difficulties that stepparents are likely to encounter. Marrying someone with children will more than likely be incredibly difficult and will require infinitely more work than would a marriage to someone who does not have children. It can certainly be done successfully, but not unless the bride or groom knows exactly what he or she is in for and is prepared to work extra hard to make the marriage, and the new family, successful.

Preparing Teens for Your Remarriage

If you want to guarantee a rocky start to your contemplated marriage, you should be sure to spring it on your teens with little or no warning. Something like, "I hope you guys don't have anything planned for next weekend, because Monica and I are getting married," is sure to set the marriage up for a rough beginning. Unless children are well prepared for one of their parents remarrying, they will generally react with considerable negative emotion to such an announcement. This is particularly true of children in their early teenage years.

The Problems

The problems start with the fact that teenagers are old enough to have known their parents for many years, forming a strong bond with them. The thought of someone trying to replace their biological parent (as they see it) is very frustrating for them. Unless the parent was extremely abusive in the past, the teens love him and want him to remain a part of their lives. With the advent of a new stepparent, the teens are unsure as to how the situation will develop and, like most people, they fear the unknown.

Teens' emotionality is another factor that causes them to resent stepparents. The teenage hormones that are preparing them for reproduction also cause them to be extremely emotional. This exaggerates the two main emotions that they feel when faced with the advent of a stepparent, which are *anger* and *jealousy*. The anger begins from the realization that their parents will now never be getting back together. Even if they already knew this on a rational level, in their hearts they almost always harbor dreams of their parents reuniting. When the dreams are finally shattered by the impending marriage, the anger begins to grow. While some of this resentment may be towards their biological parent for not making the original marriage work, the majority of the emotion is usually directed at the new parent who is seen as having purposely taken their mom or dad away from the other biological parent.

The other strong emotion, jealousy, is a result of the teens feeling that their parents love is being taken away by his or her romantic interest. Teenagers do not want to share their parents' love with anyone, much less a complete stranger. Bonnie's feelings are typical:

"He knows her for three months, gets married to her, and all of a sudden she's better than me. Then he expects me to like her."

While it is unusual for a teen to be able to articulate her feelings so clearly, Bonnie has managed to plainly state what so many of her peers also experience. They are jealous of the position that the future stepparent is about to occupy. These feelings are particularly strong if the parent has been single for a number of years. Where once they had exclusive possession of the biological parent, now the teens have to share him or her with someone outside the family. It is little wonder that the stepparent's entry into the family is greeted with a wall of resentment. What is remarkable is that so few stepparents seem to realize what they are in for. Instead of trying to understand the source of their stepchildren's resentment, they tend to react to the children's resentment with anger and defensiveness. The war is then on. The thinking seems to be something like, "Their father (mother) loves me, so the kids will too." When the teens show their emotions by being rude, refusing to talk to the stepparent or by not doing any-thing the stepparent asks them to, the new parent often tends to respond with an authoritarian approach. This is exactly the wrong thing to do.

Parental Actions

> *The most important key is to give them time to adjust to this radically different situation.*

A stepparent usually comes into children's lives over their strong objections. The stepparent is generally seen as someone who hands out chores and punishments, violates the child's space and takes the attention of the real parent away from him or her. The most important key is to give them time to adjust to this radically different situation. In addition to time, teens need a huge amount of reassurance and attention to get used to another major change in their world. As a result, the parent who is marrying needs to prepare them carefully for the remarriage. It would be nice if the other biological parent would help as well, but unfortunately this is rarely the case. The following are the key components of this preparation:

- *Tell your children before you tell anyone else. In fact, keep them in the picture from the time you realize that the relationship is serious. Discuss your intention to get remarried with them, then give them enough time to adjust to the idea. Long courtships may not be necessary for the parents, but they definitely are for the teens. Slow down the marriage plans until your teens have accepted the idea.*
- *Answer all their questions as honestly as possible. These may come up periodically throughout the betrothal period. Take the time to carefully answer even the most trivial questions. Do not assume that time alone will take care of things.*
- *Let your children see how happy you are. Tell them about your feelings, the things you love about your fiancé and how excited you both are to be building a new family.*
- *Reassure them constantly that they will still be the number one things in your life. Let them know that your love for them will not change, even though you are in love with this new person. Explain how there is plenty of room in your heart for them and a new person too.*
- *Seek your teenagers' help in planning the wedding. Let them look through the bridal books, help them shop for clothing and ensure that they have some part in the ceremony. Ask for their opinions, then follow their suggestions whenever possible.*
- *Spend extra time with them in the weeks before the wedding.*

Don't let yourself become so immersed in the wedding plans that you ignore the teens. Instead make a point of being with them more than ever. This also helps communication between you because being together stimulates conversation.

- *Pay special attention to your children's behavior. If there are any changes since the wedding announcement, such as an increase in rudeness or rebelliousness or signs of depression or withdrawal, talk to them about it. Get any problems out in the open and deal with them as quickly as possible. If necessary, postpone the wedding until the issues are resolved.*

Taking these steps may seem as if the teens come first. Many parents wonder about their own happiness and how it fits in. In fact the children should come first. If they are not happy with the situation, the marriage is doomed from the start. Parental issues can be more easily resolved because they are the adults and the mature ones. Teenagers cannot resolve their own issues. They need adult help to do this. If parents take the time to prepare their teenagers for their remarriage, the future of the new union will be much brighter than if they place their own needs first.

Building a Relationship with Your Stepteens

Even when the teens have been carefully prepared for the nuptials, once the wedding bells have stopped ringing and the stepparent is firmly ensconced in the parent's home, a whole new set of problems begin. These involve adjusting to living with each other and building a positive relationship between you and your stepchildren. Once again most adults completely underestimate the amount of time teenagers need to adjust to the presence of a new person. Not only is this new person competing for their biological parent's attention and affection, he or she is now in a position of authority over them. If this authority is not used carefully from the start, the resentment it causes can poison the relationship forever.

The Problems

The most common mistake newly minted stepparents make is not giving their relationship with the stepchildren time to develop. The modern world is a fast-paced one, with instant meals, instant pictures and high-speed telecommunications. People tend to get impatient when things do not happen instantly. Unfortunately, while there may be such a thing as love at first sight in romantic relationships, it rarely happens this way in step-relationships. It takes much more time than most people realize for the stepparent to just be accepted into the family, much less loved. This time is necessary to overcome the initial negative emotions that generally occur when a parent remarries. This is especially true when the biological parent does not have custody, and the teens visit only every other week. The length of time to develop into a family will vary greatly, depending on how well prepared the teens were for the marriage, but step-parents should expect to think in terms of years rather than mere months.

> *The biggest mistake most stepparents face is to be too authoritarian too soon.*

Another major problem that faces stepparents who want to develop a relationship with their spouse's children involves family discipline. Upon marrying the children's parent, the stepparent is immediately placed in a position of authority. How they wield this authority is vital to the development of family harmony. The biggest mistake most stepparents make is to be too authoritarian too soon. Since their presence in the family is generally already resented, being strict and controlling will only increase this resentment. The resentment is usually summed up with statements such as, "You're not my real parent so you can't tell me what to do." This defiance usually takes stepparents by surprise and they tend to react defensively. The result is arguments and shouting matches that only weaken the relationships further.

Lack of communication is also a major barrier to developing a positive relationship with stepteens. Communicating with teenagers is a difficult proposition at the best of times (See Chapter 1 for more details). For a stepparent it is even harder due to the anger and resentment that is usually present. This resentment results in the teens being even less communicative than they would be in a traditional family. As a result the stepparent must either be an excellent communicator or must learn communication skills if any dialog is to occur at all with the stepchildren.

Jealousy on the part of the stepparent is another problem that can interfere with developing a rapport with stepteens. This is often seen in the stepparent being upset when the biological parent spends time with his or her children. These stepparents insist on going everywhere with the family, never letting them have any time to themselves. Biological parents, not wanting to jeopardize their marriage, often reduce the time they spend alone with their children when they sense their partner's jealousy. The natural result is an increase in the teenagers' resentment towards the stepparent. Jealousy in anyone is a highly destructive emotion, but it is even more so when displayed by a stepparent.

Finally, stepparents can guarantee that they will never develop a relationship with their spouse's children by trying to completely replace the biological parent. Behavior such as saying negative things about the original parent, not allowing the children to discuss their absent parent, and demanding undivided loyalty and commitment from the kids will ensure that any resentment they started with will not only continue, it will increase. Children of all ages will continue to have strong feelings for their biological parent, even when that parent has been abusive or addicted. This is particularly true of teenagers, who are not only much more emotional than younger children, but are more aware of the social situation. Stepparents need to be conscious of these feelings and not try to stamp them out. They need to realize that the teens can continue to love their natural parent, and still develop a real affection for their new parent.

Tannis' Story

"I don't like my stepdad, I never have. Ever since my mom married him I have been furious at her, and now she's too petrified to have another failed marriage. She doesn't see that there is no love in this marriage. It's pointless. My mom and I would be better off if he wasn't in it. All he does is fight with her and when she gets in a fight she takes it out on my sister and I.

"On the other hand I love my stepmom. She is the only one of my four parents that I can talk to and she actually listens. My stepdad is trying to take the place of my dad. He is always making rude comments about how my dad was never there for me when I was little. Even though I would never let him take the place of my dad, it still bothers me.

> *"My stepdad and I never got along. We're always fighting and arguing about something. He thinks that just because he is married to my mom he can tell me what I can and can't do. He is always yelling at me because I don't listen to him or show him the respect he wants. He'll never get any respect from me. I moved to my dad's to get away from him. I can't stand him and I never will."*

Step-Parental Actions

A loving relationship with a stepchild can definitely be established if enough time and effort is put in by the stepparent. Unfortunately this is rarely done, usually because stepparents are completely unprepared to assume their new role. They just don't know where to start. The following is a series of actions that, if followed closely, will virtually assure that a good relationship will eventually be established with a stepchild.

- **Don't take initial rejection personally.** Stepparents must expect that, at best, they will initially be disliked. However, this dislike is not for you personally, but for the role you are assuming. Do not be afraid of this early rejection, and do not react defensively. Expect it, then forgive and forget the rudeness and negative response. Remember that they are just kids and are acting emotionally, not rationally.

- **Be patient — then be more patient.** Being accepted, and eventually loved, by stepchildren is going to take time. In fact it will probably take years. If all goes well the initial dislike will turn to tolerance, then finally to true affection. Stepparents should remember that teens need to know that they are loved and respected. They want to have a loving and trusting relationship, but they have difficulty getting over their initial fear of the unknown. Give them the time to do this by waiting patiently for their distrust to turn into a positive relationship.

- **Plan activities together.** Rather than avoiding children who seem to hate you, be active with them. Give them lots of notice, involve teens in planning, and then work at enjoying activities with them. If you are seen to be genuinely interested in their having fun, and seem to enjoy being with them, the teens will start to enjoy your company too.

- **Try to understand the nature of teenagers.** Many stepparents who are suddenly thrust into a family with teenagers do not know what to expect. The result is that many actions that are typical of all teenagers are thought by the stepparents to be directed at them. Arguing and mood swings are typical examples. The best advice is for stepparents to assume that the problem is a normal teenage one until there is solid evidence to the contrary. You still have to deal with it, but at least these are often problems that all parents face, so there is no need to take it personally. (Hint — it might be a good idea to read my first book *"Hear Me, Hug Me, Trust Me."*)

> *If in doubt, let the biological parent make the final decision, at least for the first year or so.*

- **Both parents must maintain a united front.** This is often difficult, as teenagers are geniuses at playing one side against the other. Nevertheless it is usually a good idea to check with the other parent before making a decision. For example if a teen says "Why can't I go to the rock concert? Dad always lets me," then check with dad before saying anything. In fact, if the parents happen to disagree on a strategy, discuss the issue until you can present a common opinion. If in doubt, let the biological parent make the final decision, at least for the first year or so.

- **Be a good listener.** If there is one mistake that all parents tend to make, it's that they would rather talk than listen to the teen. Stepparents will find that by learning to listen most of the time, their relationship with the teens will improve greatly. Pay attention to them and respect their opinions, even when you finally have to rule against them. Ask questions about their activities, use short questions to keep the conversation going, and really listen to the answers. Once they get talking, do not interrupt or lose concentration until they have finished.

- **Never criticize the parent you are replacing.** In fact it is important to go even further. Encourage the children to maintain a close relationship with the original parent. As hard as this may be, the teens will respect you more. They have room in their hearts for their original parent and you too, so you have nothing to lose. No matter how poor a parent the original one is, keep your thoughts to yourself.

- **Develop a firm but fair system of discipline.** This should be done as a family. Sit down together and work out a set of rules. Seek the teen's input and compromise whenever possible. Then, when a family rule is broken, enforce it by first staying calm, then handing out a consequence. It is usually best if the biological parent does most of the enforcing at first, but this is not always possible. The teens will definitely resent a stepparent's authority at first, but if you stay calm and simply enforce what the family has decided, the teenagers will come around eventually. If a stepparent finds him- or herself in a situation where the biological parent is backing off the discipline, possibly with the misguided notion that the kids should not be hurt further, then it will be necessary to sit down together and develop a united front. Teens need discipline and they know it, but how you do it is important.

- **Attend as many of the stepchildren's activities as possible.** Try to do this even if the original parent is there. Show a keen interest in what they are doing and the teens will really appreciate this attention. If you don't know anything about their activity, read up on it and learn the finer points. Don't be fooled by the teenager's apparent indifference about whether you attend or not; they always want their parents to see what they are doing, they just have to be "cool" about it. Eventually you may even want to get involved in the activity as a volunteer.

- **Join a stepparents' support group.** These organizations are invaluable for helping a stepparent weather the storms of adolescence. Just realizing that you are not the only one having problems with the stepparent role makes one of these groups worthwhile. Check the telephone book or the World Wide Web for the nearest one in your area.

There are few roles in life harder than that of a stepparent but by following the above steps and maintaining a sense of humor, the family will eventually coalesce, and your experiences will be rewarding ones.

Comments by Stepfathers

"Being a stepfather is not easy and not for everyone. It may require more patience, personal strength and character than does conventional parenting. A stepfather has to give more, and in many cases, receive less than a biological father receives. There is also something special about the bond between biological parent and child that does not exist between stepfathers and children. No matter how well you do 'the job' that closeness will not be there to see you through the tough times, and help you appreciate the good times. I am proud of the effort I am making on behalf of my stepchildren, and our family, and hope that it 'pays off' for all of us in the future."

"So far, being a stepfather has been a lot of giving and receiving very little. I have gone out of my way several times to do things for the children and didn't even receive an acknowledgement. I know it will get better."

"There are times that being a stepfather is the greatest joy and other times when it is the hardest thing I have done. There are times when I feel part of a wonderful family, and times when I feel like an outsider."
— From: Stepfamily Australia and Stepfamily Association
of South Australia

Blended Families

Blended families are a special type of stepfamilies. There are many different possible combinations, but they basically include children being brought into the marriage by at least one of the parents, plus either children from the other parent as well or a child born to the remarried couple. The result is either a "mine and yours" family, a "mine and ours" family or, the most complex of all, a "yours, mine and ours" grouping. To make a family with a stepparent work is already a major test, but these combinations bring special challenges to the stepfamily. All the rules from the articles above still apply if the new family is to be a success, but with the blended family there are yet more factors to consider.

The Extra Problems

"If I could I would change the fact that my 4-year-old brother Roger (mom and stepdad's son) gets away with blue murder. They always let him pick on me and my two other brothers."
— *Tanya*

The most common difficulty with blended families, in the opinion of teenagers, is the different treatment given to the various children. As the teens see it, mom treats her kids better than she treats dad's offspring, dad only looks after his kids and both parents treat their own child better than either their stepchildren or their own children by the non-custodial parent. Often these observations are true, but almost as often the problem may be one of perception. Teenagers are often looking for things to find wrong with their stepparent, and differential treatment is an obvious point of attack. Unfortunately, when the teens are actually being treated differently, the chances of the two families ever blending into one are virtually nil.

The main reason why parents treat their children better than their stepchildren relates to the initial wall of dislike that generally greets most stepparents when they enter a family. Although this is natural and normal, especially when the teenagers have not been properly prepared for the marriage, most stepparents do not expect to be disliked. Under these circumstances it is far easier for them to be fair and understanding to their own kids, who are acting relatively normally to them, than it is to be nice to the negative stepteens. Unfortunately a vicious circle tends to develop. The stepchildren's negative reaction to the stepparent causes the parent to react to the teens with defensiveness and anger. Often this takes the form of being very authoritarian. This in turn confirms the teenagers' opinion of the stepparent and they become even ruder and more defiant. That results in more anger from the stepparent, and the relationship continues to deteriorate. The connection between them is then truly in a downward spiral.

Another problem in blending families is simply related to the increase in numbers. Where once a parent had just one or two children, suddenly there are one or two more grown children to deal with. This requires more time and organization, and this too catches many parents off guard. There are more mouths to feed, more bodies to clothe, more activities to drive kids to and more parent-teacher interviews, recitals and athletic events to attend. Even worse, there are now two non-custodial households to have to take the kids to on visitation weekends. All this extra activity can significantly increase the stresses in a family, and that can result in shorter tempers all around.

While combining stepparents and stepchildren is always a difficult task, a blended family has an equally difficult task in having to unite two sets of children as well. Amazingly, parents usually choose to believe that this will be an easy task. They think the children will instantly become friends and will enjoy the benefits of having another brother or sister. That attitude is tremendously naïve. Instead of the children becoming friends, it is more likely that they will become rivals, competing for the time, attention and resources of their parents. If either set of children dislike their stepparent, they will immediately earn the enmity of that parent's children. If they have to share a room with their new sibling, where once they had their own, more anger will develop. Blending two sets of children is usually a very difficult job which parents have to work extremely hard at if they want the family to become a single unit.

> *"I wish my stepmom would stop favoring*
> *my stepsister over everyone else."*
> — *Cheyenne*

There is another phenomenon that occurs both in regular stepfamilies and in blended families, and that creates a tremendous amount of tension in the family. This situation happens when a natural parent is either unable or unwilling to discipline his or her own kids. Why this happens is hard to determine, but it is definitely a common occurrence. When it does happen it leaves the stepparent in a particularly difficult position. This person is usually disliked to start with and, if he or she is forced into the role of disciplinarian by default, then the children tend to detest the stepparent even more. It's almost as if the natural parent is saying, "Oh good, now I have a spouse to do the disciplining so I don't have to." This is extremely unfair to the stepparent, and to the children of the natural parent.

Blending two families together adds an extra challenge to remarriage as it creates two stepparents, with all the problems that they encounter in trying to join a family. Added to this are the problems that arise when two sets of children are suddenly put into one household. Parents who are considering remarrying someone who already has children must be aware of the potential problems and take as many steps as possible to head them off.

Extra Parental Actions

> *"I like the fact that although I live in a blended family,*
> *my stepfather treats me and my brother as their own,*
> *making us not come second best, but treating us all*
> *equal and totally the same."*
> — *Jennifer*

The first action parents need to take if they are contemplating remarrying someone with children is to read or reread the previous section on step-parenting. All the suggestions that are given for a stepparent apply to blended families as well. In fact this is doubly true as there are two stepparents in the same family. Both parents need to be aware of the challenges they face as stepparent, and not take the initial rejection personally. Perhaps the most effective action of all would be to join a stepparents' support group *well before* the marriage takes place. Awareness of the problems to be faced and some potential solutions to them will help to get the new family off to a successful start.

> *"My stepdad is really nice and he treats me like his own.*
> *A lot of the time people on my stepdad's side forget that I am*
> *not a blood relative. They all really try to include me. A couple*
> *of summers ago we had a ceremony and they adopted me into*
> *their family. It was lots of fun. I would rather be part of my*
> *stepdad's family than my real dad's family."*
> — *June-Marie*

Along with the regular step-parenting actions, parents of blended families need to take some extra steps if the family is to blend effectively. These include:

- **Treat all the children equally.** As difficult as this may be, it is vital if the family is to become a complete unit. Rules and consequences are important for teenagers in any family, and even more so in a blended one. Develop the rules together, then apply them fairly to all the children, no matter whom they belong to. Temptations exist to either favor your own children or to treat the other parent's children with kid gloves. Don't do either. Teens recognize and appreciate equal treatment, so parents need to work together to adopt a common, equal front.

- **Be highly organized.** With the sudden influx of extra children, the household can quickly become chaotic. Put a white board on the kitchen wall, and list the important events of the week. Decide on Sunday night who's going to drive who where and who is going to attend which event (if both parents can't go). Assign chores to all children then post the list weekly if there is a rotation system. If not, post it for the year. Make all lunches the night before. Buy a book on time management, then put the principles into effect.

- **Try to give each child a separate room.** In large families this may be difficult, but do the best you can. Build temporary rooms in the basement if you have to. This will give the kids a space of their own. This is particularly important for teenagers who need to withdraw from the family occasionally, and will be even more driven to do so in a blended family.

- **Keep old family traditions.** If you and your children always go to the family reunion every summer, continue to do so, at least for a few years. Do not insist on bringing the entire blended family to such events. Maintaining family traditions will help to add stability to the children's lives and gives value to the original family and its members.

- **Develop new family traditions.** Start some entirely different traditions for the new family to share together. Traditions have tremendous value in stabilizing families and some new ones, that do not remind either family of the old days, will give the blended family an identity of its own.

- **Use family meetings for communication.** Set one night a week for a family meeting. Keep these meetings short, but give every family member a chance to speak in a non-critical environment. Take note of their concerns and allow the entire family to try to find a solution. After the first year or so these may not be necessary, but they are an excellent communication vehicle when trying to blend a group of strangers into a single family.

Perhaps the most useful suggestion of all is to not use reruns of *The Brady Bunch* as your example of a blended family. TV shows tend to minimize the problems that families have and to find brilliant solutions in half an hour. This is not reality. Few blended families end up like *The Brady Bunch*. In fact, most will never become one big happy family. Start from this premise, then work very hard to make things work. Even if all the children don't buy into the blended family, hard work will at least make it a comfortable place for everyone.

Afterword

Rage, Rebellion and Rudeness has two main purposes: to explain teenagers and the behavior that is associated with this in-between period of people's lives, and to provide clear and practical solutions for dealing with some of the more difficult of these behaviors. Understanding the complex behaviors of adolescents is difficult for most parents, even though they were teenagers once themselves. However, with understanding comes a certain peace of mind, as well as a direction as to how to deal with the puzzling behavior. That's why the first three chapters of the book should be read before looking up any particular problem.

In providing solutions to specific problems, one message is repeated many times throughout the text — and that message is "Stay Calm." Nothing can ever be solved when parents lose their temper, as the emotions will interfere with rationality every time. Added to this, teenagers hate to see their parents "lose it." They want their parents to provide an example to them and to be *the adults* in any confrontational situation. While there are many components to solving problems presented by adolescents, none is more important than keeping cool.

I have tried to make this book as comprehensive as possible, but there may be problems that parents encounter that are not covered in this book due to space limitations. If you have a problem that is not in this book, feel free to e-mail me with your questions through my Web site, www.drwooding.com.

Bibliography

Amat, Paul, & Booth, Alan. *A Generation at Risk*. Cambridge, MA: Harvard University Press. (2000)

Cheng, Mei-Fang. "The ABC's of the Hormones & Behavior." *Bioscience*, V46, No. 3, March, 1996.

Davis, Jesse. *A Mother Looks at the Gay Child*. Tempe, AZ: New Falcon Publications. (1997)

Elkind, David. *Parenting Your Teenager*. New York, NY: Ballantine Books. (1993)

Empfield, M. & Bakalar, N. *Understanding Teenage Depression*. New York, NY: Henry Holt & Co. (2001)

Faber, Adele, & Mazlish, Elaine. *How to Talk So Kids Will Listen and Listen So Kids Will Talk*. New York, NY: Avon Books. (1999)

Fagan, P & Rector, R. *The Effects of Divorce on America*. Heritage Foundation of Washington. D.C. (2000)

Gallagher, Maggie, & Waite, Linda. *The Case for Marriage*. New York, NY: Broadway Books. (2001)

Hetherington, E. Mavis, & Kelly, John. *For Better or Worse: Divorce Reconsidered*. New York, NY: W.W. Norton & Co. (2002)

Houghton, Chuck. *Weekends*. www.geocities.com/Heartland/Meadows/1259/weekend.htm

Kaplan, Leslie. *Coping With Peer Pressure*. New York, NY: Rosen Publishing Group. (1993)

Popenoe, David. *Life Without Father*. Cambridge, MA: Harvard University Press. (1999)

Staal, Stephanie. *The Love They Lost: Living with the Legacy of Our Parents Divorce*. New York, NY: Bantam Doubleday Dell. (2000)

Suderman, M., Schiek, P., et al. *A School-Based Anti-violence Program*. London, ON: London Family Court Clinic.

Whitehead, Barbara. *The Divorce Culture*. New York, NY: Random House. (1999)

Wallerstein, Judith. *The Unexpected Legacy of Divorce*. New York, NY: Hyperion Books. (2001)

Wooding, Scott. *Parenting Today's Teenager Effectively: Hear Me, Hug Me, Trust Me*. Markham, ON: Fitzhenry & Whiteside Publishers. (2003)

Index

dating, 320
intoxicants, 259–60
and self-esteem, 286–87
setting, 87–89
and sibling rivalry, 195–96
and summer holidays, 90–91
telephone use, 94–97
and visitation, 343

schizophrenia, 213–14, 219–20
school performance, 33, 138–44
  skipping classes, 158–62
  underachievement, 148–54
school refusal, 166–69
selective serotonin reuptake
    inhibitors (SSRI), 220, 290
self-discipline, 32
self-esteem, 280
  and bullying, 304–05
  and jobs, 279
  and lying, 246–47, 250–51
  and obesity, 309
  parental action, 284–87
  and peer pressure, 294
  signs of low self-esteem,
    280–84
  and underachievement, 151
sex, 227–31
  and alcohol or drugs, 258
  and dating, 315–16
  handling sex education,
    231–32
  homosexuality, 261–65
  issues, 232–36
  and morality, 53
  and parental dating, 341
  pregnancy, 228–29, 237
  premarital, 65, 67
  and values, 224

sexual intercourse, 228, 229–30,
    235, 236
sexually transmitted diseases
    (STD), 66, 229, 237–38
shoplifting, 108, 238–41
siblings
  blended families, 365–66
  handling sibling rivalry,
    195–97
  rivalry, 190–94
  unequal treatment, 24, 193,
    365, 368
single parenting, 59, 325–29
  parental action, 329–32
skipping classes, 158–62
  parental action, 163–66
  school refusal, 166–69
smoking, 241–45
society, impact on teens, 58
spying, 208–12
step-parenting, 354–55, 358–61
  handling remarriage, 355–58
  handling step-parenting,
    361–64
  see also blended families
stress, 58, 61–62
  and drugs, 64–65
  extracurricular activities, 70–72
  homework, 68–69
  jobs, 72–73
  and single parenting, 326–27
  substance abuse, 257, 258
  and urban lifestyle, 69–70
suicide, 220, 251–53
  and depression, 288, 289
  and homosexuality, 262–63
  myths about, 254
  parental action, 255–56
  warning signs, 253–54